CORNISH STUDIES

Second Series

SIXTEEN

INSTITUTE OF CORNISH STUDIES

EDITOR'S NOTE

Cornish Studies (second series) exists to reflect current research conducted internationally in the inter-disciplinary field of Cornish Studies. It is edited by Professor Philip Payton, Director of the Institute of Cornish Studies at the University of Exeter, Cornwall Campus, and is published by University of Exeter Press. The opinions expressed in *Cornish Studies* are those of individual authors and are not necessarily those of the editor or publisher. The support of Cornwall County Council is gratefully acknowledged.

Cover illustration: Woodcut of Prince Rupert,
Royalist commander, at the capture of Bristol in July 1643.
Reproduced courtesy of the British Library.

CORNISH STUDIES

Second Series

SIXTEEN

edited by
Philip Payton

UNIVERSITY
of
EXETER
PRESS

First published in 2008 by
University of Exeter Press
Reed Hall, Streatham Drive
Exeter EX4 4QR
UK

www.exeterpress.co.uk

British Library Cataloguing in Publication Data
A catalogue record for this book is available from the British Library.

ISBN 978 0 85989 836 2

Typeset in Adobe Caslon
by Carnegie Book Production, Lancaster
Printed in Great Britain by Printed in Great Britain
by TJ International, Padstow

FSC
Mixed Sources
Product group from well-managed
forests and other controlled sources
Cert no. SGS-COC-2482
www.fsc.org
© 1996 Forest Stewardship Council

Contents

Notes on contributors

Graham Busby is Programme Manager (BSc Tourism Awards) and University Teaching Fellow at the University of Plymouth. He has published extensively on literary and film-induced tourism besides various facets of Cornish Studies.

Pamela Dale is a researcher based in the Centre for Medical History at the University of Exeter. Her co-authored article in this collection was developed while she was employed as a temporary lecturer in the School of Humanities and Social Sciences at Exeter. It is a sequel to a comparative study of health visiting in the South West and in the West Riding of Yorkshire that was generously supported by a Wellcome Trust Fellowship. Pamela Dale has published work on a number of twentieth-century health topics.

Bernard Deacon is Senior Lecturer in Cornish Studies at the Institute of Cornish Studies, University of Exeter, Cornwall Campus, where he is also AHRC Knowledge Transfer Fellow (leading a collaborative project between the Institute and the Royal Cornwall Museum in Truro) and director of the Master of Arts in Cornish Studies degree programme. His most recent book is *Cornwall: A Concise History* (2007).

Robert Dickinson works part-time with the Regional Council of Brittany, where he Lectures on different aspects of the European Union. He is currently completing the Master of Arts in Cornish Studies degree programme at the Institute of Cornish Studies, University of Exeter, Cornwall Campus.

Erik Grigg is a mature Ph.D. student at the University of Manchester, where he is researching medieval dykes. He currently lives and works in Lincoln, and has recently completed a study of the medieval Cornish play 'Bewnans Meriasek', shortly to be published.

Cheryl Hayden works in strategic communication for the Queensland Government in Australia. She graduated from the University of Exeter as a Master of Arts in Cornish Studies in 2002 and has just completed a Master of Arts in creative Writing at the Queensland University of Technology. Following several years in journalism, she has written and published several short stories and has completed two as yet unpublished novels, both set in Cornwall.

Jan Lokan has a Ph.D. in education from the University of Ottawa, Canada, and spent most of her working life as a professional educational researcher, first with the Ottawa Board of Education for nine years and subsequently for 23 with the Australian Council for Educational Research (ACER) in Melbourne. At the time of her retirement in 2001 she held the professorial-level position of Assistant Director of ACER. She has published many journal articles and books in the field of education. Since retiring, she has been pursuing family history research and has discovered the fascination of Cornish Studies.

Kevin Meethan is Senior Lecturer in Sociology at the University of Plymouth, and has been researching and writing about tourism for a number of years. Publications include *Tourism in Global Society: Place, Culture and Consumption* and an edited collection *Tourism Consumption and Representation: Narratives of Place and Self.* His research interests include globalization, cultural change and consumption, the cultural industries, and regeneration policy. He is also a member of the editorial boards of *Tourism Today* and *Cultural Sociology.*

Catherine Mills is a Wellcome Research Fellow in the Centre for Medical History at the University of Exeter, where she is currently exploring the relationship between respiratory diseases and the regulatory politics of clean air in post-war Britain. Her co-authored article in this collection owes its origins to her postgraduate studies on the development of health and safety regulation in the British mining industries in the nineteenth and early twentieth centuries, with particular reference to non-ferrous metals. Catherine Mills has published work on smoke abatement and a variety of health and safety related topics, with particular reference to Cornish mine labour.

Mark Stoyle is Professor of History at the University of Southampton. His particular research interest is in the 'British crisis' of the 1640s; cultural, ethnic and religious identity in Wales and Cornwall between 1450 and 1700; and popular memory of the English Civil War from 1660 to the present day. Among his many books are *West Britons: Cornish Identities and the Early Modern British State* (2002) and *Soldiers and Strangers: An Ethnic History of the English Civil War* (2005).

Peter Tremewan is a retired Local Government Officer and a long-time student of Cornish history. He has a special interest in the influence of Methodism, mining and migration on the people of Cornwall. Recently he has researched the family tree of Billy Bray, giving fresh insights into the personal life of this icon of Cornish Methodism. In 2008 he was awarded the degree of Master of Arts in Cornish Studies by the University of Exeter.

Joanie Willett is a Ph.D. student in the Department of Politics at the University of Exeter, Cornwall Campus. Previously, she completed a BSc in Combined Social Sciences at Cornwall Business School and an MA in Critical Global Studies at the University of Exeter. She is interested in 'insider' and 'outsider' perceptions of Cornwall and Cornishness, and how these impact on the Cornish economy. She is intrigued by why Cornwall has been poor for so long, and is looking for answers in Marxism, Post-stucturalism and Post-colonial political theory.

Derek R. Williams was born and brought up in Camborne in Cornwall, although he has worked as a Librarian outside of Cornwall for many years. He is a bard of the Cornish Gorsedd, for which organization he has edited *Henry and Katherine Jenner* (2004) and co-edited *Setting Cornwall on its Feet: Robert Morton Nance 1873–1959* (2007). His other publications include *A Strange and Unquenchable Race: Cornwall and the Cornish in Quotations* (2007) and *Cornubia's Son: A Life of Mark Guy Pearse* (2008).

Introduction

In early 2008 Professor David Cannadine (Institute of Historical Research, University of London) called for the establishment of a Chief Historical Advisor, to mirror UK governmental positions such as Chief Scientific Adviser and Chief Medical Officer. As Professor Cannadine explained (*History Today*, February 2008, p. 3), 'I believe Whitehall departments should have historical advisers and the government should have a Chief Historical Adviser. Historians and politicians bring very different perspectives to bear on the contemporary world and greater dialogue between them would be beneficial to the policy process'. Moreover, he argued, 'Historians can suggest, on the basis of past precedents, what might or might not work ... This would be particularly valuable in policy areas such as constitutional reform'.

On the eve of constitutional reform in Cornwall, with the County and District Councils set to disappear in April 2009, to be replaced by a unitary 'Cornwall Council', it is timely to consider the Cornish implications of David Cannadine's proposals. The 'One Cornwall' transformation plan that has managed and publicised the process leading towards the new Cornwall Council has emphasized the Council's Cornish and democratic credentials, co-opting Cornish symbolism – including the use of black-and-gold, the traditional Cornish colours, in its new logo – to stress its Cornish identity, and highlighting the role of 'community hubs' or one-stop-shops in bringing governance closer to the people. This may be in part an attempt to answer critics opposed to the demise of the existing two-tier system, who argue that in shedding one level of local government, the new structure will be less accountable and more Truro-centric, to the detriment of grass-roots democracy. But this emphasis by the One Cornwall project on Cornishness and democratic outreach is also an expression of the determination that the new Cornwall Council should be demonstrably – even radically – different from what has gone before, offering significantly enhanced services and playing a more positive role in the lives of people in Cornwall.

The avoidance of the word 'county' – always anathema to Cornish nationalists – emphasizes that the new body is not merely the old County

Council refashioned. But it also suggests that the new Cornwall Council has a quality that is aspiringly 'regional', confirming Cornwall's long-felt status as more than 'just another county' and at last giving this institutional expression. This is not the same as a Cornish Assembly – in either nomenclature or in the powers it might exercise – and it is a million miles from the Welsh Assembly, let alone the Scottish Parliament. Yet it is redolent of the language of devolution and regionalization, and Cllr David Whalley – Leader of the out-going Cornwall County Council – has argued that the new Cornwall Council should be seen as a precursor, a first-step towards a fully fledged Cornish Assembly. As he explained to the annual conference of the Cornish Constitutional Convention in Truro in December 2007, 'There is something inevitable about the journey to a Cornish Assembly'. Just how that journey is to be made – the wresting of new powers away from the tight grip of central government, the avoidance of losing existing powers to unelected 'South West' bodies – is not at all clear. But the aspiration is genuine.

At the very least, the new Cornwall Council offers a fresh start, a clean sheet on which to sketch a Cornish agenda for the twenty-first century. And it is here that Professor Cannadine's comments have a particular Cornish relevance. The Institute of Cornish Studies, as part of the University of Exeter's presence in Cornwall, has enjoyed a long and privileged relationship with Cornwall County Council, and on occasions has been able to work closely with that Council on policy and other issues – most recently in the Cornish Language Partnership. More generally, Cornish Studies as it has developed as an area of academic inquiry over the last decade or two, has been able to offer a multiplicity of insights into Cornwall's past and present, often with significant lessons for the future. History is important here, in the way that David Cannadine suggests, but Cornish Studies is inherently multi-disciplinary and inter-disciplinary, with a particular interest in contemporary issues – including those of governance. History, social science, cultural studies and other areas all contribute to the meld that is Cornish Studies, and its practitioners are by no means confined to the Institute itself – as the international team of contributors to this and earlier editions of the series *Cornish Studies* more than demonstrates. The formidable body of knowledge that comprises Cornish Studies is a significant resource for contemporary Cornwall – *vide* the hugely successful Knowledge Transfer partnership between the Institute and the Royal Cornwall Museum, or the major community linkages forged by the Institute's Cornish Audio Visual Archive project – and as we have observed before, Cornish Studies has much to offer the planners and policymakers entrusted with Cornwall's future: should they care to listen.

The establishment of the new Cornwall Council is an important opportunity to consolidate the relationship between Cornish Studies and contemporary governance in Cornwall, for exactly the reasons that David Cannadine has proposed. Whether or not the new regime might consider the appointment of a 'Chief Cornish Studies Adviser' as part of its supporting infrastructure, there is no doubt that a close relationship should be developed between the new Council and the Institute of Cornish Studies, with the latter viewed as an important reservoir of knowledge and specialist opinion on Cornwall's past, present and future. In projecting its distinctiveness and its aspirations, and in demonstrating its responsiveness to the nuances and subtleties of Cornwall's communities, it is important that Cornwall Council view the Institute as a vital resource, not merely of incidental information but of profound knowledge critical to the elaboration of its own identity and for understanding the nature of modern Cornwall.

This present volume of *Cornish Studies* makes its own contribution to that understanding, probing – as have earlier books in the series – a wide range of issues from the medieval to the modern. As part of the current upsurge in interest in the Cornish language, debate about the possible existence of a medieval Cornish Bible continues apace, with Erik Grigg entering the ring to add his voice to those who consider that there may once have been such a Bible – and, intriguingly, that one might still exist today, hidden away in some archive, library or museum, just as *Bewnans Ke* was until just a few years ago. His is a plea for John Trevisa not to be dismissed too lightly or too swiftly as possible author of a medieval Bible in the Cornish language. As he remarks, the Bible had by that time already been translated into Catalan and Czech, and Trevisa was a champion of the vernacular. William Caxton imagined that Trevisa had produced an English Bible but, as Grigg observes, could have been mistaken – it might have been in Cornish, for Trevisa had the means and opportunity as well as motivation to provide such a translation.

But Grigg's argument does not end there. He also draws attention to the hitherto overlooked Welsh antiquarian and book collector, Robert Vaughan, who between c.1616 and 1625 kept a notebook listing the owners and whereabouts of various Welsh-language manuscripts, the great majority of which he had seen and had attempted to purchase or at least copy or make notes from. Amongst these listed manuscripts was a 'Cornish Bible', said by Vaughan to be in an Oxford library. What happened to this 'Cornish Bible', if indeed it did exist, is a mystery. But Grigg points out that Vaughan was not easily fooled – as a Welsh-speaker he could tell the difference between Welsh and Cornish manuscripts, and he was also familiar with Cornish drama and so unlikely to mistake a miracle play for a Bible. His claim to have had knowledge of a 'Cornish Bible' cannot be easily ignored, therefore, and, at the very least, is deserving of further research. Erik Grigg intends his article as a spur to such research, and postulates a link between the 'Cornish

Bible' of Vaughan's notebook and the supposed Trevisa volume. As he safely concludes, there is 'no doubt that the quest for the medieval Cornish Bible will continue'.

The continuing fascination with the putative medieval Cornish Bible is mirrored in a similar interest in the exploits of the Cornish in the upheavals of the early modern period – in the rebellions of 1497 and 1549, and in the Civil War. The latter is the province of Mark Stoyle, who in a string of scholarly articles and in two major books – *West Britons: Cornish Identities and the Early Modern British State* (Exeter, 2002) and *Soldiers and Strangers: An Ethnic History of the English Civil War* (Yale, 2005) – has demonstrated the importance of Cornish particularism in explaining Cornish allegiances and behaviour in the Civil War. In his contribution in this collection, he considers the experience of the 'Old Cornish Regiments, the five Cornish infantry regiments raised on behalf Charles I in October 1642. Together, these regiments became what Stoyle describes as 'among the most celebrated military formations of the British Civil Wars', and led by their Cornish colonels – Godolphin, Grenville, Slanning, Trevanion, Mohun – they were known collectively as 'the Cornish army'. The early history of the Cornish army is well known, including the spectacular victories of Lansdown and Roundway Down and the capture of Bristol. But the stunning loss of Sir Bevill Grenville at Lansdown, together with the grievous loss of Cornish life – including Slanning and Trevanion – in the pyrrhic victory at Bristol, has led to the historiographical assumption that thereafter the Cornish army was finished as a fighting force. In his article here, Mark Stoyle offers a corrective, arguing that it was not those traumatic events of the summer of 1643 that did for the Cornish but rather the experiences of the subsequent year, culminating in the absorption of the 'Old Cornish' into the main Royalist 'Oxford' field army in December 1644.

It is this 'afterlife' that Stoyle traces here, following the fortunes of the Cornish army as it struggled to maintain both its identity and its reputation. When, in the summer of 1643, the Cornish army had been combined with the Marquis of Hertford's forces at Chard in Somerset, the newly created formation was dubbed 'the Cornish Army': a significant concession to Cornish pride and recognition of Cornish military prowess. But thereafter there were disputes over nomenclature, further suggestions of merger with other forces, and constant leadership changes, all of which to served to erode the Cornish identity of what – under Prince Maurice's command – became known officially as merely the king's 'Western Army'. Although the title 'Cornish army' continued in popular parlance for some time yet to describe the five regiments, it had now dropped out of official usage. But the Cornish continued to exert influence within the Western Army, notably in arguing for an offensive against Parliamentarian Plymouth, which posed a strategic threat to Cornwall. Exeter was captured in some style, but Plymouth proved an altogether more difficult nut to crack. Eventually Maurice gave up and the siege was raised on Christmas Day 1643. There was further fighting in Devon and in Cornwall, including the destruction of Essex's Roundhead forces near Fowey in late summer 1644, a victory in which the 'Old Cornish' shared. By now, however, Sir Richard Grenville was raising his 'New Cornish Tertia', and it appears that many of the 'Old Cornish' simply deserted to this new formation, preferring to serve under Grenville rather than Maurice. Grenville, after all, had presented himself as a Cornish leader putting Cornish interests first. The remnants of the original five regiments struggled on, badly battered at the battle of Newbury, and it was only a matter of time before they met up with the main Royalist army at Oxford, into which they were absorbed. It was the end of the old 'Cornish army'.

It may be, as Mark Stoyle has argued elsewhere, that the events of the Civil War marked the end of a Cornish identity based on rebelliousness and ethnic resistance to intrusion by the English state, with the defeat of the last Cornish rising in 1648 'the *coup de grace* for traditional Cornishness' (*West Britons*, 2002, p. 5.). But, as we know, the Civil War had also produced a new territorial sense of Cornishness, based on the territorial extent of Cornwall itself, and this helped underpin a new and equally distinctive Cornish identity that emerged during the industrial period of the eighteenth and nineteenth centuries. Mining, as it spread eastwards from its western heartlands, lent a sense of ethno-occupational unity to much of the territory of Cornwall, quite literally from Cape Cornwall to the banks of the Tamar, and widespread emigration also emphasized this culture of solidarity. At Grass Valley, Moonta, Johannesburg and scores of other destinations across the globe, individuals from St Just, Redruth, St Blazey, St Cleer and Gunnislake came together to express their common transnational 'Cornishness', not least in opposition to competing ethnic groups. Yet behind this veneer of homogeneity their remained a pattern of myriad differences – at home and overseas. Notwithstanding the pre-eminence of mining, there was a multiplicity of different 'Cornwalls' – fishing communities, agricultural districts, ports and harbours, high moors and sunken sylvan estuaries, north and south coasts, church and chapel, grand houses and the hovels of the poor. St Ives was not Torpoint; Sheviok was not Sancreed. Overseas, Cornish solidarity fragmented as new 'Cornish' communities took on lives of their own, as at Moonta in South Australia, for example, where 'Cousin Jack' identity was increasingly rooted in the locality and correspondingly remote from its origins in Cornwall. And in all this, there were the lives of individuals, of real people, all too often obscured in glib Cornwall-wide generalizations concerned to explain broad trends or to present statistics in which individuals are necessarily subsumed in the mass.

As Cornish Studies has matured, so there has been an increasing willingness to step back from such generalization, and to recognise the value of 'micro' studies which respond explicitly to this pattern of diversity. It is in this spirit that Jan Lokan offers here a detailed 'micro' case study of the experiences of her grandfather, John Goldsworthy, who emigrated from Cornwall to Australia in 1864 as an 18-year-old. A deeply reflexive piece, with a strong sense of historical continuity that binds the late nineteenth-century agricultural development of South Australia's northern Yorke Peninsula to the landscape we observe there today, this article charts the fortunes of one Cornish emigrant as he strove to achieve an ambition shared by many of his compatriots – to shake off the occupation that had drawn him to Australia in the first place, mining, and to acquire the status of an independent farmer, owning and working his own land. The survival of John Goldsworthy's diary from all those years ago provides a unique insight into the struggle to make good that ambition, and reveals the personal and other difficulties he endured as he sought to make his way on the land. As Lokan explains, the liberal-ization of South Australia's land laws in the 1860s encouraged many Cornish miners to exchange the pick for the plough. But northern Yorke Peninsula – the mining country of Moonta, Wallaroo and Kadina – lay at the very edge of 'Goyder's line of rainfull', and the expansion of the agricultural frontier in that district was marked by fearful droughts that drove many aspiring farmers from the land – including, at first, John Goldsworthy. But Goldsworthy succeeded in the end, as did the more tenacious of his neighbours who were able to hold on until better days – and wetter winters – arrived.

Jan Lokan's 'micro' approach also offers insights into nineteenth-century Cornwall itself, such as the pattern of intra-Cornwall mobility that was often a prelude to emigration overseas. As she notes, the Goldsworthy family hailed from west Cornwall, from around Crowan and Camborne, but moved progressively eastwards as the fortunes of the different mines waxed and waned, eventually emigrating to Australia. Explaining this movement, she sheds momentary light on places such as Penpillick, St Ive, Merrymeet and Pensilva, localities often unobserved or overlooked in the generalizations of Cornwall's emigration story. Her discussion of the widespread desire on northern Yorke Peninsula to forsake mining, to achieve the 'independence' and 'respectability' conferred by social mobility – not least by owning and working the land – also resonates with the condition of nineteenth-century Cornwall. Many of those Yorke Peninsula miners may have been small-holders as well as miners back in Cornwall, especially those who had come from the west where there was a long tradition of making croft and wastrel available to mining families for 'improvement' – 'improvement' of both of the land itself and the people who worked it.

Peter Tremewan, also responding explicitly to the call for 'micro' studies at a sub-Cornwall level, echoes this nineteenth-century concern for 'independence' and 'respectability', and finds in those mining communities of west Cornwall – with their small-holdings, cows, pigs and poultry – the 'collateral support' that underpinned a distinct social identity. Beginning with a brief review of Stephen King's seminal study of the relief of poverty in the period 1700 to 1850, Tremewan interrogates the generalized model which suggests a dichotomy between two 'regions' – one in the south and east of England, predominantly rural and agricultural, and one in the north and west which was more urbanized and industrial. In this latter region, to which Cornwall belonged, the poor were offered significantly less support than those in the more rural south and east. Cornwall was also part of a 'sub-region' proposed by King, including parts of Devon, Somerset and Gloucestershire, but even this level of disaggregation is unsatisfactory, argues Tremewan. Cornwall itself, as he points out, was hardly a uniform social and economic area, but rather a collection of dissimilar communities in which (it turns out) there were differing levels of support for the poor.

The Poor Law Amendment Act of 1834 was a watershed in its application of a central plan for the administration of poor relief. In Cornwall it led to the creation of thirteen poor law 'unions', which, despite their disparities in terms of population size, provide the basis from which intra-Cornwall comparisons can be made. In 1851, as Peter Tremewan shows, there was a distinct contrast between the western unions and those in the east. In the north and east of Cornwall, agriculture enjoyed what he terms a 'commanding strength', despite the eastward creep of mining to localities such as Liskeard, whereas from St Austell westwards mining was the major male occupation, except in maritime Falmouth. As Tremewan goes on to demonstrate, this distinction was mirrored in the differing levels of support offered to the poor in west and east Cornwall, with the highest in the far north-east (Stratton) and the lowest in the far west (Penzance). In a sort of microcosm of the King thesis, the more 'urbanized', 'industrialized' mining heartland of the west received significantly less support than in the mainly agricultural east. Tremewan furnishes further evidence to confirm this east–west shift, and then proceeds to seek an explanation for this marked distinction. He finds clues among the answers to the 'Rural Queries' of 1832, designed to gather information about the poor across the country, and discovers that the mining families of west Cornwall were far more likely to possess 'collateral aids' – such as ownership of cottages and land and livestock – than their labouring counterparts in east Cornwall. Such collateral support lent individuals and families their much-prized 'independence' – including non-reliance on the poor law – and engendered the self-help, 'improvement' ethos of Cornish Methodism and west Cornwall's many friendly societies, creating in turn the social 'respectability' to which many aspired. As Peter Tremewan concludes, this east–west divide reflected much earlier divisions within Cornwall, cultural as well as economic – including the Fowey–Camel line as linguistic and economic boundary – one which had 'long roots back into the early modern period'. 'Traditional Cornishness' may not, after all, have met its demise in 1648.

By the early twentieth century, however, there were those who feared that 'traditional Cornishness' of any sort had all but disappeared. The trauma of de-industrialization in the latter part of the nineteenth century, and the consequent acceleration of the 'Great Emigration' of Cornish people to destinations up-country and overseas, was reflected in a crisis of identity as the bedrock of Cornwall's industrial prowess was all but swept away. Diversification into china clay extraction, horticulture and other activities had offered some cause for optimism in the early years of the twentieth century. But the events of the Great War and its aftermath had nipped much of this in the bud, and by the 1920s Cornwall was firmly in the grip of its socio-economic 'paralysis'. Earlier in the century, Henry Jenner had secured recognition from a sometimes sceptical Pan-Celtic world of Cornwall's status as a 'Celtic nation' but by the end of the First World War the project to re-invent Cornwall's Celticity anew appeared to have faltered. As Derek R. Williams argues in his article, one response to this apparent impasse – in which, as Robert Morton Nance wrote in 1925, 'Celtic things here are literally gasping for the vital breath' – was to try to place Cornwall centre-stage in the Celtic world by inviting the Celtic Congress to hold its annual conference at a Cornish location.

As Williams goes on to show, the invitation was from the beginning fraught with difficulty. Against the background of continuing scepticism about Cornwall's claims, and what proved to be a less than tight adminis-trative regime within the Celtic Congress itself, the proposal struggled to make headway after it was first mooted in 1920. Not that it was without its supporters: D. Rhys Phillips, secretary of the Celtic Congress until 1925, argued that a 'visit to Cornwall, while Dr Henry Jenner is still hale and hearty would I think … make a wonderful impression', adding later that 'The invitation from Cornwall is open … it would be a fine thing to crown his [Jenner's] great Celtic devotion by giving them the Congress for one year'. It was a point that Phillips was not afraid to repeat – in 1923 he found himself insisting that 'Even tho' Cornwall is commercially and industrially stricken, we may never see Dr Jenner again and a brief Celtic Congress there … wd therefore be a gallant thing to do'. But gallantry aside, Nance – who was a leading advocate of Cornwall as a Congress venue – knew well that there was continuing suspicion regarding Cornish claims, and he settled down for the diplomatic long haul.

In 1924, in the aftermath of the Celtic Congress that year in Quimper, Brittany, Nance and Jenner renewed their request for the Congress to meet in Cornwall, suggesting the next year, 1925. But the 1925 Congress was held instead in Dublin, in Ireland, prompting Nance to press even more vociferously for a Congress in Cornwall in the following year, 1926. Yet it was not until February of that year that he learnt of his success and the Congress' decision to plump for Cornwall at last, a decision that left perilously little time to make all the necessary conference arrangements. Penzance was agreed as the location and a committee formed. However, the committee seemed to flounder from the first, with little idea of what was required and experiencing great difficulty in eliciting support or advice from the Congress itself. Things were not helped by the industrial turmoil that had by now gripped Britain – 1926 was the year of the 'General Strike' – and, in the face of continuing hesitancy and uncertainty in Cornwall's organizing committee, E.T. John wrote to Nance on behalf of the Congress. He suggested that, with the prospect of few delegates being prepared to brave the industrial strife to travel to distant Penzance, it might be sensible to postpone the Congress in Cornwall. It was a lifeline that was accepted with some relief. As Derek R. Williams concludes, even without the upheavals of 1926, it is doubtful whether the cultural infrastructure in Cornwall would have been robust enough to support a Congress conference. In its way, this failure was another manifestation of Cornwall's 'paralysis', at its most profound in the 1920s. Nonetheless, it was a tribute to the determination of the Cornish Celtic Revivalists to rise above this disability that they persevered in their aims, not only establishing the Cornish Gorseth in 1928 but at last hosting the much sought after Celtic Congress in Cornwall in 1932, when it was a 'complete success from beginning to end', as Nance recorded.

The socio-economic 'paralysis' of inter-war Cornwall affected many aspects of Cornish life. As Catherine Mills and Pamela Dale demonstrate in their ground-breaking discussion of public health in Cornwall in this period, health care provision was one such area. Still locked in a tradition that prioritized male health – a legacy of long-standing occupational health concerns associated with the mining industry – Cornwall appeared resistant to central government attempts to focus attention on the welfare of women and children. In 1929 the Local Government Act transferred many of the Poor Law functions to local authorities. This was the cue for the Ministry of Health to initiate detailed public health surveys of each county and county borough council, including Cornwall, with a view to assessing local services against criteria devised by the Ministry. From the beginning, the survey team identified Cornwall as 'backward', the Ministry of Health having 'long been frustrated by the apparent determination of Cornwall County Council to do as little as possible in the field of public health'. When Dr Allan C. Parsons completed his survey of Cornwall in 1931, he found that things were worse than he had imagined, not least in comparison to neighbouring

Devon and Somerset. Yet Parsons was prepared to consider Cornwall a 'special case', suffering as it was from an unusual set of circumstances and disadvantages. Remoteness from London was considered a disability, as was the 'unhelpful' dispersion of the population across the countryside instead of its concentration in more urban areas. Overall, the population was in decline – a function, it was reported, of the continuing difficulties experienced by Cornwall's staple industries – and although the number of people receiving indoor and outdoor relief was not seen as excessive, there was no doubt that Cornwall was 'poor'.

Parsons' main criticism of public health provision in Cornwall was two-fold. Firstly, Cornish 'vital statistics' – everything from maternal mortality rates to deaths from cancer – were deteriorating as those elsewhere in Britain were improving. Secondly, he found no evidence of official concern in Cornwall about this state of affairs. He criticized a lack of ambition in both health officials and councillors, especially those connected with the apparently ineffectual public health and housing committee. Staffing was a problem – there were too few health professionals, and they were under-qualified and poorly paid and badly organized – and everywhere there was what Parsons called a 'spirit of defeatism'. Specialist provision for women and children was especially weak. However, the picture was not universally bleak. The lunatic asylum at Bodmin was well managed, Parsons found, while the treatment of tuberculosis and venereal disease in Cornwall showed what could be done with imaginative use of limited resources. But health care provision was at best patchy. Ultimately the problem was political, Parsons concluded, with the now dominant agricultural interest in Cornwall reluctant to spend money and unable to appreciate the benefits of investment in public services. He may well have been right. But as Mills and Dale observe, in his 'top down' assessment of Cornwall's public health provision, Parsons had probably paid insufficient attention to what they term Cornish 'alternative traditions of independence and self-help, strongly embedded in local work cultures' – those very 'traditional' qualities identified by Tremewan in nineteenth-century Cornwall. Parsons had also missed the historic emphasis on occupational rather than public health (for example, the relative strength of tuberculosis and orthopaedic provision in the mining areas), this being a male-oriented focus which reflected Cornish culture and work practices. As Catherine Mills and Pamela Dale conclude, it was this, rather than the supposed 'backwardness' perceived by central government, which led to the paucity of provision for women and children. Moreover, they add, this 'emphasis on work and working conditions had arguably the further damaging effect of linking the health of the community to the state of its main industry, which allowed the terminal decline of the latter to overshadow attempts to promote the former'.

In the half century and more since the end of the Second World War in 1945, Cornwall has been comprehensively 're-invented'. Although today there are still issues of severe socio-economic disadvantage that Dr Parsons would have recognized in the 1930s, Cornwall in the early twenty-first century is perceived as an outstandingly desirable tourist destination, with a firmly established repertoire of attractive cultural 'difference' complemented now by the new high-quality exoticism of Rick Stein restaurants and the Eden Project. It is against this background that Graham Busby and Kevin Meethan consider the question of 'cultural capital' in Cornwall. As they explain, this cultural capital is of two types – 'personal' and 'destination-based'. The first is related to an individual's level of education, and his or her predisposition to value one cultural form over another. The second refers to the potential economic value which may be derived from the inventory of cultural 'assets' at a given tourist destination. As Busby and Meethan note, the rise of 'heritage tourism' in Cornwall has led to the deployment of both forms of cultural capital. Alighting upon Cornwall's 'church heritage' as a case study, they examine both types of cultural capital in Cornwall, and investigate where the nexus between the two might exist.

Destination-based cultural capital, it is explained, is either 'latent' (usually tangible, such as ancient buildings) or 'potential' (such as the association of a geographic locality with a famous author). In Cornwall, for example, the association of Daphne du Maurier with Lanteglos-by-Fowey, one of the 'Cornish church heritage' sites considered by Busby and Meethan, is a classic example of the latter, situating the church as apart of the wider 'du Maurier Country' celebrated in the eponymous annual festival held at Fowey. Comments from tourists in the church's Visitor Book in 2000 demonstrate the process. 'Can see where Daphne du Maurier gained some of her inspiration', wrote a visitor from Wales; 'Felt Daphne's spirit', added a tourist from Germany. In establishing the Daphne du Maurier Festival in 1997, Restormel Borough Council commodified this latent destination-based cultural capital, complementing the earlier commodification exemplified in Hollywood adaptations of du Maurier novels such as *Rebecca* but now rooting the author in one specific and easily identifiable geographic location in mid-Cornwall.

To the 'potential' cultural capital invested in places like Lanteglos-by-Fowey, explain Busby and Meethan, is added the intrinsic 'latent' cultural capital of such venerable sites. Ancient churches across Cornwall routinely draw their devotees from far and wide, including the descendents of Cornish emigrants overseas, with several ecclesiastical sites – notably St Just-in-Roseland – enjoying international reputations as 'heritage' destinations. Inevitably, such sites act as irresistible draws to tourists with strongly developed personal cultural capital, the 'Celtic' attributes of saintly dedications, ancient crosses, holy wells and so on enticing the visitors who – armed already with their Simon Jenkins' *Thousand Best Churches* or Nickolaus Pevsner's *Cornwall* guide – make their well-informed pilgrimages to these distant churches. 'Is the stained glass by Kemp, or perhaps his pupil??' was the educated guess of one visitor at Gunwalloe in 2000; 'Incredible to find the remains of original rood screen in a Cornish church' added another sophisticated *aficionado*. Here, indeed, is the nexus between destination-based and personal cultural capital, as the well-educated tourist visitors 'with their Pesvner and Jenkins guides or their du Maurier novels and Betjeman poems, seek the hidden sanctuaries of the Celtic "Saints of Cornwall" about which they have read so much'.

Robert Dickinson, in his contribution, also addresses the relationship between tourism and representations of Cornwall in travel writing. Focussing on the period 1949 to 2007, he notes, like Busby and Meethan, the commodi-fication of cultural sites for tourist consumption, pointing to the key role of travel writing in this process. In Cornwall, as elsewhere, such writings 'spin webs of colonizing power', he argues, and in the post-War era under review he detects a shift in the way the Cornish themselves have been represented in such literature: from the conquered but subdued 'Other' to the conquered but hostile 'Other'. This period was, he notes, one of profound socio-economic change in Cornwall, marked by high in-migration, persistent unemployment, and a growth in 'Cornish national consciousness' which found its way onto the political agenda. To chart the shifts in representations over time, he alights upon key travel writers, from Ruth Manning-Sanders and her *The West of England* of 1949 to Paul Gogarty's *The Coast Road* (2007), taking in along the way John Hillaby, Paul Theroux and Ian Aitch. None of these is entirely original, Dickinson remarks, in the sense that they all draw to a greater or lesser degree on earlier writings, so that 'discursive echoes of the past' continue to be heard in these modern accounts. Thus, for example, 'the Cornish in these texts are represented as inferiors, racially impure and strange, while Cornwall is remapped as partly Cornish and partly English'. The boundaries of Cornwall are themselves uncertain and confused – the Tamar is the border but the land of 'Cornwall, not-England' is encountered further west. For Manning-Sanders, for example, 'the "essential Cornwall" lies west of a line drawn from Hayle to Marazion, while England begins as the road widens east of Liskeard'.

Robert Dickinson suggests that both Manning-Sanders and Hillaby continued to represent Cornwall within the discursive space of nineteenth-century Romanticism, with Cornwall occupying an ambiguous, hybrid position – not unlike that of the English Lake District, whose own hybridity combined the threatening Celtic wildness of Scotland with a reassuring Home Counties picturesqueness. The further west one travelled in Cornwall, according to this Romantic view, the more 'foreign' in appearance were the landscape and its people, with Cornwall's 'difference' rooted in a 'foreign past' which had shaped this physiognomy. By contrast, Dickinson argues, the more recent accounts of Theroux, Aitch and Gogarty portray the Cornish as living in a 'strange present', one 'where they do things differently'. Here Cornwall is 'creepy', where the locals 'can do what they like' (as Aitch writes), a surreal, bizarre world exemplified (according to Gogarty) in the eccentricities of Cornish 'Druid', Ed Prynn. Cornwall now is not so much 'foreign', as 'strange'. Coupled to this shift in representations of Cornwall is the parallel shift in portrayals of the Cornish, who remain a 'conquered' Other but are now actively 'hostile' rather than passively 'subdued'. For Theroux, it is tourism that has 'made the Cornish nationalistic', a nihilistic xenophobia aimed at 'Englishness' rather than a positive affirmation of Cornish identity, while Gogarty's unashamedly colonialist discourse draws comparisons with Native American society, with the 'dwindling pool of indigenous inhabitants' forced from their harbourside dwellings to their 'reservation' in inland Cornwall. This inland Cornwall, it turns out, is largely off the tourist map, and is not the 'real' Cornwall of the tourist imagination. As Dickinson concludes, it is tourism that mediates portrayals of Cornwall, and during the period 1949–2007 the 'aesthetics of high Romanticism have been subverted by the economics of mass consumerism as the tourist industry becomes the dominant influence fashioning representations of Cornwall, commodifying Cornwall for urban consumption'. As he puts it: 'Gone are the sea monsters, mermaids and megaliths, replaced by Rick Stein's restaurants, the Pilchard Works and the Eden Project'.

The growth in 'Cornish consciousness' noted by Robert Dickinson is illuminated in detail by Joanie Willett, who in her piece asks whether this perceived Cornish identity is merely a 'vague notion', a slippery and inchoate phenomenon that does not lend itself to sustained analysis, or whether it is a 'social fact' – something that can be interrogated through the close application of social science methodology, both qualitative and quantitative. As she explains, it was the sociologist Emile Durkheim who first proposed the concept of 'social facts' – societal 'realities' that can be discovered through empirical research. Durkheim also suggested that such 'social facts' existed on a graduated scale, from the 'morphological fact' fully integrated and continuously visible in the everyday life of a society to the 'transitory outbreaks' that are occasionally observable as now and again waves of passion or activity break through the surface of society. In determining whether Cornish identity might be deemed a 'social fact', therefore, Joanie Willett was also concerned to discover where it might lie on this graduated scale. Noting that 'identity' is itself a complex concept, with current scholarship stressing both its dynamic quality and its tendency towards hybridization, she adds that, although there has been considerable discussion of Cornish identity in its historical context, there is only a limited social science literature on contemporary Cornish identity. Hence the empirical research reported in her article: the first, she claims, to attempt a representative cross-section of the population of Cornwall, and the first to distinguish between 'civic' and 'ethnic' conceptions of Cornish identity as well as to ask what criteria individuals deploy to decide their own (or other people's) 'Cornishness'.

Employing a blend of qualitative (focus group) and quantitative (questionnaire) methods, Joanie Willett teases out answers to a complex series of questions, and comes up with some intriguing results. For example, of the 150 questionnaire respondents, 57 per cent considered themselves Cornish, 41 per cent felt more Cornish than English (answering either 'Cornish not English' or 'more Cornish than English'), and 56 per cent considered themselves Cornish instead of British or English. These uncertain boundaries of identity were observable throughout the study; for example, in the tendency of some respondents who had not identified as 'Cornish' in answer to Question 1 of the questionnaire to nonetheless select 'Cornish' options in the subsequent question, indicating both their own uncertainty and the importance of personal 'choice' in determining individual identity. As Willet guides us through the complex world of these responses, it becomes clear that – in addition to the highly problematic relationship between 'Cornish', 'English' and 'British' identities – there are both 'ethnic' and 'civic' identities at work. The former stresses the importance of genealogical affinity, of being born in Cornwall of Cornish parentage or outside Cornwall of Cornish descent, while the latter emphasizes the socializing ability of 'Cornishness' to embrace a wider, more inclusive grouping – including, for example, in-migrants from various backgrounds who have developed a strong sense of 'belonging'. As Willett observes, it is clear from her results that contemporary Cornish identity 'is complex, dynamic, and a significant factor in the lives of the majority of people in Cornwall'. Does this make it a 'social fact'? Joanie Willett concludes that it does, and in attempting to place her results in Durkheim's scale, suggests that while Cornish identity may not be a 'morphological fact' – exhibited prominently across the full range of day-to-day life in Cornwall – it is far more than a 'transitory outbreak'. It corresponds best, she suggests, to the 'institutionalized norms' proposed by Durkheim, where local institutions refer routinely (if sometimes only superficially) to the specific identity in question, reflecting its everyday presence (if not salience) in society's deliberations.

This conclusion resonates strongly with Cheryl Hayden's article, in which – as an Australian of Cornish descent – she expresses surprise that the Cornish rebellions of the early modern period are comparatively little known and not widely understood in Cornwall, and that its leaders are not routinely celebrated here as 'martyrs' or 'heroes' as they might be in other societies. Increasingly fascinated by the gaps and silences of the historical record, Hayden decided that she should try to restore the 'subaltern voice' that had been all but erased by 'history'. In Cornwall, there is a strong tradition of historical fiction, with 'historical novels' from the pens of authors such as Sir Arthur Quiller Couch, Daphne du Maurier and E.V. Thompson deploying imaginative creative writing and the judicious application of literary license to bring alive long-past events for audiences who might not normally read 'history'. Cheryl Hayden implicitly places herself within this tradition. But her novel *A Christmas Game* is designed not merely to bring a wider appreciation of the 1549 rebellion to the reading public, but has the explicit intention of giving voice to the silenced rebels, of restoring them as significant actors in the story of early modern Cornwall. Here she explains, in another deeply reflexive article in this collection, how she accomplished this task. As she puts it, 'To create the novel I imagined, I would need to understand the relationship between history and fiction, recognize and counteract the techniques employed hitherto by "history" to ensure that the rebels remained quiet, and to locate places where echoes of their voices may still remain.'

Like Robert Dickinson, Cheryl Haydon sees in the mainstream treatment of Cornish history 'webs of colonizing power', and alights upon the 'subaltern school of post-colonial theory' – in particular the work of Ranajit Guha – as an analytical tool to help understand and deconstruct that history. Examining the historiography of the 1549 rebellion, Hayden concedes that in recent years there has been a concerted attempt by some historians – notably Mark Stoyle – to discuss the history of early modern Cornwall from a Cornish perspective. But she adds that this determined attempt to place Cornwall and the Cornish within the 'new British historiography' has largely fallen on deaf ears in the historical establishment, with Skidmore's recent *Edward VI* (2007) the latest generalized work to pay scant attention to the Cornish dimension. Moreover, she argues, such has been the unwillingness to consider the rebel voice, that several important documents that provide significant insights into that 'voice' have been regularly overlooked. Building on these, and deconstructing John Hooker's sixteenth-century 'eye witness' account of the events of 1549, Hayden rescues the 'rebels' – the 'refuse, scum, and rascals' – from the denigration of history and restores to them agency and the power of rational thought and action. As she explains, the challenge in her novel was to tell the story of 1549 in such a way that her readers would be able to enter the hearts and minds of the Cornish rebels, empathizing with them and understanding their motives and aspirations. Fictional characters such as 'Margh Tredannack', 'Kitto Trigg' and 'Jan Spargo' are the means by which such empathy and insight are achieved, articulating for the reader 'the passion, the logic, the fear and love' that surely drove these people to fight for their cause. In this way, as Cheryl Haydon concludes, it may be possible at last to give voice to those 'rebels' of long ago – and to ensure that they are heard.

The extent to which historians of Cornwall have penetrated the 'new British historiography' is also considered by Bernard Deacon in his review article of John Rule's recent collection *Cornish Cases: Essays in Eighteenth and Nineteenth Century Social History*. Like Hayden, Deacon believes that these Cornish attempts at penetration have been only marginally successful. In any case, he adds, the new British historiography is itself open to criticism on a number of grounds, not least that – despite the original vision of J.G. Pocock which envisaged a 'new British history' that encompassed the entire modern period and looked globally to a wider 'British world' – it has in practice become preoccupied with state formation processes in the British Isles in the early modern period. John Rule, in introducing the *Cornish Cases* collection, offers his series of essays – most of which have been published before – as contributions to the 'new Cornish historiography', the Cornish variant which has sought to influence and engage with the wider British history. But Bernard Deacon is not convinced. As well as noting Rule's sceptical, slightly suspicious view of the normative assumptions underpinning the new Cornish historiography, Deacon argues that Rule's real contribution lies in other directions. This is not only in the wider writing of comparative British social history, something stressed by Roger Burt in his Foreword to *Cornish Cases*, but also in the agenda-setting potential of John Rule's Cornish work presented in his book. As Deacon remarks, Rule's 'book implicitly provides a map with which we can find our way to a more nuanced historical approach that transcends those limitations [of both the new Cornish historiography and the social history tradition] and prefigures the potential shape of Cornish history'.

In criticizing Rule's 'quietism' thesis – the view that Methodism and the tribute system combined to retard the emergence of trade unions and the political Labour movement in Cornwall – Deacon finds in Rule's essays other explanatory evidence, not yet fully evaluated: the role of friendly societies, for example, or the importance of 'collateral aids' in the mining areas of west Cornwall. Renewed focus on such evidence – such as that presented by Peter Tremewan in this volume of *Cornish Studies* – would be one way ahead for Cornish historical research. This, as Bernard Deacon explains, might lead to 'an all-encompassing ethnographic history' of Cornwall in all its manifestations, a series of in-depth 'micro studies' which, deploying a deliberate 'triangulation' of methods, would seek 'new angles on old subjects'. Tragically, as John Rule remarks in *Cornish Cases*, this is exactly what Rule had planned to attempt himself had he not been overtaken by illness, a detailed ethnographic history of Cornwall's mining and fishing communities. It will now be for others to pursue that task. As Rule comments in the closing paragraph of his book, historians of sufficient imagination – 'although hardly [able to] live among those who culture they seek to understand' – can emulate the ethnographic techniques of anthropologists to ensure that 'voices' from the past can still be heard. And, as Bernard Deacon concludes in his review article, John Rule has already done much to rescue these labouring communities of eighteenth and nineteenth-century Cornwall from the 'enormous condescension of posterity', and for that reason especially *Cornish Cases* 'deserves to be on the bookshelves of anyone with a serious interest in Cornish history' – including, one might suggest, the members and officers of the new Cornwall Council.

Professor Philip Payton,
Director, Institute of Cornish Studies,
School of Humanities and Social Sciences,
University of Exeter, Cornwall Campus

I

The Medieval Cornish Bible
More Evidence

Erik Grigg

Introduction

An article by Charles Penglase in *Etudes Celtiques* has stimulated a vigorous debate in recent volumes of *Cornish Studies* about the possible existence of a Medieval Cornish Bible. Penglase argued that Tregear's Cornish translation of Bonner's *Homilies* (c.1556) contained duplicates of all Biblical quotes in an older form of Cornish because Tregear had utilized extracts from a Medieval Cornish Bible to give his work moral authority.[1] Malte Tschirschky, in *Cornish Studies: Eleven*, criticized Penglase's work, suggesting that Tregear had fabricated the archaic sounding quotes and that calls for a Cornish Bible during the Reformation confirm that no earlier medieval translation had ever existed.[2] Matthew Spriggs then unearthed further historical references to a medieval Cornish Bible, and also pointed out that during the Reformation there was actually no specific call to translate the Bible into Cornish. But Spriggs concluded, *inter alia*, that it is unlikely that there were enough literate medieval Cornish scholars to produce a Cornish Bible.[3] This article seeks to continue this debate, arguing that previous contributions have missed some important evidence and made some erroneous assumptions.

Various commentators have argued that that the failure to translate the Bible (and the Prayer Book) into Cornish accelerated the replacement of the language by English, in the process destroying the last vestiges of its status and esteem.[4] When a language is utilized as a vehicle for the 'Word of God' it gains authority, something that Cornish appeared to lack by the sixteenth and seventeenth centuries when the local gentry saw it as merely the tongue of the poor and powerless.[5] In the eighteenth century, as part of a 'revivalist' project to restore the language, Cornish scholars such as William Gwavas (1676–1741) and John Keigwin (1641–1710) advocated the production of a Bible in Cornish; in 2002, as part of the contemporary revivalist movement, the New Testament appeared in Unified Cornish Revised, to be followed two years later by a Common Cornish version.[6] These attempts to produce a Cornish Bible demonstrate that even in today's secular age a Bible translation gives credibility to a language. And, as the Bible is a large and complex book, such translation inevitably stimulates academic study of the language in question.

Evidence for a 'Cornish Bible'

Some important pieces of Cornish literature (including the only known copy of the play *Beunans Meriasek*) and a vast amount of Welsh literature (*The Book of Taliesin, Brut Y Tywysogion, The Black Book of Carmarthen* and *The White Book of Rhydderch*) only exist today thanks to the work of the Welsh antiquarian and book collector Robert Vaughan (c.1592–1667). Between about 1616 and 1625, Vaughan kept a notebook listing the owners of various interesting Welsh language manuscripts, in which he noted a 'Cornish Bible' in a public library in Oxford (by which he probably means the Bodleian).[7] It seems extremely likely that Vaughan had actually seen the volumes he had listed, as he later bought many of the items mentioned in the notebook or tried to have made notes or copies of ones he could not acquire. All the texts mentioned in his notebook still exist in some form or another, with the exception of the enigmatic 'Cornish Bible', and so are not figments of Vaughan's imagination. Indeed, some 13 of the 43 texts he noted are now in the National Library of Wales, having come from Vaughan's collection when it passed to the nation in 1909.

We know that Vaughan attended Oriel College Oxford in 1612, so if the report of the 'Cornish Bible' had been hearsay, he could have investigated it easily and struck it from his notebook. If the Bible was merely a medieval Latin Bible from Cornwall, rather than one in the Cornish language, it is unlikely that a Puritan such as Vaughan would have been interested in it.[8] It is inconceivable that he could have mistaken a Welsh Bible or a Cornish Biblical play for a Cornish Bible, as Vaughan was a native Welsh speaker and familiar with Cornish drama. A Breton Bible may have fooled a Welshman, but there is no evidence of a Breton translation for another two and a half centuries.[9] Yet if Vaughan did see a Cornish Bible in Oxford, there is no record of it in later catalogues of his collection – though these often omit the 'gems', suggesting perhaps that the family locked away the finest books when visitors perused the collection. It would have been difficult for Vaughan to make a copy of such a large work, and, although there is no sign of a medieval Cornish Bible in the Bodleian catalogues today, it would also have been difficult for Vaughan to buy a book from a public library.

The King James Bible, published in 1611, heavily influenced English literature and the William Morgan Bible, published in 1620, had a similar effect on the Welsh language. In Cornish, the effects of a medieval Bible may not have been limited to Tregear's *Homilies* as Penglase supposes. Around 1400–1450, two major pieces of Cornish literature appeared, which suggests a strong tradition of sophisticated writing in Cornish in the early fifteenth century.[10] The first was *Pascon agan Arluth* ('The Passion of Our Lord'), a poem telling the Biblical story of the Resurrection, while the second is the massive three mystery plays in one called the *Ordinalia*, a dramatization of large sections of the Bible.[11] The similarities between the themes and wording of these two works[12] could well be the result of the influence of a Cornish Bible, suggesting that if there was a Cornish Bible, it was produced around 1400 or before.[13]

Attempts to translate the Bible into Cornish in the early eighteenth century suggest that if a Cornish Bible existed, it was lost sometime after Vaughan's note. Even if the Vaughan reference is correct, Penglase's assertion that the Bible was well known ('bien connue') seems unlikely.[14] The mystery play *Gwreans an Bys*, written in 1611, contains similar material to earlier Cornish Biblical literature, but we cannot be certain that the author utilized a Cornish Bible or merely replicated sections of the *Ordinalia*.[15] Tschirschky claims that there were calls during the Reformation for a Cornish Bible, which implies that such a book did not exist already, although Spriggs has pointed out there is no real evidence for the existence of such demands at that time. During the 1549 Prayer Book Rebellion, the rebels rejected the English Prayer Book, asking that 'the Byble and all other bokes of scripture in Englyshe' be recalled and insisting upon a return to services in Latin (though perhaps they may have aspired initially to services in Cornish).[16] In 1560, both the Bishop of Exeter and an ecclesiastical petition suggested that those Cornish children who could not speak English should learn the Catechism in Cornish.[17] None of this evidence suggests a request for a Cornish Bible (such a translation would have required an Act of Parliament, and at no point was one proposed). But while there is no mention of a Cornish Bible in the sixteenth century, there is some evidence that the Cornish was used in church services in medieval times, with the Cornish language playing a major role in the ecclesiastical life of Cornwall.[18]

Matthew Spriggs has found some previously undiscovered post-Reformation references to a Cornish Bible. He cites a 1691/92 letter from John Aubrey to the Celtic linguist Edward Lhuyd, in which Aubrey recounts a meeting in a London coffee house with a Cornish gentlemen who claimed that Keigwin had a Cornish Bible.[19] Spriggs has also found two documents (dated 1740 and 1753), once owned by the Cornish antiquarian William Borlase (1695–1772), that mention acquaintances who promised to supply a Cornish Bible written by John Trevisa. There is also a reference in 1875 in the *Quarterly Review* to a Cornish Bible, translated by Trevisa, said to exist among papers once owned by Borlase.[20] The published works of Lhuyd and Borlase make no mention of such a Cornish Bible, although it is possible that Borlase could have found a Cornish Bible (not subsequently preserved with his other papers) in the period between the publication of his final book and his death. Both Spriggs and Trevisa's biographer, David Fowler, are dismissive of these reports. The coffee house conversation sounds like hearsay regarding Keigwin's own attempts to translate the Bible, some of the other reports simply suggest confusion with medieval Cornish works with a Biblical theme, and two of the three references to Trevisa having produced a Cornish Bible could have been copied from the earliest reference.[21] However, the name 'Trevisa' in the Cornish references is an intriguing detail not easily explained away.

John de Trevisa (c.1342–1402) was a Cornish clergyman (who almost certainly spoke Cornish) and a prodigious translator credited with preventing French from all but extinguishing the English language.[22] Trevisa believed that learning should be open to all and translated into the vernacular language of England various books of knowledge, including the huge general world history *Polychronico*'.[23] He studied at Oxford and was a contemporary (and friend it seems) of the early Lollards, who believed that the Word of God should be taught in the vernacular, not Latin. From the time of Caxton (1482) onwards, Trevisa was widely credited with translating the Bible, although historians cannot identify his hand in any known English Bible.[24] We know he had translated a small part of the Bible into French, as it appears painted on the ceiling of the chapel of his patron Lord Berkeley. Trevisa initially attended Exeter College, but later moved to Queens where Wycliff and some of his followers had also decamped. In 1378, Trevisa and a group of his fellows fell out with the authorities and ran off with a Bible, a Latin grammar and various Biblical commentaries (all he would need for a Biblical translation).[25] They returned the books in 1380 and Trevisa resumed his career in the Church. Trevisa had the ability, motive and opportunity to produce a Cornish Bible. The association of any other medieval Cornishman with references to a Cornish Bible might be readily dismissed. But mention of Trevisa by those claiming to have seen a Cornish Bible suggests an intimate knowledge of his life and work, a scholarly understanding rather than the empty assertions of an idle boaster, and such references are not so easily brushed aside.

In his article, Spriggs doubts if Trevisa could have managed a project the size of a Bible translation without help, and he suspects that there not were enough Cornishmen lettered in their language to justify such a project.[26] Yet Oxford University produced many Cornish scholars, some of whom Trevisa would have met, especially in Exeter College, which was set up in 1314 specifically for scholars from Devon and Cornwall. In Cornwall, literacy standards may have been higher than Spriggs imagines.[27] The Cornish play *Beunans Meriasek*, for example, contains a scene in which a drunken Grammar Master teaches his pupils Latin. The play was probably performed in the tiny village of Camborne (of which St Meriasek was patron), and the private tutoring of Cornish children in Latin must have been common enough for the audience to understand the joke.[28] The nearby College at Glasney was a significant seat of learning where very accomplished medieval Cornish literature was produced.[29]

There were contemporary parallels to the putative medieval project to produce a Cornish Bible: Catalan and Czech versions of the Bible had already appeared by Trevisa's day, indicating that the translation into vernacular languages was not unknown even at that early date. Only about 34,000 people spoke Cornish in 1400,[30] but a relatively small number of speakers has not always been a deterrent to translation. In Victorian times, for example, the Australian Methodist missionary James Egan Moulton translated the entire Bible into Tongan single-handed; the modern population of Tonga (about 116,000 in 2008) remains far less than that of modern Cornwall.

Conclusion

John Trevisa, widely credited with translating the Bible, was a Cornish translator who believed in spreading ideas in the vernacular. During 1378–80 he vanished with all the materials needed to produce a Bible, and in such circumstances it would be surprising if he had not attempted translation of at least part of the Bible into his native Cornish language. Shortly afterwards, as we have seen, some major pieces of Cornish literature on Biblical themes appeared, all of which seem to use similar phrasing suggestive of a single authoritative source. Much later, the book collector and expert on the Welsh tongue, Robert Vaughan, noted the existence of a 'Cornish Bible' in a library in Oxford. Eighteenth- and nineteenth-century references likewise mentioned a Cornish Bible, this time in relation to the collection of William Borlase (who like Trevisa and Vaughan had attended Oxford University), and specifically named the translator as John Trevisa. It is easy to dismiss each piece of evidence singly, but taken together the case seems more compelling, suggesting that John Trevisa may indeed have translated the Bible: not into English, as Caxton assumed, but Cornish.

Spriggs and Tschirschky conclude their articles in the hope that they are proved wrong and that a Cornish Bible did exist; I hope I am proved right and that such a Bible still exists today, awaiting discovery. It would be the only surviving medieval Cornish work in prose and would massively increase our lexicon of Cornish-language words. If a copy still exists it will be very difficult to find. Rare medieval books may only be ordered in libraries by readers who knows the catalogue numbers of what they seek: the British Library (which owns many of Borlase's papers), the National Library of Wales (which houses Vaughan's collection) and the Bodleian are unlikely to let members of the public behind the counter to investigate possible miscataloging. But the recent discovery of the fifteenth-century Cornish-language play *Bewnans Ke* in the National Library of Wales shows that such finds are not impossible, and no doubt the quest for the medieval Cornish Bible will continue.

Notes and references

1. C. Penglase, 'La Bible en moyen-cornique', *Etudes Celtiques*, 33 (1997), pp. 233–43.
2. M. Tschirschky, 'The Medieval "Cornish Bible"', in Philip Payton (ed.), *Cornish Studies: Eleven* (Exeter, 2003), pp. 308–16.
3. M. Spriggs, 'Additional Thoughts on the Medieval "Cornish Bible"', in Philip Payton (ed.), *Cornish Studies: Fourteen* (Exeter, 2006), pp. 44–55.
4. A.D.S. Smith, *The Story of the Cornish Language* (Camborne, 1969), p. 9; P.B. Ellis, *The Story of the Cornish Language* (Redruth, 1998), p. 13.
5. Ellis, *Cornish Language*, p. 17.
6. Ellis, *Cornish Language*, pp. 15–16; P.B. Ellis, *The Cornish Language and Literature* (London, 1974), p. 113; P.A.S. Pool, *The Death of Cornish* (Penzance, 1975), p. 17.
7. Vaughan's notebook is now in the National Library of Wales in Aberystwyth. It has also been reprinted in D. Huws, *Medieval Welsh Manuscripts* (Aberystwyth, 2000), pp. 299–302. The Bodleian Library was founded in 1602 by Thomas Bodley, an Exeter gentleman who had a great passion for languages and represented St Germans in Cornwall in Parliament.
8. Unlike most medieval Bibles, almost none of Vaughan's books was illuminated. Huws, *Manuscripts*, p. 295.
9. Le Gonidec's 1866 translation.
10. Smith, *Cornish Language*, p. 4.
11. Ellis, *Cornish Language*, p. 11.
12. J.A. Bakere, *The Cornish Ordinalia: A Critical Study* (Cardiff, 1980), pp. 103–8.
13. C. Fudge, *The Life of Cornish* (Redruth, 1982), pp. 19–20.
14. Penglase, 'La Bible', p. 241.
15. Ellis, *Cornish Language*, p. 15.
16. J. Youings, 'The South-Western Rebellion of 1549', *Southern History* 1 (1979), pp. 99–122, pp. 109, 114; M. Stoyle, 'The Dissidence of Despair: Rebellion

and Identity in Early Modern Cornwall', *Journal of British Studies* 38.4 (1999), pp. 423–44, p. 438.

17. Spriggs, 'Additional Thoughts', p. 49; Ellis, *Cornish Language and Literature*, p. 63.

18. Ellis, *Cornish Language*, pp. 8–9. Some writers claim that in the parish of Menheniot there were Cornish language services until the vicar, Dr Moreman, introduced English services in 1540; Smith, *Cornish Language*, p. 10. However, the assumption the language replaced was Cornish not Latin is probably erroneous; Ellis, *Cornish Language and Literature*, p. 60; Youings, 'South-Western Rebellion', p. 115; for the ecclesiastical influence of the Cornish language in the sixteenth century, see D.A. Frost, 'Glasney's Parish Clergy and the Tregear Manuscript', in Philip Payton (ed.), *Cornish Studies: Fifteen* (Exeter, 2007), pp. 27–87.

19. Spriggs, 'Additional Thoughts', pp. 46–47.

20. 'MS Collections at Castle Horneck', *Quarterly Review* 139 (1875), pp. 367–95.

21. Spriggs, 'Additional Thoughts', pp. 47–49; D.C. Fowler, 'John Trevisa and the English Bible', *Modern Philology*, 58.2 (1960), pp. 81–98, p. 86 fn. 26.

22. Ellis, *Cornish Language*, pp. 9–10.

23. For a thorough biography of Trevisa (to which I am indebted for much of the details of Trevisa's life) see D.C. Fowler, *John Trevisa*, Aldershot, 1993. Spriggs dismisses the idea that Trevisa could have produced a full Bible translation on his own, but Trevisa's known translations are very large works.

24. Fowler, 'John Trevisa', p. 81. John Bale in 1548 claimed Trevisa had translated the Bible into English ('*In Anglicum idioma*'), J. Bale, *Illustrium Maioris Britanniae scriptorium* (1548), p. 518.

25. Fowler, 'John Trevisa', pp. 14–17.

26. Spriggs, 'Additional Thoughts', p. 52.

27. G. Thomas and N. Williams (eds), *Bewnans Ke* (Exeter, 2007), p. xliii.

28. N. Orme, 'Education in the Medieval Cornish Play *Beunans Meriasek*', *Cambridge Medieval Studies* 25 (1993), pp. 1–13.

29. T. Peter, *The History of Glasney Collegiate Church, Cornwall* (Camborne, 1903).

30. K.J. George, 'How Many People Spoke Cornish Traditionally?', *Cornish Studies* 14 (1986), pp. 67–70.

2

Afterlife of an Army
The Old Cornish Regiments, 1643–44

Mark Stoyle

Introduction

The five Cornish infantry regiments which were raised by Sir Ralph Hopton on behalf of King Charles I in October 1642 are among the most celebrated military formations of the British Civil Wars. Led by their 'first Colonells' – Sir William Godolphin of Godolphin, Sir Bevill Grenville of Stowe, Colonel Nicholas Slanning of Maristow, Colonel John Trevanion of Caerhayes and Warwick, Lord Mohun, of Boconnoc – the five Cornish foot regiments were swiftly forged into a fighting force which became known popularly as 'the Cornish army': an army which went on to win a stunning series of military successes between November 1642 and July 1643.[1] The story of the Cornish soldiers' remarkable achievements during this period was first told by Hopton himself, in a narrative which he penned soon after the Civil War was over,[2] and ever since then the story has been told and retold by legions of historians: all of them drawing very heavily on Hopton's original account.[3] As a result, the history of the Cornish army between October 1642 and July 1643 has remained firmly in the historiographical spotlight throughout the past three centuries. Yet the subsequent histories of the five individual regiments which together made up that formation can only be said to have passed into historiographical shadow.[4] The present article sets out to redress the balance by providing the first detailed account of the military service of the five 'Old Cornish' regiments between their participation in the successful Royalist assault on Bristol in July 1643 and their absorption into the king's main 'Oxford' field army in December 1644. In the process, the article will seek to demonstrate, first, that the popular notion that 'the history of the Cornish army as a fighting unit' came to an abrupt end as a result of the heavy casualties which had been sustained before Bristol is somewhat misleading,[5] and second, that it was the events of summer 1644, rather than the events of summer 1643, which finally conspired to bring about the Cornish army's ruin.

The campaign of summer 1643

The story of the Old Cornish regiments after July 1643 can only be properly understood within the context of the merger which had taken place between the Cornish army and the forces of the Marquis of Hertford at Chard in Somerset during the previous month. At the beginning of June Hopton's army – then consisting of the five Cornish infantry regiments, '3,000 excellent foot', together with 1,000 horse – had linked up with 2,500 other Royalist troops under Hertford (whom Charles I had previously appointed as his supreme commander in the South West).[6] From the point of view of the Royalist high command, the conjunction of Hopton's force – which consisted chiefly of infantrymen – with Hertford's – which consisted chiefly of cavalrymen – had been a signal success: one which had allowed them to put 'a pretty marching army' into the field.[7] Yet from the point of view of the Cornish rank-and-file things had looked very different. In his famous *History of the Rebellion* the leading Royalist Sir Edward Hyde subsequently observed that, although 'the marquis's party' had been much smaller than Hopton's, it had been 'supplied with all the general officers of a royal army', including 'a general [i.e. Hertford himself], lieutenant general, general of the horse, general of the Ordnance, a major general of horse and another of foot'. This – together with the fact that Hertford had out-ranked Hopton – had meant that, once the two forces had been combined, there had been no senior positions left for 'the chief officers of the Cornish army', who had thus found that, 'by joining with a much less party than themselves', they had been reduced to 'the condition of private colonels'.[8]

Fortunately for Charles I, Hopton and the other senior commanders of the Cornish army had accepted their demotion with good grace. Sir Ralph had agreed to serve as field marshal under Hertford, while Grenville and the other regimental colonels had agreed to serve under the direction of Hertford's major-general of the foot: a professional soldier named Joseph Wagstaffe.[9] Nevertheless, the demotion of the Cornish commanders had caused a great deal of resentment among their troops and, according to Hyde, 'if the extraordinary temper and virtue of the chief officers of the Cornish had not been much superior to that of their common soldiers, who valued themselves high … there might have been greater disorder at their first joining [with Hertford] than could easily have been composed'.[10] In the end, it was only thanks to the direct intervention of the Cornish regimental commanders that the 'murmurings and emulations amongst [their] inferior officers and common soldiers' were stilled.[11] As I have noted elsewhere, one of the arguments that seems to have been advanced to placate the disgruntled Cornish troops at this time was that the combined Royalist force 'would continue to be referred to as "the Cornish Army"'.[12] Although Hopton's force was officially termed 'the Western Army', it was as 'the Cornish Army' that it was usually known, and this was 'the style it ... carried' in June 1643.[13] By agreeing that the joint Royalist force should retain the latter title, Hertford thus made a significant concession to Cornish pride. Nevertheless the merger of the two Royalist forces may be seen, in retrospect, as the beginning of the Cornish army's long decline. In the words of F.T.R. Edgar, it was the first in 'a series of metamorphoses' which would see 'the original structure, and with it, the animating spirit, of ... [the five] Cornish regiments ... vitiated by ... merger with other – to the Cornish, alien – units, by different forms of organisation, and above all by unfamiliar commands'.[14]

Throughout much of June and early July, Hertford's army marched and countermarched through Somerset as it attempted to get the better of the Parliamentarian forces. Then, on 5 July, Sir Bevil Grenville was killed at the Battle of Lansdown, near Bath. Grenville was not only the first of the Cornish regimental commanders to die but was also, according to Hyde, 'an excellent person, whose activity, interest and reputation was the foundation of ... [all that] had been done in Cornwall [for the king]'.[15] If the decline of the Cornish army may be said to have begun with the merger at Chard, the loss of Grenville undoubtedly accelerated that process. The story of Sir Bevill's death has been told by dozens of historians, yet this famous incident also marks the point at which their interest in the wider story of the Cornish regiments has tended to fade. Symptomatic of this is the fact that, although scholars have long been aware that Grenville was succeeded as colonel of his regiment by his 15-year-old son, John, the precise date at which John Grenville took command of his father's unit remains unclear.[16] During the 1860s R.S. Hawker forged a letter purporting to be from one of Sir Bevill's servants, which claimed that John had not only been present at Lansdown, but that, after Bevill's death, he had been placed at the head of his father's troops and had led them into battle.[17] Despite the fact that there is no contemporary evidence whatsoever to support this story, it continues to appear in general histories of the Civil War.[18] All that can be said for certain is that, in the wake of Bevill's death, his son began to assume a new eminence in Royalist circles. Later in July Sir John Berkeley – the commander of the Royalist forces which were then besieging Exeter – wrote two letters to Hopton in which he commended to him 'the consideration of Mr Greenevill'.[19] Berkeley was presumably suggesting that John Grenville should be given an honour or appointment of some kind – and it may perhaps have been the colonelcy of his father's former regiment which Berkeley had in mind. Some historians have suggested that John was already serving in this capacity when the Cornish army moved into the assault against the Parliamentarian-held city of Bristol on 26 July, but there appears to be no hard evidence that this was so.[20] On the contrary, the one eyewitness who specifically alludes to the regiment at this time refers to it simply as 'Sir Bevile Greenviles ... regiment'.[21]

Whatever John's Grenville's precise position may have been in the immediate aftermath of his father's death, the subsequent itinerary of the five Cornish regiments is clear from Hopton's narrative and has been traced in many subsequent histories. From Lansdown, the Cornishmen retreated with the rest of Hertford's forces to Devizes and from Devizes they marched out to assist in the rout of Sir William Waller's Parliamentarian army at the Battle of Roundway Down on 13 July. Hertford's forces were now triumphant and a few days later, in the words of Hyde, 'the Cornish army (for that title it deservedly kept still) ... possessed themselves of Bath'.[22] It was from Bath that Hertford's troops subsequently set out to participate in the storm of Bristol: first crossing the Avon at Keynsham on 24 July and then advancing right up to the perimeter of the city defences. It is intriguing to note that, even as the Royalist forces were taking up their positions before Bristol, the Cornish troops were continuing to insist on their preferred title being applied to the army under Hertford's command. Listing the regiments which made up what he termed 'My Lord Marquesse Hertfords Western Armye' at this time, a Royalist witness went on to observe that 'this, the Cornish [soldiers] would have styled the Cornish Armye'.[23]

Disputes over nomenclature were temporarily forgotten on 26 July when the Royalist forces moved into the attack: an attack which resulted in heavy casualties being inflicted on the Cornish army. According to the most detailed contemporary account, more than 100 Cornish officers and men were killed or wounded in an unsuccessful attempt to storm the southern defences of Bristol, while among those who died in the aftermath of the fighting were two more of the Cornish regimental commanders: Sir Nicholas Slanning and John Trevanion.[24] Other Royalist forces under the command of the king's half-German nephew Prince Rupert eventually succeeded in penetrating the Parliamentarian defences elsewhere, and as a result the garrison agreed to surrender on the following day. Nevertheless, historians have long argued, from a Royalist perspective – and especially, perhaps, from a Cornish Royalist perspective – the capture of Bristol was a pyrrhic victory.[25] This view was never more forcefully or more eloquently expressed than in Mary Coate's classic history of Cornwall during the Civil War, first published in 1933. 'The death of Slanning and Trevanion, following on that of ... Grenville [at

Lansdown] was an irreparable loss' to the Cornish Royalists, wrote Coate, 'for the life of the Cornish army had been in its leaders; they had inspired it with enthusiasm; they had given it its unity, and when they died its history ended'. In a striking peroration, which has exerted a powerful influence over historians ever since, Coate went on to aver that 'Lansdown and Bristol might be numbered among the Royalist triumphs, but for the Cornish army they were its Ichabod'.[26]

In many ways, of course, Coate was quite right. The loss of three of the Cornish army's 'first Colonells', together with several hundred other officers and men, in the actions fought at Lansdown and Bristol *did* have a terrible effect on that army's morale, and *did* mean that the formation would never be the same again. Yet Coate was wrong to imply that these losses had brought the history of the Cornish army to an end – as she herself tacitly acknowledged just a page or two later when she wrote that 'there are few episodes of the Civil War more tragic than the decline and fall of the Cornish army after ... the fall of Bristol'.[27] That Coate should have found herself in the curious position of declaring that the history of the Cornish army had ended at Bristol, even when she knew perfectly well that this was not the case, probably reflects the extent to which she – like so many other historians, both before and since – had been influenced by the Ur-text of the Cornish army's history: Sir Ralph Hopton's near-contemporary narrative of events, which was edited and published by C.E.H. Chadwyck-Healey under the title *Bellum Civile* in 1902.[28] Because Hopton's 'relation', which is so informative about the activities of the Cornish regiments between October 1642 and July 1643, virtually ceases to refer to them after the latter date, it is easy for the reader to come away with the impression that those regiments had ceased to be of any great importance. Yet, as we shall see, the disappearance of the Cornish regiments from Hopton's narrative merely reflects the fact that Sir Ralph's own connection with them had been severed immediately after the fall of Bristol. The fact that Walter Slingsby – who also composed three narrative accounts of military affairs in the West during 1643–44, accounts which were published alongside those of Hopton by Chadwyck-Healey in 1902 – *also* ended his connection with the Cornish army in July 1643 has only made it easier still for readers of *Bellum Civile* to assume that the Cornish army simply faded out of the picture after this date.[29] Yet, as soon as one turns to other contemporary sources, it becomes clear that the five Cornish regiments, though terribly battered, continued to form a vital part of the Royalist war-machine for many months to come.

The conquest of the West

In the wake of the capture of Bristol, a series of disputes broke out among the victorious Royalist commanders: disputes which were so serious that Charles I decided that he must leave his wartime capital at Oxford and travel to Bristol to settle them in person.[30] The king began his journey on 1 August and arrived in the newly captured city a day or two later.[31] His first task was to settle the argument which was then raging over who should become governor of Bristol: an argument which the king resolved by appointing Rupert as governor, and encouraging the prince to appoint Hopton as lieutenant governor.[32] Sir Ralph promptly accepted the post, and Slingsby – who was then serving as lieutenant-colonel of Lord Mohun's regiment – was subsequently chosen to act as his deputy: thus depriving the Cornish army of another of its original field commanders.[33] Charles's second task was to decide whether or not to combine Hertford's army with his own in order to create a single Royalist host. After much discussion, the proposed merger was abandoned: not least because the Cornish soldiers under Hertford's command had 'expressed a peremptory aversion to joining … with the king's army'.[34] Clearly, the men of 'the Cornish army' – as Hyde continued to refer to Hertford's force – remained determined to preserve their own separate identity.[35] It is clear, too, that Charles was desperate to keep the Cornish troops on-side, for Hyde recalls that, as well as vetoing the proposed merger, the king 'affected to make all possible demonstrations to them [i.e. the Cornish] of an extraordinary high esteem he had of their wonderful fidelity and courage'.[36] This probably helps to explain why, soon after his arrival in Bristol, Charles knighted not only John Grenville, but also another teenage Cornish officer, Captain Chichester Wrey, who commanded a company in Mohun's regiment.[37] Having decided that Hertford's army should retain its independent existence, Charles then went on to make a third critical decision: namely, that the marquis himself should no longer command it. Hertford and his Lieutenant General – Prince Rupert's younger brother, Prince Maurice – had long been unable to agree, and the king now resolved that – in order to bring this bickering to an end – the marquis should join him in his own camp, while Maurice should assume the role of General of the Western Army.[38] As a result, the Cornish troops found themselves being placed under the authority of their third general in as many months.

Upon assuming command of the Cornish regiments, one of Maurice's first priorities must have been to appoint new officers to replace those who had been killed or wounded during the previous weeks. Very little evidence survives about the military appointments which the prince made at this time, but, from a variety of sources, it has proved possible to establish the identities of the men who took over the command of the Cornish regiments in the wake of their original colonels' deaths.[39] Thus it is clear that, soon after the fall of Bristol, if not before, command of Sir Bevill Grenville's regiment devolved on his son: the newly knighted Sir John.[40] The regiment which had originally been commanded by Sir Nicolas Slanning was taken over by Thomas Bassett of Tehidy, near Redruth, while the regiment which had originally been commanded by Sir John Trevanion was taken over by a second West Cornish gentleman: Thomas St Aubyn, of Clowance.[41] Lord Mohun was still leading his own regiment at the time of Bristol's fall. However a week later, on 4 August, he was appointed 'Colonel General' of the five Western counties: a promotion which may well have been another result of Charles I's concern to demonstrate his esteem for the officers of the Cornish army.[42] Following his elevation Mohun presumably decided to resign command of his foot regiment, for a newly discovered commission, issued by Prince Maurice on 5 August, reveals that, by this date at the latest, Lord Mohun's 21-year-old brother, Sir Charles, had succeeded him to the colonelcy.[43] Thus, within two weeks of Bristol's fall, William Godolphin was the only one of the five original Cornish colonels to retain command of his regiment. It is interesting to note that, in the commission issued on 5 August, the prince chose to style himself 'Generall of his Majesties Westerne Army'.[44] There is no evidence that Maurice referred to the forces under his command as 'the Cornish army' thereafter (although, as we shall see, the title continued to be used unofficially to refer to the Cornish regiments for some time to come). This in turn suggests that the prince was rather less willing than Hopton and Hertford had been to flatter the particularist sentiment of the Cornish soldiers.

The Cornish rank-and-file may have lost the long-running battle over the official title of the king's army in the West, but they still possessed sufficient influence to help shape the strategy which that army would adopt. As we have seen, it was protests from the Cornish soldiers which had been one of the crucial factors in persuading Charles I to abandon the idea of merging Hertford's army with his own. Not content with this, the Cornishmen now demanded that they should be allowed to return to the West in order to reduce the Parliamentarian garrison of Plymouth – which posed a pressing threat to the peace and security of Cornwall itself. It soon became apparent to the king that, if the Cornish troops 'were compelled to march eastwards, to which they were not inclined ... they would moulder so fast away that there would be little addition of strength by it'.[45] He therefore decided to send Maurice's army back into Devon and Dorset to conquer the remaining Parliamentary garrisons there. At the beginning of August, Charles ordered the Earl of Caernarvon to advance on the Roundhead stronghold of Dorchester with the cavalry of the Western Army and Maurice to follow him 'with the foot'.[46] It is clear that these orders were swiftly obeyed, for, on 7 August, news was received in Oxford from Bristol that 'Prince Maurice with the Cornish forces ... was gone towards Devonshire'.[47] This report was clearly no more than the literal truth and although the lack of a detailed contemporary narrative has led to a plethora of contradictory statements about the subsequent activities of the Cornish foot appearing in later histories – that the Cornish troops had 'withdrawn from ... operations', for example; that they had gone to Oxford; that they had accompanied the king to Gloucester; or that many of them had stayed behind with Hopton in Bristol[48] – it is evident, in fact, that virtually all of the Cornish foot-soldiers who remained in arms at Bristol in August 1643 set off for Dorset with Maurice.

Once their march back to the West had begun, the Cornish troops made rapid progress. Caernarvon swiftly persuaded the people of Dorchester to surrender and Maurice himself was quartered in the town by 10 August.[49] The Western Army next moved on to Honiton in East Devon and from there to join the Royalist forces under Sir John Berkeley which were besieging Exeter.[50] One of Berkeley's officers, Colonel Joseph Bampfield, later recalled that Maurice arrived before Exeter with 'about 3,000 Cornish foot'.[51] Bampfield's statement is significant, not only because it shows that he had continued to regard the Western Army as a predominantly Cornish force – a view which other contemporaries plainly shared[52] – but also because it suggests that almost as many Cornish infantrymen had returned to Devon in August as had marched out of that county two months before. It may well be that the casualties which the five Cornish regiments had suffered during the fighting in Somerset and Wiltshire have been exaggerated, then, or, perhaps, that further drafts of recruits had arrived to reinforce them in the meantime.[53] By 27 August, Maurice was established at Polsloe, just outside Exeter, and making plans for a full-scale assault on the city.[54] This attack was finally launched on 3 September and pressed home at dawn the following day when the Cornish troops took part in a successful storm of the city's southern defences.[55] Henry Manaton, then serving as a lieutenant-colonel in one of the Cornish regiments, received a serious leg-wound during this attack: a wound which incapacitated him for the rest of the war.[56] No doubt many other, more humble, Cornish officers and soldiers were killed and wounded at the same time.

The capture of Exeter was one of the greatest triumphs of the Cornish army, and although this fact has tended to be lost sight of by later historians, it was clearly recognized at the time.[57] Indeed, there can be little doubt that it was the Cornishmen's success at Exeter which prompted Charles I to issue his famous declaration to the inhabitants of Cornwall on 10 September 1643, in which he thanked them for 'their zeale for the Defence of our Person' and promised to reward them for the 'many strange Victories' which they had won 'over their and our Enimies'.[58] With Exeter secured, Maurice swiftly moved on to besiege Dartmouth: now the only town in Devon apart from Plymouth which continued to hold out for Parliament. Soon after arriving in South Devon, the prince fell seriously ill and it was therefore left to his subordinates to co-ordinate operations against Dartmouth.[59] They eventually resolved to storm the Parliamentarian defences, just as they had done at Exeter, and on 4 October the Royalist troops moved into the attack. It is evident that the Cornish regiments played a crucial role in this assault for, in the heavy fighting which followed, the new commander of Lord Mohun's former regiment, Sir Charles Mohun – described contemptuously by one Parliamentarian pamphleteer as 'young Moone' – was slain.[60] Sir Charles was the fourth regimental commander of the original Cornish regiments to have been killed in action, and his death must have cast a pall over the men under his command. Nevertheless, the attackers had succeeded in taking several vital outworks and on the following day the demoralized Parliamentarian garrison agreed to surrender the town.[61] The capture of Dartmouth was thus added to the Cornish army's long series of military successes.

Over the next few days, Maurice's troops refreshed themselves in the vicinity of Dartmouth. Large quantities of arms and ammunition had been taken from the Parliamentarian forces in the town, and these were now gathered up and redistributed to the Royalist soldiers. It is fascinating to note that – according to a recently discovered list of all the munitions which were supplied to the Royalist forces at this time – no fewer than 300 muskets and 34 powder barrels were delivered 'to the Cornish Army'.[62] That this particular title should have been used by the document's author is highly significant for it shows that, as late as 22 October, nearly three months after Hopton's former infantry regiments had been taken over by Maurice, those regiments continued to be collectively known as 'the Cornish Army'. The fact that the weapons distributed to the Cornishmen headed the list, moreover – and that they received nearly half of all the muskets which were supplied – strongly suggests that the Cornish regiments continued to form the most important single element of Prince Maurice's force. That this was so is confirmed by a report which appeared in the Royalist court journal *Mercurius Aulicus* on 13 October. Having informed his readers that Maurice was preparing to move against Plymouth, the editor of *Aulicus* boasted that the prince would swiftly take the pertinacious sea-port 'for the Cornish foote, being the men put upon it, will not easily be perswaded to leave one town untaken, having been conquerors over all the rest'.[63] Here again, the perception that it was the Cornish infantry regiments whom Maurice chiefly relied upon – and that it was they who had been the true 'conquerors' of the West of England for the king – was made very clear.

Towards the middle of October, Maurice and his army set off to reinforce the small Royalist force under Colonel John Digby which was already besieging Plymouth. Digby was a brave, resourceful officer who had served as a cavalry commander in the Cornish army during 1642–43, but who possessed no infantry regiment of his own.[64] This probably helps to explain why it was he who now assumed command of Lord Mohun's former regiment in place of the dead Sir Charles, thus becoming the unit's third colonel.[65] Soon after they had taken up their quarters before Plymouth, the five original regiments of the Cornish army underwent yet another change of nomenclature when they began to be colloquially referred to as 'the Old Cornish regiments': presumably in order to distinguish them from the other, newly raised, Cornish infantry regiments which had joined them in the Royalist siege-camp.[66] Within a fortnight of their arrival before Plymouth, the Old Cornish had won further battle-honours. Basset's regiment is known to have been one of the three royalist foot regiments which took part in the successful assault on the Parliamentarian fort at Mount Stamford on 7 November and the fact that Bassett, Digby and Wagstaffe all signed the Royalist summons which was sent in to the town from there a few days later suggests that the other two regiments may well have been Old Cornish ones too.[67] Yet the capture of Mount Stamford was to prove the besiegers' last major success. Over the following weeks, a whole series of Royalist attacks was beaten off by the Parliamentarians and on Christmas Day 1643 Maurice finally gave up and raised the siege.

According to a contemporary account, the prince then 'drew off from Plimmoth with Sir John Greenvill's, Colonel Godolphin's, Colonel Bassett's and Colonel St Aubin's regiments ... and marched to Tavistocke, where hee quartered with those four regiments' throughout the following winter. Digby's regiment was apparently left behind at Plympton with some other 'forces ... under the commaund of General Digby', who had been charged with blocking up the Parliamentarian garrison.[68] The failure to take Plymouth must have been a bitter blow for the men of the Old Cornish regiments. This was the first out-and-out defeat which they had suffered for more than a year, and it seems very likely that more Cornish troops had been killed or wounded – or had succumbed to disease – during the long-drawn out siege of Plymouth than had fallen in the engagements fought at Lansdown and Bristol a few months before. To make matters worse, Plymouth was, as we have seen, the town which the Cornish soldiers had been most determined to reduce because it posed a serious threat to Cornwall itself. Now the Cornish soldiers were forced to confront the galling fact that, despite their great series of victories, Plymouth remained as defiant as ever – and during the following year Plymouth's continued resistance was to have an increasingly malign effect on both the morale and the military performance of the Old Cornish regiments.

The campaign of summer 1644

In March 1644 a popular insurrection broke out against the Royalists in East Devon: an insurrection which had been encouraged by the Parliamentarian garrison of Lyme in Dorset.[69] Maurice realised that there could be no peace in East Devon while Lyme remained defiant and he therefore set off to besiege the little port. Once again the Old Cornish regiments formed the heart of Maurice's army, but this time only four of those regiments accompanied him: Godolphin's, Grenville's, Bassett's and St Aubyn's.[70] Mohun's former regiment was left behind at Plympton with its new colonel, John Digby, who had been ordered to maintain a blockade of Plymouth.[71] Maurice's decision to leave Digby's regiment behind may well have been taken partly in order to reassure the other Cornish soldiers that Plymouth would be contained by their comrades during their absence. Nevertheless, this was the first time that the Old Cornish regiments had found themselves being split up and deployed in two quite separate theatres of war: another sign of how the collective identity of the former 'Cornish army' was gradually being eroded.

On 7 April, Maurice arrived in the Dorset town of Beaminster. He remained here until 14 April, when the little town was practically destroyed by a fire which had been started 'by reason of a falling out between the French and the Cornish' soldiers under his command.[72] Six days later Maurice's army appeared before Lyme, the prince's strength being put at anything between 2,500 and 6,000 men. The four Old Cornish regiments, which continued to form the core of Maurice's infantry force, were placed in the very centre of the besiegers' position, to the north of the town and over the next few weeks, the Royalists launched a series of desperate assaults on the Roundhead defences. A Royalist officer later noted that 'the falling on was for the most part on the Cornish side, where they [i.e. the Parliamentarians] were strongest ... contrary to the advice of the best experienced souldyers'. Maurice apparently decided to adopt these risky tactics because 'the Cornish ... [were] more terrible to them [i.e. the Parliamentarians]' than were any other Royalist soldiers.[73] Yet, despite their fearsome reputation, the Cornish troops were unable to prevail. The defenders of Lyme proved as tenacious as those of Plymouth had done before them and in May the advance of Parliament's main field army, under the Earl of Essex, forced Maurice to abandon the siege altogether 'with his whole army beinge lesse by one halfe at least then when he first sate downe before Lyme'.[74] Once again, the unsuccessful siege of a fortified town had taken a terrible toll on the Old Cornish troops.

From Lyme, Maurice retreated to Okehampton where he spent much of July. Towards the middle of that month, most of the Royalist infantry units which had been left behind to maintain the blockade of Plymouth – including Digby's regiment – were ordered to leave their positions before the town and to march to reinforce the prince.[75] The five Old Cornish regiments were thus re-united, though they now found themselves divided up into two separate 'tertias' or brigades. A surviving list of Maurice's foot – which was probably drawn up when his troops were assembled at Crediton on 27 July – lists Digby's regiment as being in Sir Henry Carey's tertia alongside the other regiments from Plymouth. There were 600 men in Digby's regiment at this time. The other four Old Cornish regiments were grouped together in a single tertia, which consisted of 400 men under 'Colonel [Thomas] Bassett'; 200 men under 'Colonel [John] Greenvile'; 400 men under 'Colonel [Thomas] St Albons'; and 500 men under 'Colonel [William] Godolphin': a total of 1,500 men in all.[76] Thus the total strength of the Old Cornish regiments in July 1644 was 2,100 men: still a formidable number, though well down from the 3,000 men they had mustered during the previous summer. Digby had been badly hurt in a skirmish before Plymouth in June, so it was probably soon after this that the teenage Sir Chichester Wrey assumed command of Mohun's former regiment (in which, as we have seen, he had long served as an officer).[77] Certainly, a Royalist officer was able to describe Wrey as 'a Colonel of the foot' soon afterwards.[78] On 27 July Charles I himself – who had by now arrived in Devon with his own army to reinforce Maurice – knighted Henry Carey, Thomas Bassett and Joseph Wagstaffe at Crediton.[79]

As Charles and Maurice linked hands in Mid-Devon, the Earl of Essex and his Parliamentarian army – whom the prince had earlier side-stepped in order to join forces with his uncle – were marching triumphantly into Cornwall. From the point of view of the Old Cornish soldiers, the fact that Essex had got between them and the Tamar bridges and invaded Cornwall itself can only have been seen as a disaster, and they must surely have clamoured for an immediate return to the West. The combined Royalist armies at once set off in pursuit and by mid-August, Charles I and Maurice – assisted by a scratch force of local troops known as 'the army for the defence of Cornwall' which had been hastily assembled by Sir Bevill Grenville's younger brother, Sir Richard – had pinned the Roundhead forces down in the countryside around Fowey.[80] During the next fortnight, the Old Cornish regiments continued to serve in the very forefront of the fighting. On 24 August, for example, Sir Thomas Basset's tertia was sent to St Blazey to cut off the Parliamentarian forces from the west.[81] A week later, Basset's men returned to fight against Essex's troops in the entrenchments at Castle Dore and the Old Cornish shared in the Royalist triumph when the entire Roundhead infantry force finally surrendered at Fowey on 2 September. The Old Cornish troops had fought with great tenacity during the campaign of summer 1644, and that campaign had been crowned with splendid success: Charles I himself crying out elatedly to the sheriff of Cornwall in the wake of Essex's defeat, 'Now Mr Sheriffe, I leve Cornwall to yu safe and sound[!]'.[82] Yet no sooner had this great victory been won than clear signs began to emerge that all was not well with the Old Cornish regiments.

A crisis of identity?

On 5 September the king marched out of Cornwall and back into Devon again. That night, he quartered at Tavistock, where, his secretary later reported, he was 'obliged to stay [for] some time ... to get his army together, especially that of Prince Maurice, which consisted most of the Cornish, who were gone home to rejoice with their friends for their deliverance'.[83] That many of the Cornish soldiers should have decided to temporarily abandon their colours at this time in order to celebrate their recent victory is perfectly understandable, but, already, some English Royalists had started to suspect that the absentees were unlikely to return. On 6 September a correspondent of Prince Rupert's wrote to him from Tavistock, observing that 'I believe we shall not be able to carry many of your brother's men with us'.[84] Two days later, Charles I directed his forces to move against Plymouth. Hyde's remark that the king's decision to advance upon Plymouth was taken partly because 'so far it might be presumed that the Cornish troops ... would attend him' not only provides yet another example of the Cornish tail wagging the Royalist dog, but also underscores the point that Charles was finding it extremely hard to cajole the Cornish soldiers into accompanying his forces back across the Tamar.[85] Over the following days the Royalist assembled all of the troops that they could muster in preparation for a storm of Plymouth but, in the end, Charles decided that Plymouth's defences were simply too strong to attempt; on 14 September he ordered that the attack should be abandoned and the Royalist forces evacuated the positions which they had occupied before the town.[86] Plymouth had survived once again, therefore – and once again, it was Cornish Royalist troops who were left with the thankless task of containing the Parliamentarian garrison. On the day of his departure, Charles appointed Sir Richard Grenville, with the remnants of the small army which he had brought out of Cornwall, 'to lye at Plympton, and make workes to stop them from foraging into the country'.[87] As we shall see, this was a decision which was to have fateful consequences for the Old Cornish regiments.

Meanwhile the king himself had returned to Tavistock, from where he resumed his efforts to round up the missing Cornish troops. On 16 September Charles sent a letter to the Sheriff of Cornwall complaining that 'divers officers and souldiers of the regiments of foote' in the armies of Sir Richard Grenville and Prince Maurice had 'gonne home without licence'. He therefore ordered the sheriff to 'immediately publish our pleasure throughout that county that all officers and souldiers of Sir Richard Greenviles forces doe instantly upon payne of death repaire to theire collers, and then that you give afterwards the like order to all officers and souldiers of our deare nephew's army'.[88] Having issued these instructions, the king left Tavistock and set off for East Devon on the following day: accompanied both by his own army and by that of Prince Maurice. Unfortunately for Charles, the orders which he had sent into Cornwall took little effect: at least as far as the Old Cornish regiments were concerned. Of the 4,600 foot soldiers whom Maurice had led into the field in late July, barely 2,000 remained by the end of September.[89] As the five Old Cornish regiments *alone* had mustered 2,100 men when they were assembled at Crediton on 27 July it can scarcely be doubted that those units had suffered a dramatic decline in numbers since. Indeed, if one assumes that the Cornish element of Maurice's infantry force had wasted away at roughly the same rate as the non-Cornish element – an assumption which probably underestimates the extent of desertion among the Cornish troops[90] – it may be calculated that the total strength of the Old Cornish regiments had fallen to *circa* 900 men by the time that the prince's army arrived back in East Devon. Sir Edward Hyde later admitted that 'few of the Cornish marched outward with the king' and other contemporaries made similar comments.[91] But why should the five regiments which had once made up the 'Cornish army' – regiments which had shown such courage and determination in the king's service hitherto – have started to waste away so rapidly in the aftermath of Charles's great victory in Cornwall?

Hyde himself later wrote that many of the Cornish foot soldiers who had deserted their colours at this time had been 'impatient to be at their harvest' – and this may well have been so.[92] Yet gathering in the harvest would scarcely have detained the runaways for more than a week or two, so it seems hard to believe that this factor alone can explain the decline in the strength of the Old Cornish regiments. Far more significant was surely the fact that, after going home for a few days – either to assist with the harvest or to celebrate Essex's defeat – many of Prince Maurice's soldiers had chosen not to return to their old colours but to enlist themselves under Sir Richard Grenville instead. By 28 September, it had clearly begun to dawn on the Royalist high command that many of the Cornishmen who were coming in to strengthen Grenville's forces before Plymouth were deserters from Prince Maurice's army. On that day, the king sent a letter to Grenville telling him that 'wee must still put you in mind to use your utmost endeavours to send uppe all the straglers of our Armee and that upon no pretence you admit any that have been in any Regiments of ... our Nephews Army to stay behinde or put themselves under any other command': a missive which one of the king's servants bluntly described as a 'letter ... to Greenvile to send away the Prince's foot'.[93] Yet there is no evidence to show that Grenville ever responded to this letter – or that he ever sent back any of the soldiers who had deserted from Maurice's army. Instead, he employed the deserters – together with many fresh levies – to build up five new Cornish infantry regiments of his own: units which swiftly became known as the 'New Cornish' regiments, to distinguish them from the 'Old Cornish' regiments which were serving under the prince.[94]

Hyde was later to attribute the sudden waxing of Sir Richard's forces – and the equally sudden waning of Prince Maurice's – chiefly to the machinations of Grenville himself, but, while it is clear that Sir Richard did indeed do all he could to attract men to his banner, he was only able to achieve the success he did because so many Cornish soldiers had previously deserted the prince. The question therefore remains: what can have prompted the veteran Cornish soldiers who had fought so stoutly under Maurice thus far to abandon him in droves during August-September 1644? It is impossible to provide a definitive answer to this question, but it does not seem too far-fetched to suggest that the Old Cornish troops may have been growing increasingly disillusioned with the prince's leadership during late 1643 and early 1644: first, as a result of the bloody repulses which they had suffered before Plymouth and Lyme; second, as a result of the progressive erosion of collective Cornish identity within the Western Army and third – and, perhaps, most important of all – as a result of that army's spectacular failure to protect Cornwall itself from invasion. Maurice's decision to dodge past Essex's army during late July and to link up with the king – thus leaving the defence of Cornwall to Grenville's scratch forces – may have made sense from a purely military perspective, but from the point of view of the prince's Cornish soldiers it must have seemed uncomfortably like a betrayal. Maurice's actions had underscored the fact that the defence of Cornwall was not the Western Army's prime concern – and this in turn may well have caused many of the prince's Cornish soldiers to wonder if serving in that army was really the best way of protecting their homes and families.

It is against this backdrop that the dramatic decline in the strength of Prince Maurice's Cornish infantry regiments after the Lostwithiel campaign must surely be understood. As I have argued elsewhere, Grenville was to appeal to Cornish particularist sentiment with considerable skill during July–September 1644: presenting himself as a Cornish leader who would put Cornish interests first.[95] After Charles I had given Sir Richard the task of containing and, if possible, capturing Plymouth on 14 September, moreover, Grenville's ability to reach out to the Cornish rank and file must have become stronger still for, as we have seen, the capture of Plymouth had been one of the prime concerns of the king's Cornish soldiers since mid-1643, if not before. Compared to Grenville, Maurice can no longer have seemed an even faintly plausible champion of the Cornish interest – especially as he was now preparing to march his forces far away to the east – and as a result the Cornish people may finally have abandoned the notion that Maurice's army was in any sense a 'Cornish army' and focused all of their hopes on Grenville's forces instead. This would certainly help to explain why so many soldiers deserted from the Old Cornish regiments during August-September 1644 – and, indeed, why the stout fighting spirit which had previously distinguished those regiments became so much less evident thereafter.

End game

As the concluding part of this article will show, the final months of 1644 were bleak ones for the Old Cornish. During the first half of October, Maurice's army – with what remained of the Old Cornish regiments still at its heart – marched eastwards through Dorset and Wiltshire alongside the king's main field army.[96] On 18 October Charles prepared to launch a surprise attack on the Roundhead general Waller at Andover, but, although, the king's army were at the rendezvous at the time appointed, a Royalist officer complained, 'Prince Maurice's foot ... came up not so timely, it being past 11 o clock before they were there ... [which] questionless was the cause we did not totally rout Waller'.[97] As one historian has observed, such comments reveal a growing perception that the performance of Maurice's foot 'left much to be desired'.[98] Worse was soon to come. By 26 October, the prince's infantry were quartered at the village of Speen, near Newbury. In order to safeguard their position against the Roundhead forces who were gathering nearby, they threw up a strong entrenchment on Speen Hill, just to the west of the village, behind which they mounted several pieces of cannon.[99] Towards the end of the following day, Parliamentarian troops launched a violent attack on the Royalist entrenchments.

A vivid account of the subsequent battle was penned by the Roundhead Colonel Norton, who observed that the Royalist infantry 'were held to be as good foot as any in the world, and to help them they had fortified themselves with ... good brestworkes ... soe that they were as confident as men could be'. Nevertheless, Norton continued, the Parliamentarian foot 'fell on, and with a greate deale of resolution ... beate them from one work after another till they beate them from all their ground'.[100] Driven from their earthworks, Maurice's foot were pushed back through the village until they finally rallied near Newbury.[101] Roundhead sources suggest that something like panic had broken out among the Royalist infantry on the hill, one writer alleging that 'the Cornish souldiers ... most fearfully threw down their armes and ran away crying out, *Devils, Devils, they fight like Devils!*'.[102] This may well have been an exaggeration, but the fact that a Devon Royalist later claimed that 'the loss we then had fell on Prince Morrice his quarters, by disorder of our owne men' makes it hard to doubt that the Western foot had indeed performed badly in the battle.[103] It is clear that the Old Cornish were roughly handled during the fighting. Sir John Grenville himself was left for dead on the field, while, according to Parliamentarian reports, 'about 200 of the Cornish [soldiers] which fled thence' ran as far westwards as Marlborough.[104] The Roundheads may still have believed Maurice's infantry to be 'as good foot as any in the world' on the morning of the battle, but by nightfall this proud reputation – a reputation which had been founded on the previous successes of the Cornish army – lay shattered once and for all.

After the engagement at Newbury, the Royalists initially retreated towards Oxford but then moved onto the offensive again. On 6 November Maurice's forces were present at the Royalist rendezvous on Shotover Green, and from here they advanced to take part in the relief of Donnington Castle on 9 November.[105] From Donnington, the Old Cornish presumably marched back towards Oxford with the rest of Maurice's army. On 25 November the Royalist general Sir Jacob Astley reported that he had received a letter from Sir Thomas Basset at Wantage, asking for 'a thousand waighte of musquet bullites', and a day later Astley noted that Maurice's forces had received orders 'to march toward Woodestock'.[106] Presumably these orders were obeyed and presumably the Old Cornish spent the next few weeks quartered in the countryside near Oxford. Evidence about the movements of the prince's foot regiments during this period is tantalisingly slight: perhaps, in part, because they had by now dwindled away to such an extent that their passage excited little attention. All that can be said with confidence is that, towards the end of December, Prince Maurice 'laid down his commission' as general and 'the remnants of the Western Army were absorbed by the royal army'.[107] With their numbers severely depleted and their reputation in tatters, the surviving officers and men of the Old Cornish regiments had finally been forced to accept that merger with the main Royalist field army which they had successfully resisted a year and a half before. The remnants of the Old Cornish would continue to fight on in Charles I's cause – and indeed it would only be a matter of days before they would find themselves part of a semi-autonomous military formation once more[108] – but they would never again bear the proud title of 'the Cornish army' which they had carried throughout the first half of the Civil War.

Notes and references

1. For the description of these five individuals as the Cornish troops' 'first Colonells', see A.C. Miller (ed.), 'Joseph Jane's account of Cornwall during the Civil War', *English Historical Review* (hereafter *EHR*), 90 (January 1975), p. 101. For brief accounts of Grenville, Trevanion and Slanning, see *New Dictionary of National*

Biography (hereafter *New DNB*). For brief accounts of Godolphin and Mohun, see P.R. Newman, *Royalist Officers in England and Wales, 1642–60: A Biographical Dictionary* (New York and London, 1981), pp. 159–60, 257.

2. Bodleian Library, Oxford (hereafter Bod.), Clarendon MSS, Volume 23, Numbers 1738 (1) and (4); printed in C.E.H. Chadwyck-Healey (ed.), *Bellum Civile: Sir Ralph Hopton's Narrative of his Campaign in the West* (Somerset Record Society, 18, 1902), pp. 1–60.

3. See, for example, E. Hyde, Earl of Clarendon, *The History of the Rebellion and Civil Wars in England* (ed. W. Dunn Macray, six volumes, Oxford, 1888); M. Coate, *Cornwall in the Great Civil War and Interregnum, 1642–1660* (1933, reprinted Truro 1963), chapters 5–7; A.H. Burne and P. Young, *The Great Civil War: A Military History of the First Civil War, 1642–46* (1959, reprinted Moreton-in-Marsh, 1998), chapters 3, 6; J. Stucley, *Sir Bevill Grenville and his Times* (Chichester, 1983), chapters 10–13; S. Reid, *All the King's Armies: A Military History of the English Civil War, 1642–51* (Staplehurst, 1998), chapter 4; J. Barratt, *Cavaliers: The Royalist Army at War, 1642–46* (Stroud, 2000), chapter 10; and T. Royle, *Civil War: The Wars of the Three Kingdoms* (London, 2004), chapter 5.

4. The only historians to have examined the later history of the five Cornish regiments in any depth are me and Malcolm Wanklyn. See M.D.G. Wanklyn, 'The King's Armies in the West of England, 1642–46' (unpublished MA thesis, University of Manchester, 1966), pp. 62, 65, 74–7; M. Stoyle, *West Britons: Cornish Identities and the Early Modern British State* (Exeter, 2002), pp. 158–60, 164–5; 198–207, 210–12; and M. Stoyle, *Soldiers and Strangers: An Ethnic History of the English Civil War* (Yale, 2005), pp. 175–80, 196.

5. Coate, *Cornwall*, p. 100.

6. Chadwyck-Healey, *Bellum Civile*, p. 47; Hyde, *History*, III, p. 77.

7. P. Young and N. Tucker (eds), *Military Memoirs: Richard Atkyns and John Gwyn* (Hamden, CT, 1967), p. 12.

8. Hyde, *History*, III, pp. 78–79.

9. For Hopton's position as field marshal, see F.T.R. Edgar, *Sir Ralph Hopton: The King's Man in the West, 1642–1652* (Oxford, 1968), p. 93; and C.H. Firth, 'The Siege and Capture of Bristol, by the Royalist Forces in 1643', *Journal of the Army of Historical Research* (hereafter *JSAHR*), 4 (1925), p. 195. For Wagstaffe, see Newman, *Royalist Officers*, p. 394.

10. Hyde, *History*, III, p. 77.

11. Ibid., p. 78.

12. Stoyle, *Soldiers and Strangers*, p. 175.

13. Ibid; and Hyde, *History*, III, p. 75.

14. Edgar, *Hopton*, p. 93.

15. Hyde, *History*, III, p. 92.

16. For John Grenville, see *New DNB*.

17. Stoyle, *West Britons*, pp. 175–9.

18. See, for example, Reid, *All the King's Armies*, p. 51.

19. R.W. Cotton, 'Naval Attack on Topsham', *Devon and Cornwall Notes and Gleanings*, 1, 10 (15 October 1888), p. 154.

20. See, for example, Edgar, *Hopton*, p. 115.

21. Firth, 'Siege and Capture of Bristol', p. 195.

22. Hyde, *History*, III, p. 107.

23. Firth, 'Siege and Capture of Bristol', p. 195.
24. Ibid., pp. 195–6.
25. See, for example, Hyde, *History*, III, p. 113.
26. Coate, *Cornwall*, p. 100.
27. Ibid., p. 102.
28. Chadwyck-Healey, *Bellum Civile*, pp. 1–84.
29. Bod., Clarendon MSS, Volume 23, numbers 1738 (2), (3) and (7); printed in Chadwyck-Healey, *Bellum Civile*, pp. 90–103. Until July 1643 Slingsby had served as Lieutenant Colonel of Mohun's regiment, see Chadwyck-Healey, *Bellum Civile*, p. 92; and Newman, *Royalist Officers*, p. 347.
30. Hyde, *History*, III, pp. 120–4.
31. British Library, Thomason Tracts (hereafter E.); 65 (13), *Mercurius Aulicus*, No. 31 (30 July to 5 August 1643), pp. 412, 417.
32. Hyde, *History*, III, p. 124.
33. Newman, *Royalist Officers*, p. 347.
34. Hyde, *History*, III, p. 127.
35. Ibid., p. 126.
36. Ibid., p. 127.
37. On Grenville, see *New DNB*; and Newman, *Royalist Officers*, p. 165. On Wrey, see I. Roy (ed.), *Richard Symonds's Diary of the Marches of the Royal Army* (Cambridge, 1997), p. 61; J.L. Vivian, *The Visitations of Cornwall* (Exeter, 1887), p. 564; and Newman, *Royalist Officers*, p. 423. According to Vivian, Wrey was knighted on 3 August.
38. Hyde, *History*, III, pp. 127–9.
39. I first set out the identities of these men in Stoyle, *West Britons*, Appendix 4, pp. 193–212.
40. A.R. Bayley, *The Great Civil War in Dorset, 1642–60* (Taunton, 1910), p. 138.
41. Devon Record Office, Exeter (hereafter DRO), QS/128, petition of Andrew Heywood; and Bayley, *Civil War in Dorset*, p. 138. On Bassett and St Aubyn, see Newman, *Royalist Officers*, pp. 19, 323; and Vivian, *Visitations*, p. 438.
42. Newman, *Royalist Officers*. p. 984.
43. DRO, 312M/FY95 (commission to Captain Arthur Bassett). See also C. Hammond, *Truth's Discovery: Or the Cavalier's Case Clearly Stated* (London, 1664), p. 22.
44. DRO, 312M/FY95.
45. Hyde, *History*, III, p. 126.
46. Ibid., pp. 127–8, 157.
47. E.65 (26), *Mercurius Aulicus*, No. 32 (6–12 August 1643), p. 427.
48. C.V. Wedgwood, *The King's War, 1641–47* (1958, reprinted London, 1983), p. 249; M. Bennett, *The English Civil War* (Harlow, 1995), p. 44; J.L. Malcolm, *Caesar's Due: Loyalty and King Charles, 1642–46* (London, 1983), p. 107; and Edgar, *Hopton*, p. 132.
49. Bayley, *Civil War in Dorset*, p. 100; Hyde, *History*, III, pp. 158–9; Wiltshire Record Office (hereafter WRO), Bullen Reymes MSS, 865/393 (commission to Captain Bullen Reymes).
50. J.W.R. Coxhead, 'Honiton Churchwardens' disbursements for 1642, 1643 and 1646', *Devon and Cornwall Notes and Queries*, 29, part 8 (January 1964), p. 226.
51. J. Loftis and P.H. Hardacre (eds), *Colonel Joseph Bampfield's Apology* (London, 1993), p. 40.

52. A. Pritchard (ed.), *Abraham Cowley: The Civil War* (Toronto, 1973), p. 98.

53. There can be no doubt that some modern historians *have* exaggerated the casualties which the Cornish troops suffered at Lansdown and Bristol. See, for example, Coate, *Cornwall*, p. 81 (where the author makes the fantastical claim that 1,700 Royalist soldiers were killed at Lansdown alone!); and I. Gentles, *The English Revolution and the Wars of the Three Kingdoms, 1638–1652* (London, 2007), p. 182, where it is stated that '500 of the choice Cornish infantry' were slain at Bristol. In fact, Hyde states that 500 Royalist soldiers *in total* were killed during the assault, while the most detailed contemporary accounts put Cornish casualties at something over a hundred, see Hyde, *History*, III, p. 113; Chadwyck-Healey, *Bellum Civile*, pp. 92–93; and E. Warburton (ed.), *Memoirs of Prince Rupert and the Cavaliers* (three volumes, London, 1849), II, p. 259.

54. R.W. Cotton, *Barnstaple and the Northern Parts of Devonshire during the Great Civil War* (London, 1889), pp. 212–14.

55. M. Stoyle, *From Deliverance to Destruction: Rebellion and Civil War in an English City* (Exeter, 1996), pp. 82–4, 198–201.

56. Magdalene College, Cambridge, Pepys MSS, 791, 795 (petitions of Henry Manaton).

57. As Ronald Hutton has observed, one of the main reasons why so many later historians have failed to note the Western Army's success in storming Exeter is because Sir Edward Hyde – who disliked Prince Maurice – made no mention of the attack in his influential *History*, see R. Hutton, 'Clarendon's History of the Rebellion', *EHR*, 97 (1982), pp. 76–8.

58. Stoyle, *West Britons*, p. 160; and E.669, f.7, 37, *His Majesties Declaration to all his Loving Subjects in Cornwall* (10 September 1643).

59. Hutton, 'Clarendon's History', p. 78; and Loftis and Hardacre, *Apology*, p. 41.

60. For Mohun's death, see E.71 (24), *The Scottish Dove* (13–20 October 1643), p. 3; E.71 (32), *Certain Informations* (16–23 October 1643), p. 309; Bod., J. Walker MSS, C.6, f. 106r; and Vivian, *Visitations*, p. 326.

61. E.A. Andriette, *Devon and Exeter in the Civil War* (Newton Abbot, 1977), p. 97.

62. DRO, 3799, Add. 3 (Maiden Bradley Papers), Box 2, No. 285. I am most grateful to the Senior Archivist at the DRO, Mr John Draisey, for alerting me to the existence of these papers.

63. E.72 (1), *Mercurius Aulicus* (8 October to 14 October 1643), p. 579.

64. For Digby, see Newman, *Royalist Officers*, p. 109; and Chadwyck-Healey, *Bellum Civile*, p. 42.

65. Hammond, *Truth's Discovery*, p. 22.

66. WRO, Bullen Reymes papers, 863/395 (order signed by Anthony Kempson, 16 November 1643).

67. T. Gray and M. Stoyle, 'A Cavalier Cartographer', *History Today*, 44, 3 (March 1994), p. 5; DRO, QS/128, petitions of Laurence Elliot and Robert Spray; and E.31 (15), *A True Narration of the most Observable Passages ... at the late Siege of Plymouth* (1644), p. 17.

68. Bod., Clarendon MSS, 23, 1738 (8), f.186.

69. M. Stoyle, *Loyalty and Locality: Popular Allegiance in Devon during the English Civil War* (Exeter, 1994), p. 51.

70. Bod, Clarendon MSS, 23, 1738 (8), f.186.

71. Bayley, *Civil War in Dorset*, p. 138.
72. Ibid., p. 136.
73. Ibid., p. 139.
74. Ibid.
75. DRO, Seymour MSS, 1392M/1644/48.
76. BL, Harleian MSS, 6804, f. 199. This list is printed (though with no indication of its source) in P. Young, 'King Charles I's Army of 1643–45', *JSAHR*, 18 (1939), p. 36.
77. For the wounding of Digby on 24 June, see BL, Add MSS, 35297 (The Day Book of John Syms), ff. 34r–35.
78. Roy, *Symonds's Diary*, p. 61.
79. Ibid, pp. 2, 54. It may well be that these men were the three tertia commanders of the prince's army.
80. A.C. Miller, *Sir Richard Grenville of the Civil War* (London, 1979), p. 86.
81. Basset's tertia still consisted of four regiments and 1,500 men at this time, see J. Rushworth, *Historical Collections* (eight volumes, London, 1721), V, pp. 700, 702; E. Walker, *Historical Discourses Upon Several Occasions* (London, 1705), p. 68; and Hyde, *History*, III, p. 400.
82. Coate, *Cornwall*, p. 155.
83. Walker, *Discourses*, p. 82.
84. Bod., Firth MSS, C.7, f.164.
85. Hyde, *History*, III, p. 417.
86. Historical Manuscripts Commission (hereafter HMC), 15th Report, Appendix 2 (1897), *Hodgkin Papers*, p. 100; and M. Stoyle, *Plymouth in the Civil War* (Devon Archaeology, 7, Exeter, 1998), pp. 29–30.
87. Roy, *Symonds's Diary*, p. 82; Hyde, *History*, III, p. 425.
88. House of Lords Record Office (hereafter HLRO); Sir Edward Walker's Papers, R.H. Whiteing Deposit, no. 4.
89. Walker, *Discourses*, p. 98.
90. At least one Royalist commentator implied that the mass desertion which began to afflict Maurice's army at the time of Essex's defeat was especially marked among the Cornish troops: see Walker, *Discourses*, p. 82.
91. Hyde, *History*, III, p. 425. See also E.10 (7), *The Kingdomes Weekly Intelligencer* (17–24 September 1644), p. 590.
92. Hyde, *History*, III, p. 417.
93. HLRO, Sir Edward Walker's Papers, R.H. Whiteing Deposit, no. 18; and HMC, *Hodgkin Papers*, p. 102.
94. On the New Cornish, see M. Stoyle, 'Sir Richard Grenville's Creatures: The New Cornish Tertia, 1644–46', *Cornish Studies*, 4 (1996), pp. 26–44.
95. Ibid, p. 28; Stoyle, *West Britons*, pp. 95–9; and Stoyle, *Soldiers and Strangers*, pp. 177–9.
96. Walker, *Discourses*, pp. 98, 106; and Roy, *Symonds's Diary*, pp. 124, 128.
97. Walker, *Discourses*, p. 106. See also Hyde, *History*, III, pp. 428–9.
98. Wanklyn, 'King's Armies', p. 76.
99. S.R. Gardiner, *History of the Great Civil War* (four volumes, 1893, reprinted Adlestrop, 1991), II, p. 48.
100. J.W. Webb (ed.), *Military Memoirs of Colonel John Birch* (Camden Society, New Series, 7, 1873), p. 215.

101. Walker, *Discourses*, p. 111.
102. John Vicars, *The Burning Bush Not Consumed* (London, 1646), p. 59.
103. Kent Archive Office, Sackville MSS, C.285, Sir Ralph Sydenham to the Earl of Bath.
104. E.16 (9), *The Kingdom's Weekly Intelligencer* (29 October to 6 November 1644), p. 705.
105. Roy, *Symonds's Diary*, p. 147. That the Western infantry were present on this occasion is made plain by a sketch map of the Royalist order of battle, which shows 'Prince Maurits foot' in the field alongside 'the King's foot', see BL, Add MSS, 16370, ff.60–1. It is perhaps worth noting that this is the only contemporary depiction of the Old Cornish foot which appears to survive.
106. Bod., Firth MSS, C.7, ff.236–7.
107. B. Whitelocke, *Memorials of the English Affairs* (London 1682), p. 117; and Wanklyn, 'King's Armies', p. 77.
108. For the subsequent history of the Old Cornish regiments, see Stoyle, *Soldiers and Strangers*, pp. 179–80, 196.

3

From Cornish Miner to Farmer in Nineteenth-Century South Australia

A Case Study

Jan Lokan

Introduction

In recent years the historiography of Cornwall's nineteenth-century 'Great Emigration' has taken several important new turns. In addition to the desire to 'fill in the gaps' in the story (for example, Latin America) or to apply more theoretical approaches borrowed from elsewhere in the academic world of emigration studies, there have been attempts at synthesis and overview, alongside vigorous quantitative analyses designed to offer a more reliable estimation of the size and shape of Cornish emigration over time. There has also been a call for 'micro' case studies, with the recent recognition that there are many 'Cornwall's' – rather than just one homogenous territory named 'Cornwall' – mirrored in an insistence that the Cornish emigration experience was likewise many and varied. Issues of gender, family, place, time, climate, motivation, occupation and identity assume a new significance when viewed at a 'micro' level, as do the experiences of individual people. The lives of individuals are worthy of study for their own sake but they can also be exemplars of wider experiences, and thus may be of wide comparative interest, allowing us to generalize about broader aspects of the human condition – in this case, emigration from nineteenth-century Cornwall and settlement in colonial South Australia.[1]

This article presents one such 'micro' case study. About three years ago, my grandfather's diary, covering the period from 1872 to 1892, was found in an old box, where it had remained undisturbed for well over a hundred years. My grandfather, John Goldsworthy, emigrated from Cornwall to Australia as an 18-year-old in 1864. Material from the diary is used in this article as a means of describing one young Cornishman's endeavours to establish himself as a farmer on South Australia's northern Yorke Peninsula, after spending some years down the mines in both Cornwall and Australia. It is well documented that many miners became farmers in this area, particularly as the mines' fortunes waned after initially successful years in the 1860s and early 1870s. Some, who had accumulated capital from working on good, productive lodes in the copper mines or who had had some luck on the Californian or Australian goldfields, accomplished the transition easily. Others found the process difficult. As the article reveals, my grandfather was one of the latter.

Cornish emigration to South Australia

Australia was one of the principal destinations for the emigrant Cornish throughout the nineteenth century, with the goldfields of Victoria, New South Wales and (later) Western Australia proving important magnets for the Cornish. However, the copper mining districts of South Australia were most especially associated with the large-scale settlement of Cornish families and the transplantation of Cornish culture as well as Cornish technology. Kapunda and Burra Burra, together with smaller mines in the Adelaide Hills, were developed in the mid-1840s, and later in 1859–61 there were further rich copper discoveries on the 'ill-shaped leg' of Yorke Peninsula, in a district soon to be known as 'Australia's Little Cornwall' or the 'Copper Triangle', comprising the towns of Moonta, Wallaroo and Kadina.[2]

The rise of Australian and other overseas mines created an international demand for skilled Cornish labour at precisely the moment that Cornwall found itself in economic difficulties. Philip Payton has described the 'widespread hunger and want' in Cornwall that resulted from the potato blight of the 1840s and the further crises that confronted Cornwall in the 1860s and 1870s, with the 'crash of Cornish copper in 1866 and the subsequent faltering of Cornish tin'.[3] He has also documented the extensive departure from Cornwall in the century after 1815,[4] illustrating the depopulation suffered by many Cornish mining parishes: the population of Breage and Germoe fell by 27 per cent between 1841 and 1851, for example, while the populations of Tywardreath and St-Just-in-Penwith fell by 29 and 27 per cent, respectively, between 1861 and 1871.[5]

This departure was mirrored in arrivals abroad. Some 2,000 Cornish emigrated to South Australia in the late 1830s and early 1840s, shortly after

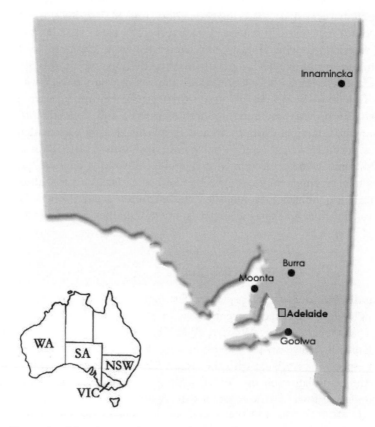

Figure 1. Map showing location of places of interest within Australia
and South Australia (SA).

the colony's foundation.[6] In a further wave, 4,775 'government emigrants' sailed
for South Australia from Cornwall between 1846 and 1850, comprising 71 per
cent of Cornish migration to Australia during that period. A further 5,177
emigrated to South Australia during the 1850s and another wave gathered
momentum during the 1860s to satisfy the demand for skilled miners to work
the newly discovered Yorke Peninsula copper fields. Among this latter group
were members of my family, including my great-grandfather and grandfather,
who were part of the population drift from Tywardreath in the 1860s.

The family in Cornwall

In Cornwall, the Goldsworthys were mostly miners from as far back as can be traced, though an occasional branch took up farming in the vicinity of Wendron, Trewennack and Releath. My great-great-grandfather, also John Goldsworthy, was a resident of Crowan parish and mined in Camborne, where he was married in 1805. Whether he was the John Goldsworthy born in Camborne in 1785 or the one born in Wendron in 1782 is uncertain, but his marriage certificate, which says 'both of this parish', implies the former.[7]

John Goldsworthy and his wife Mary had eleven children, ten of whom survived, and three of whom came to Australia between 1855 and 1870. My great-grandfather James was their eighth child, born in 1822 at St Stephen-in-Brannel. Where the family lived and when can be traced from the places of birth of their children, the Goldsworthys like other mining families migrating to different parts of Cornwall as the prospects of the various areas rose and fell. They moved from Camborne to St Stephen somewhere between 1815 and 1820. Soon after, John Goldsworthy appears to have found work at the Lanescot copper mine, for that was the address given for his children born in the mid 1820s. This mine, opened up in 1817, was located in the valley between Tywardreath and St Blazey in mid-Cornwall. Three neighbouring mines combined to become the Fowey Consols mine in 1822, and by 1827 the Lanescot and Fowey Consols mines together were second in output only to the Consols mine in Gwennap.[8] By 1830, when their youngest child Stephen was born, John and Mary were living in St Blazey itself. Sometime after 1835 the family moved to Penpillick, a village a few miles from Tywardreath, where they were living at the time of the 1841 Census, in which John is still listed as a copper miner. Both John and Mary died in the Tywardreath area, John in September 1843 and Mary in November 1851.

My great-grandfather James would have spent his boyhood and adolescent years in Lanescot, St Blazey and Penpillick, and probably had some schooling, given his accomplishments in later years, there being schools at Tywardreath at that time.[9] James married his wife Mary, born in Lanlivery in 1823, at Tywardreath in August 1843, just before his father died. In the 1851 Census James and Mary are recorded as living in Middlehill, in the vicinity of St Ive, near Liskeard, while in 1861 they were resident in nearby Merrymeet. In both of these censuses James is listed as a lead miner. For some of the years between these two censuses, as the birth records of two of their children show, they lived in the Silva Down Cottages near Pensilva. Mary died at Merrymeet in 1862.

Australia bound

James and Mary Goldsworthy had eight children in Cornwall, one of whom died as a baby and one as a four-year-old. All but one of the surviving family embarked for Australia in May 1864, after James, who was then over 40 and not eligible to emigrate unless he was wed, married his housekeeper Johanna, eleven years his junior. The mines of mid-Cornwall were by now declining and were considered increasingly unhealthy.[10] James was no doubt influenced by such considerations, and also by the emigration agents who worked on South Australia's behalf, recruiting Cornishmen to swell the numbers of skilled miners on northern Yorke Peninsula in the 1860s. He was probably also influenced by his brother Stephen and his nephew Thomas, both of whom had come to Australia nine years earlier to work in the Burra mine, Thomas moving on to Moonta with his family in 1862. James and family were classified as 'remittance' passengers, paying a fee of £4 10s for the whole family of parents and five children, the youngest of whom was 9 years old. Rachel, the oldest child, was 20, already married, and did not come to Australia until 1865.

My grandfather John Goldsworthy was James's eldest son, and was 18 years old at the time of emigration. He and his 16-year-old brother James jr were both listed as miners, along with their father James, and travelled separately from the family in the single men's section of the ship. Given that James jr was already listed as a miner at age 13 in the 1861 Census, it is reasonable to assume that John also went to work in the mines at an early age, particularly as he was the oldest son in a growing family. In the 1861 Census the younger daughters, aged 12 and 6, and the youngest boy, aged 9, were listed as scholars. In 1851, aged 5, John was recorded as a scholar, and his diary is evidence that he knew something of the 'three Rs' by the time he arrived in Australia. In addition to attending school for a few years, he would almost certainly have attended the Sunday chapel schools in Cornwall wherever the family was living. In the shipping list James Goldsworthy and family are listed as 'Dissenters' and are recorded as having been 'of good conduct' during the three-month voyage.

First years in Australia

On arrival in South Australia in August 1864, the family first went to the Burra but was at Moonta within a few months (James and Johanna had their first child there in April 1865), although John – my grandfather – stayed on at Burra for about five years.[11] It was probably easier for a single 18-year-old to obtain work in the Burra mine at that stage than it would have been for his 42-year-old father, particularly as the Burra mine had encountered hard times in the early 1860s.[12] Further, it is 'family folklore' that John and his older sister Rachel were not comfortable with the fact that their father had married his housekeeper, which would have been an added incentive for John to stay separate from the family and its new stepmother. James built a stone cottage for his family at Moonta Mines, and presumably was working in the mine by 1865.

John came to Moonta eventually, somewhere between 1869 and 1871, possibly working in one of the mines and perhaps living initially at home with his father's family. 'Family folklore' has it that one day during 1871 he rode off from Moonta on his horse, taking his dog with him, heading for Ballarat in the Victorian goldfields. John's cousin, Thomas Vial Goldsworthy, had already gone to Ballarat with his wife Grace and their five children to try his luck in 1868, and no doubt encouraged him to join them.

Meanwhile, James Goldsworthy was working hard at escaping the role of mineworker, initially by dabbling as a small-time mining capitalist. He was part of a group that formed the Wilkawat Mining Company, which applied for and was granted a mining lease of 156 acres in June 1866, on a site about two miles south-east of Moonta.[13] Their reasoning was that the area they leased was in a line with other known lodes and they held high hopes that it would yield good returns for them. Sadly, this turned out not to be the case, and the lease was forfeited a year later.[14] Others had bought shares in the company, which was listed in the Adelaide *Register* newspaper during 1866 together with its share price that decreased steadily throughout the year. Government records of mining leases granted at about this time show that a large proportion of these were forfeited after a year or two, no doubt resulting in many dashed hopes.

Following this chastening experience, James opened a licensed school during 1867, where he remained until 1874.[15] Now that the 1875 Education Act (which provided compulsory schooling) was imminent, James considered it unlikely that he would given a job in the new government schools, as he had no formal teacher training.[16] In late 1874 he began working as a draper in Moonta, where he stayed until gaining an appointment in 1878 as the inaugural teacher at a new school in Greens Plains West, a township in a wheat-growing area about fifteen miles from Moonta. He bought a 240-acre farm there to supplement his teaching income, and taught at the school until his death in 1887.

James and Johanna had a total of eight children between 1865 and 1878, only four of whom, all daughters, survived to adulthood. The 1870s were not good years for children in Moonta, poor sanitary conditions leading to typhoid and diphtheria epidemics. Three of James' and Johanna's children died as very young infants and another, aged 4, drowned in their backyard tank.[17] Yet despite such tragedies, James remained energetic and optimistic, and played his part in the civic development of Moonta township. He was a founding member of the 'Duke of Edinburgh' Freemason's Lodge in Moonta, becoming its Worshipful Master in 1871–72, as the display board in the lodge shows to this day. He was also elected to Moonta's Council during its early years, and was unsuccessfully nominated for Mayor in 1876.[18] He was captain in 1873 of the Copper Valley mine[19] (later known as Kooroona[20]); and was appointed joint auditor in Greens Plains West in 1881.[21]

By contrast, my grandfather John Goldsworthy seems to have been a considerably lesser ray in the family spectrum. He appears not to have had the confidence of his father James. Neither did he have a skilled trade, unlike his two younger brothers: James jr was a carpenter and wheelwright, working mainly at the mines, and William Henry was a very successful coachbuilder and blacksmith in Moonta, successful enough to send some of his sons to school in Adelaide and also to become Mayor of Moonta and a Justice of the Peace. All of James's sons were quick to follow their father's example in taking up occupations healthier and more attractive than underground mining. But my grandfather John is the one who seems to have had the most difficulty in following such a path, as his diary reveals.

The diary

The diary in question is approximately B5 size, with lined blank pages rather than pages with dates. Some of John Goldsworthy's entries are in ink, but most are in pencil and are sometimes hard to decipher. The writing is generally neat, sloping to the right, with well-formed letters. Scriptural text, no doubt copied, mostly has correct spelling, but John's own writing often has phonetic spelling, e.g. 'wether' for 'weather'. He was not very methodical, as he used the book from the front and the back, seemingly indiscriminately, and there is sometimes an upside-down page that is otherwise within a sequence. Further, there are several loose bits of pages and other pages where pieces have been torn off, probably when he needed a piece of paper on which to write a note. Occasional pages or part pages are covered in doodles, mostly of his signature, practised many times over (and in different writing styles). Also there are miscellaneous names which he seemed to be using to practise his writing, including what may have been fantasies about possible partnerships with other local personalities, e.g., 'Goldsworthy & Gummow', 'Harris & Goldsworthy', 'Goldsworthy & Harris'.

One interesting feature of the diary is that it was purchased in Ballarat: the stationer's stamp shows clearly on the flyleaf, substantiating the 'family folklore' that had John ride his horse from Moonta to the Victorian goldfields. After several pages of beautifully hand-written scriptural and religious texts, the first actual entry is dated November 1872. The religious texts have grand headings such as 'Trinity', 'Omniscience', 'Omnipotence', 'Original Sin', 'Atonement' and 'Total Depravity of Man'. Perhaps these reflected attendance at Bible classes, although it seems likely in later entries of this kind that John had become a class leader and was planning the classes in his diary.

For the six weeks during which he made daily entries in November and December of 1872, it is clear that he was having a tough time on the Victorian goldfields. He started cheerfully enough, giving daily bulletins about the weather and the state of his health, plus references to whether he received anything or 'paid away' anything. A typical entry at this point is from Friday 15 November: 'First Class as Regards Health. Received nothing Neither Paid away nothing. Beautifull Wether all day'. A tally of receipts and 'payings away' during the six-week period shows that he received £13 17s 9d and paid out £9 16s 9d, including board of £1 per week and 8s for 'Padocking' his horse. One poignant entry says 'spent one shilling and that is one to much'. By mid-December the state of his health had deteriorated to 'well as to Regards Bodely Health, but verry bad in mind and when I shall get better I cannot tell'. Shortly after this he stopped writing daily entries.

He obviously endured the goldfields for several more months, as the diary next picks up on 12 May 1873, when he began an account of his seventeen-day journey back from near Clunes[22] to Moonta. Although written in the composition style of a mid-primary level student, John's description of his journey back to Adelaide nevertheless makes interesting reading, especially as he took what would now be regarded as an unusual route.[23] Times were by then difficult for gold-diggers. As Geoffrey Blainey has noted, between the late 1850s and the late 1870s gold output was quartered, although until 1874 it remained a more valuable export than wool.[24]

South Australian land development

Into what kind of country and society had my grandfather come to live? In several respects the settlement of South Australia was unique, particularly in relation to how farmland was made available, and John Goldsworthy's attempts to become a farmer on Yorke Peninsula need to be understood against this distinctive background.

The colonization of South Australia had been planned in Britain several years before European settlement commenced. There were to be no convicts, nor any shiploads of paupers such as Britain had sometimes sent elsewhere.[25]

The colony was planned by pioneers such as Edward Gibbon Wakefield, Robert Gouger and George Fife Angas, names familiar as the 'founding fathers' of South Australia. These three and their supporters believed that other British colonies had been poorly established, with little or no systematic planning to ensure that the distribution of land proceeded in an orderly way.

One of their basic principles was that land should not be granted freely to settlers; rather, it should be sold at a fixed and uniform price. A certain amount should be sold initially to those who could afford it, and the proceeds of these sales would then be used to bring out from Britain people of 'desirable character' to work on the land. It was crucial to their scheme that 'the supply of Labourers be as nearly as possible proportioned to the demand for Labour at each Settlement; so that Capitalists shall never suffer from an urgent want of Labourers, and that Labourers shall never want well-paid employment'.[26] All land was to be surveyed before it could be sold. Eighty-acre blocks were proposed, at a minimum of £1 per acre, and, of great importance, in contiguous blocks for any individual purchaser. People of desirable character to work the land were specified in the South Australian Colonization Act of 1834 as 'adult persons of the two sexes in equal proportions and not exceeding the age of 30 years'.[27]

The first settlers arrived in South Australia at the end of 1836 and the colony was proclaimed on 28 December. At this time no surveying of land for purchase had been done and Colonel William Light, the first Surveyor-General, had not only to select the site for the first town (where Adelaide is now) but immediately to begin to survey one-acre town blocks and larger blocks for farming, so that the advance purchasers in Britain could claim their allocations. Light faced serious difficulties in these early days through lack of equipment and trained staff and it was many months before the surveying of farm sections on the Adelaide plains, both to the east of the city and south to the coastal town of Goolwa, could begin to catch up with demand.[28] The land was first to be divided into counties, then 'Hundreds' (areas of approximately one hundred square miles) within counties, then Sections (areas typically of eighty acres) within Hundreds, except for land within the Hundreds to be used for towns, where the blocks were much smaller.

The somewhat Utopian ideas underpinning the settlement of South Australia had come unstuck by 1840 when the supply of labourers outstripped the colony's ability to employ them gainfully. Until then, funds from London had been used to set up government works, such as the construction of public buildings to employ newly arrived immigrants, but these funds had dried up.[29] Land surveys had still not been able to keep ahead of demand for property, and so land sales fell off by 1841. Emigration, which was funded from land sales, was forced to slow down dramatically. In the way that pendulums swing, sales of land suitable for farming quickly picked up after more efforts and resources were put into carrying out the surveys in the early 1840s. Acreage of wheat sown in South Australia grew from 1,059 in 1840 to 23,000 in 1843, and there was soon a shortage of labour to work the expanding farmlands.[30] Emigration to the colony began again in the mid 1840s, and increased rapidly for many years thereafter.

One of the original intentions of the planned 'systematic colonization' of South Australia was compromised by pastoralists who had spread their sheep flocks beyond the surveyed areas within the first few years of settlement. By 1842, the government provided for annual Occupation Licences, typically at £5 a year for the licence and a penny a head for sheep,[31] which gave the pastoralists an element of tenure. Pastoralists were understandably not satisfied with this measure, and were rewarded in 1851 by a change to 14-year leases, though these were one-sided in that the land could be resumed at six months' notice if it was required by the government for sale. Further, the leases had to be surveyed and the rental was assessed as either 10s, 15s or £1 per acre depending on the rainfall area in which the lease was located.[32] By this time pastoral leases had extended to the Lower Flinders Ranges (in the mid-north of the state) and the South-East towards the border with Victoria, and the great majority of the colony's sheep and cattle were kept on leases beyond the boundaries of the already surveyed lands.[33]

Although it caused severe short-term hardship because a large number of workers went off to seek their fortunes, the gold rush in Victoria was eventually useful to South Australia's development. Some of those who joined the rush in the early 1850s returned with sufficient money to buy the land they were leasing and the large influx of people to Victoria ensured a good market for South Australia's wheat, flour and other produce. During the 1850s the acreage of wheat sown expanded substantially, rising from almost 54,000 acres in 1851 to almost 176,000 acres in 1857. As Ronald Gibbs commented, 'Many a farmer on the Adelaide plains did better than most of those who sought fortunes on the diggings'.[34] Development slowed down, however, in the 1860s, blocked by a combination of factors, including the large amounts of land involved in pastoral leases, the need for more areas to be surveyed, and the less hospitable mallee scrub lands[35] beyond the settled grasslands. In 1864 there was a major drought, with consequent large stock losses. By 1865 it had become more difficult to sell South Australian wheat to neighbouring colonies, and much of the land had in any case become 'wheat sick' because holdings were usually too small to allow for fallowing. Emigration stopped again by 1867, due to a combination of these factors.[36]

These were the conditions with which my great-grandfather James Goldsworthy and his family were confronted in 1864. If they had had any ideas of taking up farming soon after their arrival, they would quickly have learned that the time was not opportune. They reached Australia in the years when Cornish immigration came to a head – 'when most ships arriving at Port Adelaide carried sizeable Cornish groups'[37] – and the copper mines on Yorke Peninsula were then a much better prospect than farming. However, as Payton has noted, the new mining towns also acted as catalysts for the opening up of Yorke Peninsula for farming purposes, in order to supply the rapidly growing population.[38] The first wheat on Yorke Peninsula was grown at Greens Plains West, about fifteen miles from Moonta, but this was not until 1866. Before that provisions for the area were either brought by sea from the capital city, Adelaide, or overland by bullock wagons from Clare in the mid-north.[39]

The County of Daly, and the Hundreds of Kadina and Wallaroo within it (which incorporated the towns of Kadina, Moonta and Wallaroo), was proclaimed in 1862,[40] though the agricultural lands around the towns were not opened up for several more years. Surveying of agricultural lands beyond the Adelaide plains accelerated during the second half of the 1860s. The drought in 1864–65 had prompted the then Surveyor-General, George Goyder, to map out a 'line of rainfall', based on actual data, beyond which he considered the rainfall conditions not reliable enough to justify using the land for anything other than pastoral grazing. Given that Goyder had control over which lands were chosen to be released, it is not surprising that the lands surveyed in the ensuing years for farming were mostly south of his line of rainfall.[41]

It is interesting to note that Kadina and Wallaroo are clearly north of Goyder's line, while Moonta appears to be only slightly above it.[42] However, Goyder must have thought these locations close enough to the rainfall demarcation line for the survey into Sections to proceed, which happened in the late 1860s. The first land in the district to be offered for selection was not notified in the South Australian *Government Gazette* until 1869. Meanwhile, the terms under which land was made available were evolving in interesting ways. For small farmers of limited means, the main way to be involved in farming before 1866 was to rent land from a wealthier capitalist. Act 21 of 1866, the 'Scrub Lands Act', provided an alternative means in that now land which had not sold at auction could be leased for 21 years, at a minimum rental of 10s per square mile, with the right to purchase at any time at £1 per acre. The cost of clearing was reckoned at £2 per acre, but only one-twentieth of the land had to be cleared in the first year.[43]

A broader system was introduced in January 1869, when, after much parliamentary debate, the 'Waste Lands Amendment Act', known colloquially as 'Strangways Act' after the member who proposed it, was passed. Under the provisions of this act, the maximum area of land that one purchaser could bid for in most circumstances was 320 acres. Intending purchasers had to lodge their bids in writing, which determined the selling price, with a minimum fixed at £1 an acre. The land was available only on credit, with an initial deposit of 20 per cent and the remainder paid over four years.[44] The Act was designed to give the small farmers more opportunity to obtain their own land in competition with the better-off pastoralists, who had acquired all of the previous five Hundreds north of Clare when they were released.[45] The Strangways Act was not popular with pastoralists, who felt it discriminated against them, especially as it meant that many of their leaseholds were resumed for sale and they were forced to move to land further away.

It so happened that the early 1870s were bumper years for wheat crops, which led would-be purchasers to lobby the government to release land well north of Goyder's line. Their lobbying was successful, and an amendment to the Act in 1872 allowed for all but the north-western-most lands in South Australia to be surveyed for potential sale, even as far to the north-east as the outback settlement of Innamincka. Further amendments to the Act were made to liberalize the credit terms, so that selectors could have a longer time to pay off their land. The first crop year of 1869 was a poor one, and many of those who had obtained the earliest selections after the Act was passed experienced difficulties in meeting their payments. The amended Act allowed for purchase after five years, but also permitted an extension for three more years with interest of 5 per cent per year paid in advance.[46] Land obtained by credit selection had to be improved to the value of 12s 6d per acre, such as clearing, fencing and cropping, and there was a requirement for the selector to take up residence on the land.[47]

John Goldsworthy's transition to the land

The first record of my grandfather's obtaining land is that indicating that he was granted Section 130 in the Hundred of Wallaroo, almost two miles north of the Moonta township, on credit selection. The section comprised 123 acres, later re-measured as 124, for an offered amount of £187 11s 6d and the application was granted on 13 July 1876.[48] His address at the time of application was given as Moonta Mines, as it was when he returned from the goldfields in 1873, and his occupation was given as 'Carter'. There were at least two other people of the same name resident at Moonta Mines at the time, but the reference to his occupation and also various notes in his diary confirm that he was certainly the person involved in this transaction. In 1876 he would have had to pay the 10 per cent deposit up front for the land, with a further 10 per cent in three years' time.

John Goldsworthy's diary indicates that, prior to this acquisition of land, he was working as a carter, and possibly also as a timber-cutter, both of which required licences. He may have held such licences, although the earliest record

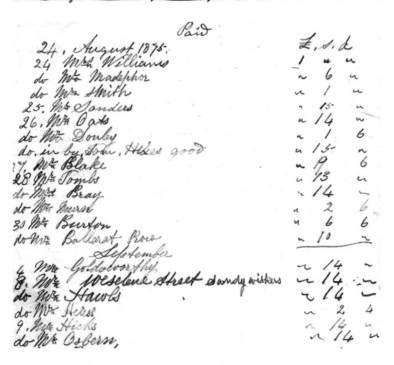

Figure 2.   Sample records of orders and payments in 1875.

of his doing so is dated 1876. His copious diary entries relating to carting wood, fence posts, tank posts, pine, wire, sand, clay, stone, watter, dongue [dung], furniture, people ('pasengers to the beach'), a dog and so on began in July 1873 and continued fairly steadily until the first half of 1876. There are also sporadic entries to carting in later years, right up to 1892 when the diary ends. The entries concerning carting consist of pages of orders, lists of moneys paid to him and lists of moneys 'howed' to him. Some of the last-named are crossed out and annotated 'Paid', but many are not. There are occasional references to spending the day 'out to the pinery', 'out for pine' or 'out for tank poles', presumably collecting wood on other people's behalf.

Some of the amounts charged for various types of loads appear anomalous. Loads of wood varied from 10s to 14s, but a load of stone varied only from 1s 6d to 2s 6d. One can only surmise that stone was difficult to move and therefore the loads were smaller, though he annotated one page to say that loads of stone needed two horses. A load of clay was 1s 6d and needed only one horse. On another page there is a list of charges: stone at 1s 3d per load; 'skimpons' at 2s 6d per load; wood at 12s per load; pine at 4½d each; bages [bags] at 5s per load; and dongue at 3s per load. An average of his takings over six months shows that he made less than £3 a week from these travails, interspersed with an occasional bonanza week when he carted many loads of stumps to the Moonta or the Yelta mine and made up to £8 in the process. It was hard manual work for what seem like rather meagre returns. Examples of some of these entries from 1875 are shown in Figure 2.[49]

Occasional lists of his domestic purchases at the time put the above earnings into context. If his lists are at all representative, he lived mostly on meat from the butcher, about a pound a day at about 6d per lb, and bread, using 23 loaves over a 6-week period. Other purchases during this period included a tin of jam, two tins of cocoa, flower [flour], sugar, tobacco (at 1s 1½d), a mouthpice [mouthpiece] for his pipe (2s 6d), a shirt (8s), a fryingpan, a candlestick, a plate, a glass and a and Cup & suser [saucer]. At the top of one page he has written 'One month's Provisions £2 15s 2d'. He mentioned settling his accounts with John Lawery (baker) and James Rutter (storekeeper), and scrawled across the page 'howing [owing] for nothing'. At these rates he had some surplus, perhaps £40 to £45 per six months on average, to help pay for the equipment he needed to run his carting activities, but details presented later in the paper suggest that he would have found it very difficult to save the deposit for the land he obtained by credit selection.

It is not clear whether he was living with his parents at this stage, or perhaps boarding, or even renting some land himself. The former seems unlikely unless he had some kind of separate hut on their land, given the purchases mentioned above. After his father had moved into the Moonta township in 1875 he, my grandfather, sometimes refers to paying board, perhaps to someone else in Moonta Mines. After he obtained his own land in 1876, he supposedly constructed some kind of dwelling and occupied it, to satisfy the conditions of purchase. A letter he drafted in his diary in 1879 is headed 'Rosworthy [Roseworthy] Farm', which must be the name he used for Section 130, and seems to imply that he was living there.

For his carting business, he listed in October 1874 that he had six horses – Vilet, Noble, Jack, Gipsy, Gurtie, Darky – and also a wagon and a 'bugy'. Some indicative costs that he provided in July 1873 are shown in Table 1. Later that year he purchased the wagon for £30 (he must have sold the horses he had in 1873, as listed in the table, and acquired others by 1874). The total displays a rare addition error, as he usually added money correctly.

Table 1.   Initial set-up costs in July 1873 for carting business

	£	s	d
York	32		
Dutch	41		
Bets	25		
dray	18	10	
Harness	8	15	
?	1	2	6
Axes		18	
nailes		12	
Batton		5	3
Collar		7	6
Backchain		3	
	128	13	9

Figure 3 shows that he wrote of transactions involving horses in 1874 and 1875, the first of which seems likely to be a purchase, though he does not name the recipient of the 'cheaque'. The 1875 transaction was definitely a sale.

From July to October 1875 he recorded a list of expenses as horse feed £6, Grubbing £5 9s 8d, Bran & Chaff £1 11s 6d, Shuing [shoeing] 10s, Repairing harnes 2s 6d, plough sheirs £2 2s 2d, nailes 4s 6d and Gathering up Butes (?) & sticks 14s. As well as these, he paid wages at the rate of 7s 6d per day to John Ralph 'about the stable', totalling £16 2s 6d for the same

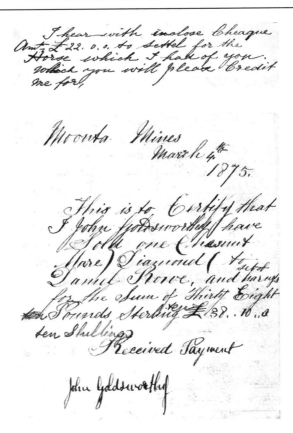

I hear with inclose Cheaque Amt £22. 0. 0. to settle for the Horse which I had of you. which you will please Credit me for,

Moonta Mines March 4th 1875.

This is to Certify that I John Goldsworthy have Sold one Chasnut (Mare) Diamond to Daniel Rowe, and harness for the Sum of Thirty Eight Pounds Sterling £38..10..a ten Shillings Received Payment

John Goldsworthy

Figure 3.
Transactions involving
horses.

four-month period. Together these expenses amount to about £32. As noted before, his average carting income was £10 to £12 a month and his living costs were about the same as one week's income, and thus, given what he spent on equipment, he would have had little opportunity to save during this period. He must have had other periods when he could accumulate some savings, as he felt himself ready to lodge an application for land by credit selection in 1876.

Section 130

His diary entries are less frequent during the time he worked on Section 130 (see Figure 6 for this section's location in relation to Moonta), but there are enough of them to show that his life continued to be difficult financially and also personally to some extent. Again, he began optimistically, recording several more purchases made early in 1877, such as a Mawer [mower] £15, a Reeper £5 10s, a dray £14, a horse £25, Chaff £4 10s, water £1, and a window frame 15s. He completed the list with the entries 'Intrest £17 10s 0d', 'goin Behind £26' and the total of £109 5s 0d. By this time he must have borrowed money on which he had to pay interest, and also had bills, yet unpaid, for £26. In the next few years there are scattered entries that he owed 'Hintrest' to two local individuals, John Northcott and Joseph Morgan, as he recorded when he paid back some of these amounts. The mention of the window frame is notable because it implies that he had some kind of dwelling on the section, as required by the conditions for land acquired by credit selection.

As noted earlier, it was also a requirement that improvements be made to the land each year. Table 2 reproduces, in tabular form, a list of John's activities from part of April 1877, which reveal that he had already cleared enough of the section to warrant sowing wheat. Note that, in good Cornish Methodist fashion, Sunday is omitted, as it is throughout his diary, even during his time at the goldfields.

Table 2.   Some tasks undertaken in April 1877*

Date	Day	Task
2)	Monday	Carried Strutes around the Section and two load of dongue and spread it over the ground.
3)	Tuesday	Carried Seven Load of dongue over the ground and ploughed some ground
4)	Wensday	Carried Struts. ploughing & down to the township after wire Carried one Coil over by the tank
5)	Thursday	four load of dongue, and spread it over the ground. but through to the tank for post plowing and went to the township for a horse
6)	Friday	Carried four load of dongue and went round the Section and Numberd the posts
7)	Saturday	aload of Pine Mr Bennetts storekeeper township. brought out some Chaff and Bran
9)	Monday	township after weat and pickling and harroing in some
10)	Tuesday	Harring and pickling and preparing for the Bald hills†
11)	Wensday	Harring Carrying Seed weat around the ground and preparing for Bald hills

* John's spelling and expressions are transcribed here as he wrote them, except that he did not set them out as a table with headings and columns.

† This may have been work undertaken for someone else; the Bald Hills are near Moonta, but not where John's own property was.

Clearly he continued valiantly with making improvements to the land. In February 1878 he mentioned paying out money for haroing [harrowing] £4 4s 0d, horse Racking 6s, fifty Posts £1 10s, pulling wire and straining it 17s 6d, cleaning of Rubish £1 18s 0d, two Days Horse Dray & Man £3 15s 4d, two Days for a Man 7s, and two ax andles (amount not given). Most likely because he was continuing his carting as he tried to earn some income, and because the work of improving 124 acres of mallee scrub was more than one person could reasonably manage, he had been paying out significant amounts to others for a variety of activities between March and June of 1878. For 'improvements on the Section' he recorded payments of one guinea to each of Richard Madron and James Gummow, four guineas to William Green, £6 5s to Charles Green and £5 10s 6d to Madron & Son. Other amounts he 'paid away' at this time are shown in Table 3.

Table 3.   'Money paid away for wood Cuting and other Labour'*

	£	s	d	
R Madron	5	18		Cuting wood
S Smith	4	1		do
W Gummow	1	6		do
R Madron	2	7		Grubbing & Cutting wood
	1			Repairing waggon & Harnes
S Smith	7	4		Driving teem
	1	6		for Rains, sheir plough & swingle trees (?)
Greens	7	2		Cutting wood
two Greens	8	8		Grubbing
R Madron	7	18	6	Grubbing & tank
	9	10		Plough & ? Malie trees
		11		two padded colars
R Madron	3			Grubbing
	59	1	6	

* John's spelling and expressions are transcribed here as he wrote them.

He referred to selling 'Black Malie' at £4 2s a ton, and 'White Malie stumps' at £2 18s a ton, but at this stage, in the first few months of 1878, did not give any lists of deliveries. The first time he mentioned receiving money is in June 1878, when he listed items totalling £48 14s 6d, but £14 of this

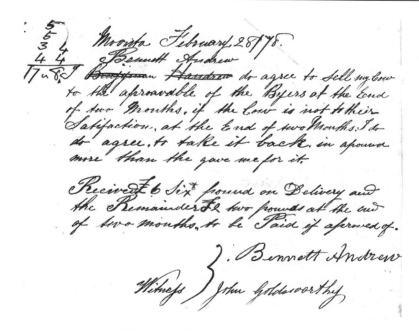

Figure 4. Transaction involving a cow.

was from 'Macklingham Banker', which sounds like a further loan. Of the amounts received, £6 12s was from the Road Board – perhaps he was doing some contract work for them. He also gave a list of amounts owed to him, totalling £17 7s, £3 1s 9d of which was due from the Road Board. Offsetting this income, however, is a long list of expenses for 'Labour & Chaff & Bran and other things', including seed, a whip handle, horse brands, hair cut (1s) and eight amounts adding to £13 16s 9d paid to 'Union'. Were these perhaps interest amounts paid to the Union Bank? The total of his expenses was £45 4s 10½d.

In February 1878 he also recorded purchasing a cow. There is an entry stating that 'This is to Certify that I, Benjamin Handrew, do agree to Sell one Cow to John Goldsworthy' which clarifies the (possibly somewhat unusual) transaction shown in Figure 4.

But by the time he bought this cow, things were already coming unstuck for him financially. On 17 January 1878 he drafted an elaborately worded 'Memmorandom of an agreement Entered into this day Between John Goldsworthy & John Nankivell of Moonta About Section 130 in the Hundred of Wallaroo County of Daly', in which he proposed that they would work the section on equal terms, and 'each to have Equel Intrest in the same', except that nothing was to be sold without his consent and the block was to be his until it was paid for. He also took up about half a page specifying what should be done if something should happen to either one of them. It seems that nothing was done about this proposal at the time, as the next entry, in February, recorded that 'James Gummow was out to me about the Section, about Transfering it to Mr Mathews from Kadina'. He commented that at this stage he was 'Out of Pocket £107–11–6'.

Somehow he managed to keep going with the Section and must have entered into an agreement with John Nankivell during 1878, as attested by the following announcement which appeared in the *Yorke's Peninsula Advertiser* on December 13 of that year:

NOTICE. – Any PIGS, GOATS or FOWLS found trespassing on the Farm of MESSRS GOLDSWORTHY AND NANKIVELL, on the Port Wallaroo Road, will be destroyed, or Impounded.

By 1879 John was delivering many loads of mallee stumps for 8s per load, often making several deliveries on the same day. He bought more equipment, including two more horses named Clyde and Eliot, for £50 and £40, respectively, two more wagons, another dray, two tanks at £4 10s each, a stone pick for 15s and several grubbing picks at 7s each. Including an unexplained amount of £60 4s 6d for 'Land', he tallied up his expenses during some of 1879 as £277 15s. In July 1879 he recorded that he had about seventy 'acers' under Crop, fourteen of these being 'out for hay', which had yielded ten tons, and fifty-six under wheat, from which he had obtained ninety bushels. These yields are low, but possibly not for a first crop and also in light of the below average rainfalls and yields experienced in South Australia from 1876 to 1878 (see the Appendix).

On a personal level, loneliness comes through in some of his diary entries in the late 1870s. He drafted letters to three different women in 1879 and 1880, indicating that he was now 'of a settled age' and had been looking around for a lengthy period 'in order to settle myself' and requesting them to consider him. Whether these letters were ever sent is not known, but he did not marry until 1898 and none of these three became his wife. He appears to have had an inferiority complex in relation to his brother William Henry, as he signed one of these letters with his name and the annotation 'A brother to William Henry'. Also, he had practised the signatures 'John W H Goldsworthy' and 'J W H Goldsworthy' many times on his doodle pages and began using these on correspondence by about 1880.[50]

The struggle to keep his head above the financial water continued and he sometimes had trouble finding money to pay for labour, as shown in Figure 5.

He tried a new way of gaining some income in 1881 – the diary lists the

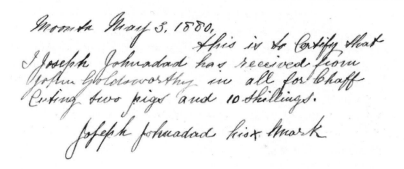

Figure 5.   Record of partly 'in kind' payment.

names of many people with whom he made appointments for his stallions to service their mares. He gives no indication of income derived from this, and may not have persisted with it beyond the few months covered by the diary entries. As the time approached when he would have to pay the remainder of the money owing on the section he gave up, and formally applied in October 1881 to transfer the section to John Nankivell, on the grounds of ill health (whether the ill health was real or not is not known; however that, and absenteeism, were the most common grounds on which the many transfers applied for at the time were requested). His application was granted on 18 March 1882.

In limbo

We know little of where John Goldsworthy was or what he did in the 1880s after the tragedy of losing his land. There is a John Goldsworthy listed as a farmer at Greens Plains West in the *South Australian Directories* of 1884 and 1885, and there is a draft letter in the diary with Greens Plains West given as his address in 1883. This suggests that he probably went to live on his father's property, helping to develop the farm there while his father taught at the local school. His obituary[51] states that he went to Broken Hill for two years, which was most likely to have been between 1886 and 1888, joining the exodus of Moonta folk to this important new mining town. However, he continued to be listed as 'farmer near Moonta' on the electoral roll for the South Australian House of Assembly throughout the latter years of the 1880s. In April 1889 his diary states that he 'started to work with Mr John Clark'. There is also a diary entry in 1890, in which he drafted a note to the Postmaster in Moonta, Mr Clark, requesting that the bearer (W. Nankivell) be permitted to collect mail for him. Otherwise there are no further entries until 1892.

Poona Farm

Perhaps John Goldsworthy had managed to save some money in Broken Hill, as he applied for and was granted a 'Lease with right to purchase' on 181 acres of land near Moonta in June 1890.[52] This arrangement was another option that had been provided for in Clause 39, Act 18 of 1872 to help ordinary citizens to acquire land. The area he leased is shown on the map in Figure 6[53] as the blocks marked 1275 to 1286, at centre right in the top part of the map:

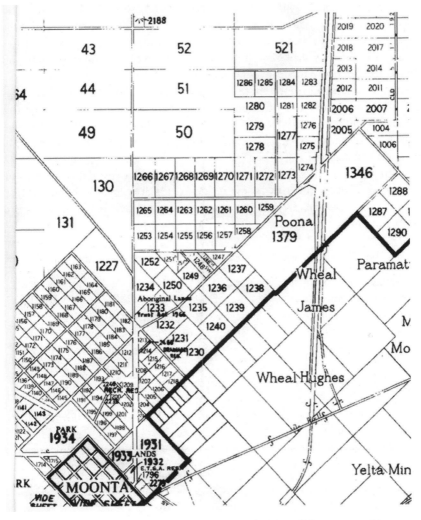

Fig. 6. Map showing relevant sections in relation to Moonta township.

The purchase price, which, at the time of purchase, could be paid any time up to twenty-one years later, was £248 17s 6d and the cost of the lease was £6 4s 5d per year. For several years after this the South Australian *Government Gazettes* listed the amounts owing for leases and when they were due, and so it was possible to check how well John kept up with his payments. He paid the first six on time, but by 1899 was three years in arrears (probably because he was paying for a house to be built from 1897). From 1899 to 1901 he paid the annual amount and in 1902 paid the annual amount plus an extra half of one year's payment. His payment record must have been just satisfactory enough for him to retain the lease, as he remained on the property and finally purchased it in 1921, with the aid of a mortgage. Once again the dice were against him with his timing for establishing a farm, as there was a severe drought in South Australia in 1891 and a resulting economic downturn in the 1890s.[54] And once again he looked for further ways to generate income.

In this regard, his diary contains a draft Tender, dated 29 October 1892, to the Kadina Council for 'Contract No 5 – grubbing and Clearing from the NE of Sec 1.091 to the NW corner of Sec 1.090 Hundred of Wallaroo: and from the NE corner of Sec 525 to the NW corner of Sec 528 at per Chain', but unfortunately the rest of the page is torn off. There are references in 1892 to carting hay or chaff for others, plus being paid for deliveries of stumps or harrowing work for several Moonta residents. He attempted to obtain a lease to graze his stock on Section 51, which adjoins his leased land (see Figure 6), in this intriguing memo:

'To the Chairman of the District Council Kadina & Councelors

Gentlemen would you let me Part of known as Moonta Park No 51 Section for a term of 7 years, for grasing & Cultivation, I would Securely fence it in with Post & wire and leave the fencing at the experation of term in good Order or to your satisfaction and would give £1.0.0 a year rent Beside securely fencing the block. As it is now it is no use to any one. But a Plague to they whom it join and a arbour for Vermon. In the offer I make to you fine in one Section out of the two in a Proper manner, and also clear say the most of the Scrub, and if you want say 10 or 20 ac left for Pick Nick Parties it could be don and that would be enough for that Purpus.

Hoping it will meet with your aprovell. if you cannot comply with my request kindly inform me what you will do.

Belive me to be your Servent. Yours Faithfully John Goldsworthy, Moonta'

As Payton wrote in 1987: 'The only ones who benefited from the difficult days of the 1890s were those who managed to last out ... Those who did survive were lucky for, with the return of brighter economic conditions and wetter winters, Yorke Peninsula became established in the early years of this [twentieth] century as a principal wheat-growing district'.[55] Somehow, my grandfather John Goldsworthy was one of the survivors of that difficult decade, but he did not have an easy time. It is known in the family that he continued his carting activities for many years in order to make enough money to keep the farm going. The farm he started in 1890 is still in the family today and horse and dray teams, such as John used for carting, were also used for work on the farm until the early 1950s. The four-room stone house that John had built for him in 1897 endures, albeit with some additions such a proper bathroom and lavatory, enclosed back verandah and front porch. Prior to having the house built, he is said to have lived in a makeshift shack under a large pepper tree that is still on the property, not far from the house. He eventually married in 1898, when his insecure personality showed through again, on his marriage record: he gave his age as 48 when in fact he was 52. He died in 1923, aged 77.

Conclusion

Like many other Cornish miners in the 1860s, John Goldsworthy had been enticed to South Australia by the demand for skilled hard-rock miners to develop the colony's rich copper deposits at a time when the workings at home in Cornwall were faltering. Again, like many Cornish miners, he came to South Australia as part of a family group (the head of the family was his father, James Goldsworthy), which in emigrating overseas anticipated new opportunities for 'betterment' and socio-economic advancement. For many this aspiration included the eventual shedding of their occupational status as miners, with a desire to set up business as artisans or to acquire land for farming. The miner-turned-farmer became a familiar figure in nineteenth-century South Australia, especially on northern Yorke Peninsula after 'Strangways Act' and other measures to liberalize land availability had encouraged small men of limited means.

The Goldsworthy family was broadly successful in its aim of abandoning mining but, as his diary shows, for John Goldsworthy it was never an easy task. The properties he acquired were at the very edge of Goyder's line, the frontier then between the 'good earth' that could be cultivated for wheat and other crops, and arid bush country fit only for grazing. He joined the rush of Cornish miners-turned-farmers who took up land in the optimistic mid-1870s but, alas, was also among the many forced off their properties in the early 1880s. But he did not give up. By 1890 he was back on the land in his own right, establishing a new farm in what turned out to be one of the most difficult decades of the period, harsh drought conditions once more driving many former miners from the land. Yet somehow he won through, and like others who had done likewise, by the early twentieth century had settled into a more secure existence as a reasonably successful farmer.

As a 'micro' case-study, the story of my grandfather, John Goldsworthy, and his diary is a revealing insight into the trials experienced by many similar Cornish mining families which attempted to take up farming on the South Australian frontier in the closing decades of the nineteenth century. It is also evidence of the tenacity and determination to succeed in the face of multiple setbacks that motivated many of these Cornish emigrants in their desire to secure socio-economic advancement beyond the world of underground labour. Ultimately, John Goldsworthy was successful in his quest to become a farmer on northern Yorke Peninsula, and his experience stands as an exemplar of the many others who sought to do the same, whether successful or not.

Postscript

Today, the Goldsworthy farm is much larger than the original core of 181 acres. Good years after the Second World War meant that the family was able to add to its holdings in the 1950s and early 1960s by purchasing the blocks numbered 1266 to 1274, Sections 50 to 52 and Section 521. Before my grandfather died, he had obtained a 21-year lease on Section 1379, (labelled Poona on the map), and also on Section 1346. These leases were renewed for further periods of 21 years on two occasions. Eventually, during the 1970s (and just before the Act was changed) my uncle took advantage of a clause that allowed long-term lessees to buy out the land they were leasing, and purchased Section 1379. He chose to keep Section 1346 on a renewable lease basis, perhaps because some old shafts of the Poona mine were on this land and there was always the possibility that the land could be resumed if the mine were to be reactivated.

The Poona mine itself was productive for some years in the nineteenth century, sending away 'a considerable quantity of marketable ore', but was 'one of the very many small mines that ceased work during the depression in the copper market in the '70 decade'.[56] The lode was discovered when a cutting was being made for the Moonta and Wallaroo Tramway. James Pryor, father of the well-known local author Oswald Pryor, was appointed underground captain of this mine in 1873.[57] Interest was shown in re-opening Poona in the 1890s, and an inspector who checked it out recommended in 1900 that 'a main shaft be sunk, some distance W and slightly to the N of the old one, to the depth of at least 320 ft ... It may be regarded as a fair legitimate mining venture, and, with the necessary amount of capital, has every reasonable chance of success'.[58]

Yet the Poona remained idle until the mid 1980s, when the Australian company Western Mining Limited discovered an extension to the original lode about one hundred and sixty metres long and up to six metres wide, with an average width of three to four metres.[59] Subsequently, the Amalg Resources company from Western Australia bought out the lease for Section 1346 in 1987, and the Poona operated as an open-cut mine from 1988 to 1991. Between 1988 and 1993, from Poona and neighbouring Wheal Hughes together, 'about 17,000 tons of copper were recovered as chalcocite-rich concentrates,' typically grading 30 per cent copper and about 7 grams per ton of gold.[60] Some of the copper extracted from Poona was of a quality known as 'black copper', which is about 80 per cent pure.

Mining at Poona has now stopped, probably forever. The land in Section 1346 will never again be used for farming, as it was excavated as a very large open-cut pit, through which the Wheal Hughes mine tour now runs a small sight-seeing train.

Acknowledgements

I should like to thank Liz Coole of the National Trust of South Australia, Moonta Branch Resource Centre, for assistance in locating some of the material used in this article. An earlier version of the article was presented at the 'Cornish Migration to Australia' biennial seminar organized by the Cornish Association of South Australia and held in Kadina as part of the 2007 Kernewek Lowender Cornish festival.

APPENDIX

Table A.1   Average wheat yield per acre in bushels and pounds
of selected counties and the rainfall in inches at Adelaide,
from 1863 to 1882

	Rainfall	*Yield per acre*		
Year	*Adelaide*	*Adelaide*	*Daly*	*Robe*
1863	19.76	13.27	–	10.24
1864	16.04	10.49	–	15.30
1865	13.03	9.19	–	22.30
1866	17.93	14.28	12.00	23.00
1867	14.28	2.41	11.01	15.00
1868	14.04	9.46	6.04	19.25
1869	9.26	6.16	2.34	14.24
1870	18.04	12.08	11.47	8.56
1871	14.18	6.00	5.18	13.39
1872	16.57	13.14	12.25	11.17
1873	14.17	5.43	10.13	8.43
1874	14.13	11.56	12.17	10.39
1875	20.14	10.57	12.47	9.19
1876	8.80	5.44	2.21	3.32
1877	15.19	5.34	6.56	6.49
1878	12.27	5.42	6.46	7.48
1879	13.83	10.46	10.06	8.21
1880	13.74	5.25	5.22	3.54
1881	12.91	8.15	4.40	4.46
1882	11.63	7.38	3.54	3.33

Source: Adapted from G.L. Buxton, *South Australian Land Acts 1869–1885*, Appendix
D.

Notes and references

1. Philip Payton, *The Cornish Overseas: A History of Cornwall's Great Emigration* (Fowey, 2005); Sharron P. Schwartz, 'Migration Networks and the Transnationalization of Social Capital: Migration to Latin America, A Case Study', in Philip Payton (ed.), *Cornish Studies: Thirteen* (Exeter, 2005), pp. 256–87; Sharron P. Schwartz, 'Cornish Migration Studies: An Epistemological and Paradigmatic Critique', in Philip Payton (ed.), *Cornish Studies: Ten* (Exeter, 2002), pp. 136–65; Gary Magee and Andrew Thompson, 'Remittances Revisited: A Case Study of South Africa and the Cornish Migrant, c.1870–1914', in Philip Payton (ed.), *Cornish Studies: Thirteen* (Exeter, 2005), pp. 288–306; Bernard Deacon, ' "We don't travel much, only to South Africa": Reconstructing Nineteenth-century Cornish Migration Patterns', in Philip Payton (ed.), *Cornish Studies: Fifteen* (Exeter, 2007), pp. 90–116; Bernard Deacon, 'In Search of the Missing "Turn": The Spatial Dimension and Cornish Studies', in Philip Payton (ed.), *Cornish Studies: Eight* (Exeter, 2000), pp. 213–30.
2. Ern Carmichael, *The Ill-Shaped Leg: A Story of the Development of Yorke Peninsula* (Adelaide, 1973); Philip Payton, *Making Moonta: The Invention of Australia's Little Cornwall* (Exeter, 2007)
3. Philip Payton, *The Cornish Overseas* (Fowey, 2005), p. 15.
4. Payton, *Cornish Overseas.*
5. Payton, *Cornish Overseas*, p. 28.
6. Payton, *Cornish Overseas*, p. 258.
7. His age at death does not confirm either of these birth years, but is closer to agreeing with 1785.
8. Jim Lewis, *A Richly Yielding Piece of Ground: The Story of Fowey Consols Mine Near St Blazey* (St Austell, 1997), p. 35.
9. Cornwall Federation of Women's Institutes, *The Cornwall Village Book* (Newbury, 2nd edn, 2000).
10. Lewis, *Fowey Consols Mine*, p. 123, citing C. Schmitz, 'Cornish Mine Labour and the Royal Commission of 1864', in *Journal of the Trevithick Society*, No. 10 (1983): 'The Commission ... was supplied with figures from the Registrar General's Office showing that at age 35, a Cornish miner was about three times more likely to die within the next 10 years of life from consumption or lung disease than a man employed in the better ventilated coal mines of Durham, Northumberland or Staffordshire, and by age 45 the likelihood was a factor of over four.'
11. The *People's Weekly*, 28 April 1923.
12. Philip Payton, *The Cornish Miner in Australia: Cousin Jack Down Under* (Redruth, 1984), p. 39: 'the Burra was plunged into decline in 1862 through an unfortunate combination of slumping copper prices and an unusually wet winter which made it difficult to keep the mine dry'. Payton also explains that 'a wide variety of new exploratory work' began at Burra in 1865 (p. 40).
13. Microfiche records held at the South Australian State Records Office, reference GRS 3130.
14. South Australian *Government Gazette*, 13 June 1867, p. 556.
15. T. Vinson, C. Warn, J. Harbison and J. Winders, *Moonta Primary School 1878–1978: A Centenary History of Education at Moonta Primary School and the Surrounding Area*

(Adelaide, 1978), p. 8 and pp. 52–3 documents that James's school was located in the vestry of the Bible Christian Church and gives enrolment numbers per year, which ranged from about 80 to about 130. The *Yorke's Peninsula Advertiser and Miners' News*, 11 September 1874, reported that James's resignation had been accepted by the Education Board.

16. However, he is listed as a Licensed Teacher in the *South Australian Directories* for the years he was teaching in Moonta Mines.

17. *Wallaroo Times*, 12 February 1870.

18. *Yorke's Peninsula Advertiser*, 17 November 1876.

19. *Yorke's Peninsula Advertiser*, 8 April 1873: 'there is little doubt that the Moonta lodes run through the property, and therefore the adventurers resume the work of the mine with every prospect of success.' This was false optimism, as confirmed in H.Y.L. Brown, *Record of the Mines of South Australia*, (Adelaide, 4th edn, 1908), p. 46.

20. Brown, *Mines*, p. 46.

21. South Australian *Government Gazette*, Volume 2, 21 July 1881, p. 241.

22. A town, near Ballarat, which was a productive gold-mining area for many years.

23. A transcript of his account has been submitted for publication to *The South Australian Genealogist*, the journal of the South Australian Genealogy and Heraldry Society.

24. Geoffrey Blainey, *The Rush That Never Ended: A History of Australian Mining* (Melbourne, 2nd edn, 1969) p. 60.

25. Douglas Pike, *Paradise of Dissent: South Australia from 1829–1857* (Melbourne, 1957), pp. 39 and 41. Pike commented that the pressure of population was a serious problem in England in 1827, when there were 'nearly 100,000 persons on parish relief'.

26. Elizabeth Kwan, *Living in South Australia: A Social History* (Adelaide, 1987), p. 11.

27. Atlas of South Australia: Organizing a Colony, p. 1. On www.atlas.sa.gov.au

28. R.M. Gibbs, *A History of South Australia: From Colonial Days to the Present* (Blackwood, 2nd edn, 1990) p. 36.

29. Gibbs, *History*, p. 46.

30. Gibbs, *History*, p. 66.

31. Carmichael, *Yorke Peninsula*, p. 5.

32. Carmichael, *Yorke Peninsula*, p. 37.

33. Atlas of South Australia: 1850: The Province Established, p. 1. On www.atlas.sa.gov.au

34. Gibbs, *History*, p. 69.

35. Mallee trees are unusual eucalypts with low-growing branches that come from the stumpy roots. They can withstand drought conditions and grow anywhere from 1.5 to about 6 metres in height, and be in dense or sparse clusters, depending on how much rainfall they receive. They are *very* hard to remove from the ground.

36. Gibbs, *History*, pp. 70–1.

37. Philip Payton, *The Cornish Farmer in Australia* (Redruth, 1987) p. 20.

38. Payton, *Cornish Farmer*, p. 76.

39. Payton, *Cornish Farmer*, pp. 73, 81.

40. Carmichael, *Yorke Peninsula*, p. 76.

41. D.W. Meinig, *On the Margins of the Good Earth: The South Australian Wheat Frontier 1869–1884* (Adelaide, 1988), p. 46.
42. Kwan, *Living*, p. 102.
43. G.L. Buxton, *South Australian Land Acts 1869–1885* (Adelaide, 1966), p. 3.
44. Buxton, *Land Acts*, p. 11.
45. Carmichael, 1973, p. 80.
46. Buxton, *Land Acts*, p. 24.
47. South Australian *Government Gazette*, 9 January 1873, p. 49.
48. South Australian Lands Department records, Application No. 969.
49. An extensive table listing people to whom deliveries were made, in which year, and what was delivered can be obtained from the author (email lokan@acer.edu.au). Sometimes a diary entry indicated the location of the recipient's house, which has also been included in the table.
50. This was never his name. The person who sent information about him to the 1988 *Biographical Index of South Australians* must have been someone with connections back to people in Moonta who knew of him when he was using this as his name, as that is the way it is listed, erroneously, in that Index.
51. *People's Weekly*, April 28 1923.
52. South Australian Lands Department records, Lease No. 1437.
53. This map was obtained from the South Australian Lands Department.
54. Payton, *Cornish Farmer*, p. 86.
55. Payton, *Cornish Farmer*, p. 87.
56. Brown, *Mines*, pp. 120–1.
57. L. Coole and J. Harbison, *Mine Captains of the Copper Triangle, Yorke Peninsula, South Australia* (Moonta, 2006), p. 43.
58. Brown, *Mines*, p. 121.
59. J.L. Keeling and K.J. Hartley, *Poona and Wheal Hughes Cu Deposits, Moonta, South Australia* (Adelaide 2005; CRC LEME, c/– Primary Industries and Resources South Australia), p. 2.
60. K.F. Bampton, 'Copper Mining and Treatment in South Australia', *MESA Journal* 28 (January 2003), p. 42.

4

The Relief of Poverty
in Cornwall, 1780–1881

From Collateral Support to Respectability

Peter Tremewan

Introduction

In his stimulating article on the need to research differences at a sub Cornwall level, Bernard Deacon calls for 'some thinking about the spatial aspect of the Cornish Studies project'.[1] Responding to this suggestion, this article addresses the geography of the relief of poverty under the Poor Law in Cornwall from 1780 to 1880. While uncovering important differences in patterns of poor relief at a district level, it will also claim that within the attitudes of both administrators and the poor we can find expression of a Cornish 'identity', moulded by long-lasting economic and social circumstances.

Steve King, in his major study of the relief of poverty in England during the period 1700 to 1850, provides an apposite starting point. King contends that throughout these years significant differences persisted in the attitudes adopted by those implementing the provisions of the existing poor laws, and that this disparity manifested itself regionally. He draws a line running from the East Riding, through Lincolnshire, central and east Leicestershire, south Warwickshire, and east Somerset to Exeter. To the north and west lay a more urbanized and industrialized economy, where the poor were offered significantly less support than those living to the east and south, where the economy relied on arable or mixed farming. Within the broad north and west region King additionally creates a sub-region in which Cornwall, parts of Devon, Somerset and Gloucester form a discrete unit. In this far west sub-region he notes that, 'mean pensions ... fluctuated within the range 1s 2d and 1s 6d by the early nineteenth century, and entitlement was narrow and inflexible'.[2] However, this is a simplification. Cornwall, although only a small part of the area, was itself hardly a uniform social or economic unit, but rather a collection of dissimilar communities.

The operation of the Poor Law in Cornwall has not attracted great attention from historians, although Gill Burke has examined the attitudes and experiences of the community represented by the Penzance Poor Law Union in the crisis decade of the 1870s.[3] Her paper concludes that the Guardians sought to protect the general ratepayers of the area from the worst of the consequences of depression by adopting a strict compliance with the provisions of the 1834 Poor Law Amendment Act, offering to the poor 'minimal provision of both indoor, outdoor and (later) charitable relief in conformity with the "less eligibility" principles of the Act'.[4] Burke suggests that this provides an insight into the response offered by other Cornish mining areas. However, no research has examined the attitudes adopted by other unions within Cornwall or drawn comparisons between Cornish districts in either the extent of poverty or its relief.

The Poor Law – and Cornish communities

The implementation of the Poor Law Amendment Act of 1834 constituted an administrative watershed with its aim to extend central control over parish provision for the poor. The existing link between parish management of funds and the relief of the poor was seriously weakened as groups of parishes were brought together to form unions. The control of disbursements to the poor, previously one of the functions of the parish vestry meeting, now passed to an elected Board of Guardians responsible for the administration of the Act throughout all the parishes of the newly created Union.

All thirteen Cornish unions were formed during 1837. At the 1841 Census the populations in the unions ranged from 8,063 at Camelford to 50,109 at Penzance. This disparity reflects the objective of the Commission to create unions with a central place to build a workhouse within reasonable reach of each of the constituent parishes.

The Act also infamously introduced a provision whereby able-bodied persons were only permitted to receive relief in a workhouse. These institutions were purposefully constructed and intended to operate in a manner providing less favourable conditions than a labourer could expect to achieve from employment outside. No concession to this rule was contemplated even where no employment was obtainable, although in Cornwall temporary unemployment was often experienced in the seasonal demands of the agricultural, mining and fishing industries. The effect upon those employed in these three predominant industries was potentially calamitous. An example

Map 1.   Poor Law Union populations: Cornwall, 1841.

Source: Census Statistics, B.P.P.1841, Session 2(52)

of the difficulties which could arise was highlighted when it was pointed out that when the Mount's Bay fleet had not been able to put to sea 800 men had presented themselves to claim relief and that removal from their normal place of employment, notionally to the Union workhouse, would certainly damage their future prospects of work.[5] Similar reasoning was applied to those involved in mining and agriculture. Such examples no doubt formed part of the overall contention that local circumstances were better countered using local knowledge and decision-making. 'In principle local people were familiar with local poverty problems, and administrators had to tread a fine line between the demands of the poor for welfare and the ability and willingness of the ratepayer to supply the funds.'[6]

Throughout the nineteenth century the two major economic sectors were agriculture and the extractive industries of mining and quarrying. Agriculture and mining for the most part occupied discrete geographic areas, agriculture dominant in the north and east of Cornwall, and mining confined to distinct districts in the middle and western areas. There were outposts at Camelford

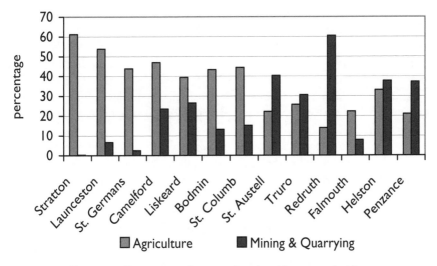

Figure 1.   Percentage of occupied males, 14 years and older,
in selected industries in Cornwall in 1851.

Source: Census enumerators' books 1851 (CFHS database).

for slate quarrying, in the St Austell district for mining and the china clay industry, and at Liskeard and in the Tamar valley, where there were emerging mining communities.

The Unions represented on the horizontal axis in Figure 1 are placed in a loosely geographic arrangement moving from east to west. The commanding strength of agriculture in the north and east and mining in the west is clearly demonstrated. In seven unions in the east between 40 per cent to 60 per cent of the labour force were engaged on the land, whereas in the west only in Helston, which includes the Meneage and Lizard farming districts, were 30 per cent employed in agriculture. In contrast, mining was the major employer in all the unions from St Austell westward, apart from maritime Falmouth. The two exceptions to this pattern are Camelford and Liskeard, where special circumstances applied.

The effect of the Poor Laws on the labour force of these two industries is a matter of debate. The movement of labour between the two, with the pressure on wage rates that this might have imposed, had its effect on the policies of the parish vestry meetings and later, the Boards of Guardians. Polanyi, cited in Boyer, writing of the late eighteenth century, maintained that outdoor relief to the able-bodied was a response by the countryside to an increased demand for labour in the cities. 'In order "to prevent the draining off of rural labour" parishes adopted outdoor relief policies, which raised the income of agricultural workers "without overburdening the farmer".[7] In those parishes where farmers dominated the poor law policy they contrived to retain a pool of labour in the parish for the labour intensive periods such as harvest. Digby, writing of rural Norfolk, contended that labour hiring farmers controlled parish government and that they responded to the seasonal nature of grain production by 'exploiting their position as poor law administrators to pursue a policy with an economical alteration of poor relief and independent income for the labourer'.[8]

Direct evidence for this practice in Cornwall is scarce, however, although, as will be proposed later, the higher per capita poor rate in the agricultural unions may suggest this to have been the case. Similar pressures were not experienced in the mining areas where there was a mobile pool of labour and employers were not faced with a major labour shortage.[9] The presence of miners and their effect on the wages paid in other industries has been viewed in different ways. In some areas the presence of 'slingers' (fishermen and miners temporarily out of work) offering their labour to farmers allegedly kept the agricultural labourers' wages artificially low. Conversely, the opportunities offered to farm labourers by the mining industry forced farmers to raise their wages to prevent a shortage of labour for the busy periods of the agricultural calendar. The balance of these two factors is difficult to assess and there is little evidence of a significant effect on the agricultural wage rate in Cornwall. Indeed, for the period 1833 to 1845 the wage rate for agricultural labourers in Cornwall is given as 8s 10d, compared with 12s 6d for Kent, 9s 10d for Hampshire, 8s 7d for Somerset and 8s 10d in Devon.[10] These statistics fall short of showing that the presence of the mining industry raised wage rates in agriculture.

The provision of relief

With the formation of the Unions it became the duty of the Board of Guardians to ensure that relief to the able-bodied pauper was confined to support in the workhouse. The previous practice of supporting able-bodied paupers in their own homes, known as out-relief, was energetically discouraged. The harshness of these provisions was an attempt to control the number of able-bodied poor receiving relief; a response to the widely held belief that many of those applying could find work but chose not to. The restrictions placed on the Board of Guardians were draconian, and many engaged in extraordinary stratagems to avert the full provisions of the statute, in effect protecting their parishioners from the worst consequences of the Act. The rules to be adopted in relation to the payment of outdoor relief to the able-bodied were detailed in the Outdoor Relief Prohibitory Order of

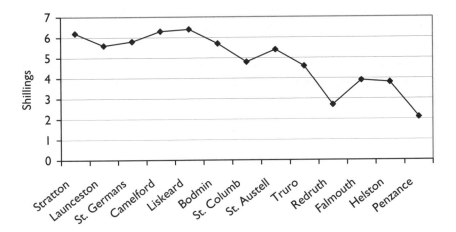

Figure 2. Average Cost of Poor Law Relief per Inhabitant in Unions:
Cornwall 1841–1881.

Source: Calculated from Poor Law Returns B.P.P. 1847/48(466), 1843(144), 1862(3037), 1870(280C) 1871(140C), 1880(66C), 1880(60C) and Census Statistics B.P.P. 1861[2846], 1871[C.381], 1881[C.2955].

1844. Although this set forth detailed restraints, the absence of any definition of 'able-bodied' was exploited by the Guardians who used such terms as 'temporary incapacity' to avoid their obligations. In Devon and Cornwall, according to an Assistant Commissioner, relief was given under 'the plea of sickness where it did not really exist'.[11] Despite these provisions, throughout the years following the appointment of the Guardians the data for poor relief in Cornwall after 1834 do not indicate any radical changes in the pattern which could denote any major effect of altered policies.

The annual reports of the Poor Law Commission, later the Poor Law Board, which was created by the Poor Law Amendment Act, provide the major source of the post-1834 data used in this article. Data have been extracted for the years 1841, 1847, 1861, 1871 and 1881. The decadal pattern is broken for the year 1851 due to the absence of suitable data. The year 1847 has been chosen as an expedient, being the closest for which appropriate statistics are available.

How far did the expenditure of poor law relief differ across the thirteen unions in the county? Figure 2 shows the average overall cost of relief to the poor per capita in each Union for each of the five years, 1841, 1847, 1861, 1871 and 1881.

The chart reveals an emphatic pattern of poor law expenditure per inhabitant; highest in the eastern part of Cornwall and lowest in the west, falling relatively uniformly. Only the three unions of Camelford, Liskeard and St Austell deviate upwards from the trend while one, Redruth, is markedly lower.

Table 1 below sets out the individual cost for each Union for each of the five years, confirming and accenting the disparity in expenditure between unions.

Table 1.   Cost of Poor Law Relief per Inhabitant:
Cornwall, 1841 to 1881

Union	1841	1841	1861	1811	1881
Stratton	7s 5d	7s 9d	4s 4d	5s 11d	5s 8d
Launceston	6s 4d	6s 6d	4s 10d	5s 2d	4s 11d
St Germans	6s 10d	8s 3d	4s 9d	5s 4d	3s 10d
Camelford	6s 10d	6s 10d	5s 0d	6s 0d	6s 7d
Liskeard	6s 10d	8s 0d	4s 3d	5s 10d	6s 10d
Bodmin	5s 10d	7s 8d	4s 9d	5s 6d	4s 11d
St.Columb	6s 7d	6s 0d	3s 7d	3s 9d	4s 0d
St Austell	4s 11d	5s 9d	4s 5d	6s 3d	5s 7d
Truro	4s 9d	4s 8d	4s 0d	5s 0d	4s 8d
Redruth	3s 6d	3s 7d	1s 10d	2s 4d	2s 5d
Falmouth	4s 11d	5s 2d	2s 3d	3s 8d	3s 5d
Heiston	3s 7d	4s 2d	2s 7d	4s 2d	4s 4d
Penzance	2s 11d	2s 4d	1s 1d	2s 1d	1s 11d

Source: calculated from B.P.P. as for Figure 3.

The noteworthy feature of the table relates to the Redruth and Penzance Unions. Throughout the period both have a consistent and significantly lower rate of expenditure, even when compared with other mining areas in the west of Cornwall. The uniformly low rate of 1861 suggests the presence of either some county-wide economic factor or external pressure on the poor law administrators, but is not a matter relevant to this project.

The overall effect was the maintenance of an east to west pattern of expenditure per inhabitant over the fifty years covered by the data. But the lower levels of relief expenditure in the west of Cornwall are not evidence either that there was less poverty in those districts or that the Boards of Guardians adopted a more stringent regime of support for the destitute. Two other factors could influence this statistic: first, the number who apply for

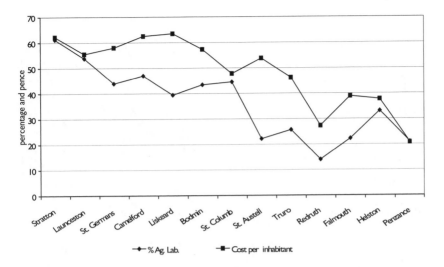

Figure 3.   Average Cost of Poor Law Relief per Inhabitant 1841–1881, and the
per cent of Agricultural Labourers in Unions in 1851: Cornwall.

Sources: calculated from BPP as for Figure 2 and Census Enumerators' Books, 1851
(CFHS database).

relief and were either supported at a minimum level or rejected; and second,
the number of those who, although poverty stricken, chose not to seek relief
for reasons of independence of spirit or cultural or religious convictions. The
gamut of motives underlying such a decision may be seen to derive from the
cultural and social structure of a community, involving both material and
emotional considerations, each defying objective quantification.

Figure 3 draws together the information shown in Figures 1 and 2, and
uses the same arrangement along its horizontal axis. It suggests a well-defined
correlation between the cost of relief and the proportion of agricultural
labourers employed in the individual unions. The apparent relationship is
confirmed by the application of Spearman's rank order correlation, which
gives a coefficient of 0.73 at a confidence level of 99 per cent; indicating
a positive relationship between the cost of poor law relief and the level of
agricultural employment in the district. However, this does not indicate a
direct interdependence between the presence of agriculture as the primary
industry and a higher expenditure on relief of the poor, but is rather a
symptom of the presence of some underlying factor or factors.

An additional perspective on the attitudes which surrounded the
stewardship of the poor may be derived from a consideration of the ratio of
paupers to inhabitants of a Union area and is shown in Figure 4.

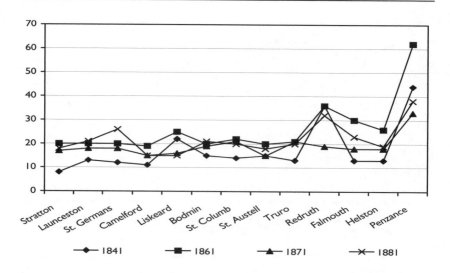

Figure 4.   Ratio of Inhabitants to Paupers in Unions: Cornwall, 1841–1881.

Source: calculated from Census Statistics B.P.P. 1861[2846], 1871[C.381], 1881[C.2955], 1847/48(466) and Poor Law Reports B.P.P. 1843(144), 1860(383B.1), 1871(140B), 1881(60B), 1880(66C), 1881(60C).

The number of paupers is that recorded as receiving relief on the first day of January in the relevant year and the number of inhabitants extracted from census statistics. Although no suitable data are available for 1847 the four years reviewed in the graph show a remarkable uniformity. The western mining districts, particularly Redruth and Penzance unions, exhibit a high ratio or relatively low numbers of paupers to population. From east to west the first nine unions recorded ratios of between 10 and 26, with an average figure over the four years of 18. The final four districts, three of which may be said to be mining areas, showed ratios of between 13 and 62, with an average figure of 29. In 1871 the Redruth ratio, consistently high in the other years, fell back to the level of the central and eastern areas. At Helston, the ratios over the years, whilst greater than those in the agricultural eastern unions, remained close to that of Liskeard and significantly both shared a similar proportion of miners to agricultural workers. At Penzance the ratio was consistently much higher than the rest of the county, ranging from 33 to 62 and must be seen to be related to the lower levels of relief expenditure shown in Table 1 for that Union.

These data reveal a distinctive and enduring pattern of poor law expenditure throughout much of the nineteenth century. The disparity between the unions occupying the areas in the east and west was present from 1841 (see Figure 2).

Though there was a correlation between poor law costs and the percentage of agricultural labourers over the years from 1841 to 1881, we cannot yet say whether this was a product of the new Poor Law or whether it reflects an older pre-existing pattern. In the following section the administration of poor law relief prior to the implementation of the 1834 Act will be examined for the possible origin of these spatial differences.

The relief of poverty under the old Poor Law

The period from 1784 to 1834 recorded a striking increase in the cost of the relief of the poor. The average expenditure on poor relief in Cornwall for the three years 1783, 1784 and 1785 amounted to £28,531, whereas by 1803 this figure had risen to £57,696, an increase of over 100 per cent.[12] Some of this increase can be accounted for by a 50 per cent rise in the cost of living during that period,[13] but nevertheless there remained a substantial sum to be met by the local ratepayers. Historians have offered a range of explanations for the increases in expenditure. These include the effects of the Gilbert Act in loosening the purse strings on out-door relief, the loss of common land due to enclosure, and the decline in cottage industries, which had previously provided some income for women and children. The level at which any or all of these reasons are relevant to the Cornish situation is problematical and will be discussed later.

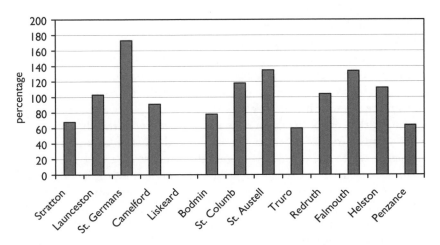

Figure 5.   Percentage increase in Poor Law Costs: Cornwall, 1784–1803.

Source: Calculated from Poor Law Returns B.P.P. 1803–04(175).

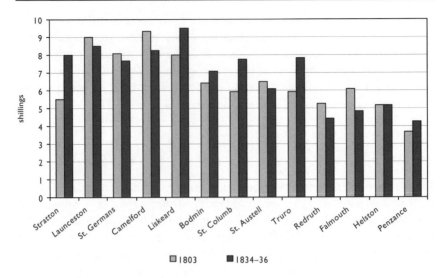

Figure 6.   Cost of Poor Law Relief per Inhabitant in Unions:
Cornwall, 1803 and 1834–36.

Source: Calculated from Poor Law Reports (B.P.P. 1803–04(175)), (B.P.P. 1801–02(9), (Higginbotham, 2004)

The increase in overall Cornish poor law expenditure from 1784 to 1803 was not uniform throughout Cornwall. Figure 5 shows, for each of the thirteen Union areas, the calculated percentage increase in poor law expenditure for the period. The 1784 figure is the average for 1783, 1784 and 1785.

No useful data are available for the Liskeard Union. Patently these bald statistics make no allowance for any demographic or social changes which may have taken place over the twenty year period. The increase for St Germans Union is quite remarkable, and may be associated with an increase in the population of the area in connection with the prosecution of the war with France. Contrarily, the rise in costs in Truro barely accounted for the increase in the cost of living over the period. Otherwise the changes do not reveal a pattern related to either the agricultural areas of Cornwall or those districts in which there had been a growth of industrial activity.

The lack of any usable reliable population census data for the late eighteenth century makes it impossible to draw a comparison of the cost per inhabitant in 1784. However, it is possible to compare the per capita expenditure in 1803 (based on the 1801 Census) with that of 1834–36.[14]

Figure 6 demonstrates that in 1803 a clear, and by now familiar, pattern of poor law expenditure per inhabitant existed in Cornwall. The highest costs were to be found in the east and the lowest levels in the extreme west.

Reading Figure 5 and Figure 6 together the conclusion must be that the rises recorded in Figure 5 were therefore superimposed on a previously existing pattern to form the basis of the spatial differences of the nineteenth century. Either, in many of the agricultural areas of Cornwall, Stratton being a notable exception, at some time in the past a relatively generous poor relief policy had been adopted, or, for yet unexplained causes, the costs of the support of the poor in the industrial regions of the west had been contained at a low level. The question remains whether this pattern of higher costs in the agrarian east could have emerged as a result of political pressure from the farming community. It is clear that the east/west pattern, which had pre-existed the Gilbert Act of 1782, was maintained beyond the Poor Law Amendment Act of 1834.

However, it is the overall uniformity of the pattern in Figure 6 which is the noticeable feature. The five mainly agricultural districts to the north and east of Cornwall shared a comparatively high cost per inhabitant, averaging 8s, whereas the eight more industrialized and/or urban districts in the centre and west gave just 5s 7d per capita to the poor. The mining districts of Redruth, Helston and Penzance had the lowest per capita rate, at an average of 4s 8d. These plain figures offer no recognition of the local factors which had influenced both the administrators and the poverty-stricken before making decisions within the Poor Laws. However, the presence of influential parochial factors were recognized as significant to the condition of the poor by the Royal Commission of Inquiry into the Administration and Practical Operation of Poor Laws.[15] They became the subject of some of the 'Rural Queries' addressed to parish authorities throughout England in 1832.

The 'Rural Queries' of 1832

The 'Rural Queries' circulated by the Commission to rural parishes in England posed a series of queries regarding the administration of the existing Poor Laws, with the intention of gathering information concerning the condition of the poor in their parish. An assessment of the full data received by the Commission is both confusing and daunting. While accepting the overall value of the resource, it is necessary to have regard to the Commission's own statement that, 'its great length must, however, render it inaccessible to many of those into whose hands the report is likely to come'. Nevertheless, the information present in the answers to 'Rural Queries', when critically assessed, remains a valuable resource for historians. The evidence adduced gives an insight into the background circumstances which existed before 1834, revealing factors lying behind the geographical contrast we have identified, especially with regard to local customs on a labourer's ownership of land.

Thirty Cornish parishes responded, although few replied fully to the 58 questions. No parish in either Stratton or Camelford Union areas submitted a return. For the purpose of this research, the returns of thirteen parishes have been reviewed, each Union being represented by at least one parish. Of the 58 questions posed, only the responses which give an insight into the underlying causes of the pattern of poor relief in Cornwall have been analysed. Four areas of interest were identified. First, the wage rates available in the area, together with the availability and continuity of work for women and children; second, a range of questions concerning the level of collateral aids, particularly the ownership of cottages and land; third, the parish policy regarding the type and level of relief which might be expected for the able-bodied applicant in the event of the threat of destitution; and fourth, the per capita rate of expenditure on poor relief.

In response to the question on wages there was consensus at 9s per week, with only tutworkers in Gwennap receiving 10s. Of equal importance to the labourer, particularly those with large families, was an opportunity for a supplementary income for the wife and children. In the report the possibility of employment for women and children warranted a discrete question. 'What in the whole might a labourer's wife and four children, aged 14, 11, 8 and 5 years respectively (the eldest a boy), expect to earn in the year obtaining ... an average amount of employment?' Understandably, the answers often express a difficulty in providing specific and reliable information; seven of the thirteen selected parishes failed to answer the question. Of the six remaining, one, a parish in which both mining and agriculture were significant, estimated an income of £45 per annum; two agricultural areas reckoned £15; two mining districts calculated that £10 and £9 were possible; and the last agricultural area placed the family income at £3. These examples highlight the unreliable nature of the data, seemingly based on hearsay and possibly a misunderstanding of the question, where at least one reply seems to include the labourer's income. Certainly the expectation would be that the 14-year-old boy and the 11-year-old child would be employed full time at a mine at a pay rate of, say, 6d per day, earning £15 per annum. However, the small sample does reflect a difference between the mining and agricultural communities. There was a consensus that it was common practice for the wives and children of agricultural labourers to work in the fields, especially during harvest time, although the implication was that their employment was far less constant than that of their mining counterparts. Some answers confirm that miners' wives were not usually employed at the mines, but acknowledged that young men and women could find work in the industry.

Significant differences emerged in the answers to the question, 'Are there any cases in your parish where the Labourer owns his own cottage?' In the agricultural areas it was stated that either 'few or none owned a cottage', whereas in the three mining parishes, St Agnes, Gwennap and Kea, it was reported that 'many' miners were in possession of a cottage, frequently with an additional piece of land. The Commission's interest in the availability of land as a collateral support is further revealed in the questions, 'Whether there were gardens with the labourer's cottages?', and 'Whether any land was let to labourers?' Only one parish recorded that no land was let for this purpose and one declared that 'all' labourers kept potato ground. Otherwise, the parishes confirmed that most agricultural workers received a piece of potato ground as part of their employment, whereas miners either owned or rented a parcel of land or utilized an area of wastrel ground for that purpose. This difference between the agricultural and mining communities parallels the previously identified correlation linking the cost per inhabitant of poor relief and the percentage of agricultural workers in a Union.

As a reflection of the widespread concern on the payment of relief to the able-bodied labourer the Commission enquired, 'Have you any, and how many, able-bodied Labourers in the Employment of individuals receiving allowance or regular relief from your parish on their own account, or on that of their families: and if so on account of their Families, at what number of Children does it begin?' Two parishes claimed to offer no relief; three gave support in return for work on the parish roads; seven accepted that wage rates were too low to support a large family and gave help, either at the third or fourth child. One part-paid for an able-bodied man to work for an individual, but two refused to do so. However, the answers do not reveal any pattern of parish practice which could be associated either with the major industry of the area or its geographic place in Cornwall.

Given the autonomy of the individual parishes at this time, even the limited uniformity of the responses to these selected 'Rural Queries' is surprising. The answers to the questions concerning the policy and practices supposedly adopted by the parishes when dealing with paupers show a level of correspondence. This is in direct contrast to the views expressed by contemporary commentators who were critical of the lack of equality of poor relief, even between adjacent parishes. However, the most noticeable dissimilarity appears in the per capita expenditure. Here the rate, calculated as an average for the four years 1803, 1813, 1821 and 1831, varied from 4s 2d in the three western parishes of St Buryan Deanery to 11s 4d in Lanreath and Gwennap, with a mean figure of 8s 6d and a median figure of 7s 9d. The conclusion, therefore, must be that the per capita rate is governed, not by the vestry's declared scale of rates for paupers, but by the number of paupers making application who complied with the parish policy. One mining parish noted that 'few miners receive relief', suggesting that the collateral aids of cottages, land and supplementary income from family employment were factors in determining the number of claimants. It is noticeable that those parishes which declared a high proportion of labourers owning their cottages and land were situated in unions where the per capita rate was below average; furthering an hypothesis that the collateral support available to certain classes of labourer was an underlying factor in the eventual per capita expenditure for the parish.

A distinct pattern of poor law relief already existed in Cornwall prior to the introduction of the 1834 Act. The replies to the 'Rural Queries', in response to the declared policies and practices adopted by the individual parishes, go some way to account for the differences observed. The presence of a greater concentration of labourers with access to land in the western mining areas of Cornwall coincides with lower poor rate expenditure in those areas, perhaps explaining the previously identified correlation between poor law costs and the dominant occupation. The higher per capita expenditure in the east of Cornwall may be associated with the agricultural industry's desire to retain a pool of labour for use during the peak periods of employment. Cornwall was not alone in this endeavour. The agricultural labourer's wages in the Cornwall were similar to those in south-western counties, reflecting the concerns of the industry to retain their employees. The other factor, that of the availability of employment for women and children, is not so clearly defined in the answers to the 'Rural Queries'. There is, however, sufficient information to suggest that such opportunities were present more frequently and with greater constancy in the mining areas rather than in the farming community. In the main women and children worked on the land during the seasonal harvesting of crops, whereas mining families, especially the children, could expect a more constant income. It is suggested that these two elements, the access to land and the availability of work for wives and children, made significant contributions to the disparity of poor law expenditure which had emerged during the eighteenth century to produce a distinctive pattern which was sustained through the nineteenth century.

Collateral support and 'independence'

Throughout the period under review the provision of a potato allotment or gardens and small plots of land included with the labourer's own cottage continued to offer a measure of independence. The opportunity to grow vegetables and perhaps raise a pig or poultry placed the labourer in a more favourable position during times of economic hardship. This, and the opportunity of an additional income from family members, was means of avoiding recourse to the poor law.

In the responses to the 'Rural Queries' there was a clear distinction in cottage and land ownership between the generally agricultural parishes in the eastern part of Cornwall from those in the more industrialized mining areas in the west. These replies are fully supported by contemporary commentators. In the 'The Poor Law Report of 1834' it was noted that, 'In Cornwall, the miners have a practice of purchasing from three to six acres of rough land, on three lives'.[16] Moreover, Rose, citing B.P.P. 1888, XXII, Q.7062 confirms that, 'a little house is a favourite investment with the Cornish miner who has saved a few pounds'.[17] In the 1892 Royal Commission Report on Labour Chapman reports, 'The miners are said to be extremely fond of their holdings and cling to them with utmost tenacity'. He continues, 'The agricultural labourer on the other hand have very few small holdings'.[18] Throughout the century, therefore, there existed a strong consensus concerning the frequency and extent of miners having ownership of cottages and land, in stark contrast to the circumstances and attitude of the agricultural labourer.

The acquisition of the plots, seemingly, to the casual observer, beyond the financial capability of the ordinary labourer, is neatly explained in the last phrase of the quote from the Poor Law Report of 1834, 'the miners ... are a distinct class, having great advantages over the ordinary labourer'.[19] Historically, Cornish miners had adopted the practice of engaging in dual occupations, frequently combining employment in the mines with work on their own smallholding or in the pilchard industry. This facility to have time to produce crops from his own land was a significant factor in the subsistence available to the miner. Often these properties had been purchased by virtue of a particularly rewarding tribute contract, an event often quoted as happening only once or twice in the lifetime of a miner. However, 'A tributer, if he has had a good venture, will often invest his gains in a house'.[20] Over the decades successive generations of miners had, by this means, accumulated family holdings. Additionally, a substantial number of cottages and land were acquired through the reclamation of wasteland. The latter practice was particularly prevalent in the Camborne and Redruth area, on the Tehidy lands of the Basset family. The leases, determined on three lives, were granted on the understanding that a cottage would be built and three acres of waste land cultivated. On the successful completion of that enterprise, the landlord would grant a lease on a further three acres, thus creating a substantial piece of collateral support. Basset held the view that there were, 'moral and economic benefits of granting smallholdings to miners'.[21] By 1841 it was estimated that one quarter of all miners inhabited cottages built on such allotments.[22] Later Chapman reported in 1892 that 'there are an immense number of smallholdings in the district, held by miners, who take from four to five acres or even more on leases for lives and reclaim the land from the moors. Between Chacewater and Truro there are several hundred of such holdings.'[23] It was reported that in the first fifty years of the nineteenth century some two thousand people had been provided with homes in the Camborne/Redruth area by the granting of three life leases on waste lands.[24] In that area, together with the St Agnes mining district, Rose asserts that 'there was one smallholding of less than five acres for every five adult male miners'.[25] For miners in the westernmost district there were alternative forms of collateral support. The joint ownership of cows was a common practice in the area, giving a family access not only to dairy products but also providing supplementary feed for the keeping of a pig.[26] The area was also well known for a collaboration between the farming community and labourers exchanging household manure for a potato allotment.[27]

Although the resource of a plot of land as a collateral aid is not accurately quantifiable, 'the contribution of the average smallholding to family subsistence, a holding of three acres with a cow, a pig and a vegetable garden might have produced potatoes and other vegetables, milk butter, cheese and bacon in sufficient quantities to feed an "average" family'.[28] Reflecting on the character of the people who occupied their own cottages and a piece of land the responses to the Poor Law Commission's 'Rural Queries', from St Agnes and Calstock, reported that 'those who occupy cottages with a portion of land attached, are very industrious, or most industrious';[29] a comment which may well be extended to have included the virtues of prudence, thrift and respectability.

The mere cultivation of potatoes alone was of great importance and its significance to the Cornish labourer's family cannot be over emphasized. Combined with the availability of cheap fish, particularly pilchards, the average family could survive at least temporary downturns in the economy without immediate recourse to the poor law. A representative illustration of the contribution made by the potato to the economy of Cornwall, and in particular to the Cornish labourer, appeared in 1846 in the Twelfth Annual report of the Poor Law Commission.[30] The household budget of a family of seven, living at Tywardreath in the mid century, was there recorded in some detail. The family subsisted on a total income of approximately £30 per annum. Included in the outgoings were items of £2 10s rent for 50 yards of potato ground, and 10s for 700 pilchards and the salt to cure them, that is 10 per cent of the total budget. The potato ground provided for the family and the pig. The pig, which weighed about 200 pounds when killed, fed the family, without beef or mutton, for seven months and the pilchards, together with some other fish, lasted throughout the year. The potato, however, remained the key factor both as a staple of their diet and a major contributor to the family's supply of meat.

It has thus been possible to draw together evidence for the potential underlying causes of the spatial comparisons observed earlier. Throughout the eighteenth and into the nineteenth centuries there was a distinction between the collateral support available to the agricultural and mining labourer. The frequent ownership of cottages and land, which was revealed in the survey to be a feature of the mining areas, distinguished miners from agricultural labourers. The dual employment of the miner, particularly in the early part of the period, was a factor as was the possibility of income from regular employment for women and children. These elements provide evidence that the social structure of some communities limited prospective applicants for poor law relief, resulting in a distinctive pattern of expenditure and a continuing spatial difference within Cornwall.

Community and respectability; Methodism and friendly societies

Although community, as a concept, is difficult to define it exhibits tangible qualities which derive from both historical and contemporary sources. The development of an identity of a community is influenced by a number of factors. Economic reliance upon a single industry by a majority of the populace, especially where that community is set in isolation, creates strong internal links capable of either resisting incoming cultures and ideas or accommodating them in a modified form suitable to the preservation of its identity. Within such communities, kinship groupings and people sharing common interests form powerful networks, which create the basis of a solidarity of purpose with distinctive attitudes, moral and ethical standards. In Cornwall, the fishing villages and mining areas epitomize communities structured on these principles. In particular miners saw themselves, and were perhaps seen by others, as a class apart, an elite of the labourers, yet not fully outside that description. Their mode of employment, with its apparent freedom of bargaining, the ever-present possibility of a windfall from a successful tribute and their plot of land set them apart. White detected 'the "improved" qualities of the Cornish miner ... you will see ... a marked difference between miners and field labourers. The intelligence gleaming in their eyes, and their general expression, denote a habit of thinking for themselves.'[31]

Two institutions provided a niche for this community identity. These were Methodism and friendly societies. The role of the first of these is well known. The message of universal salvation, and the opportunity to express themselves in the pulpit and church office was enthusiastically embraced by the labouring population. The strength of the ethos of Methodism was substantially more influential in the western mining areas, particularly in the isolated close-knit communities dependent upon a single industry for its livelihood.

Table 2.   Methodist membership in eastern and western circuits:
Cornwall, 1768–1841

Year	Eastern circuits	Western circuits
1768	543	1495
1778	718	1430
1788	818	3007
1798	1060	4637
1841	6390	19212

Source: (Rule, 1971, 217)

As Table 2 indicates, Methodism grew earlier and most rapidly west of
Truro. Although membership expanded exponentially over Cornwall after the
great revival of 1799, the ratio of members to population remained 40 per cent
higher in the west. In the mining areas the Methodist Church became a
significant influence on community, mirroring and enhancing the nationwide
move to a more civil society. Commenting on the condition of the church
in the 1830s Shaw writes, 'The whole of Methodism moved – slid – into the
orbit of Victorian respectability'.[32] Although the Methodist church, in its
later temperance and teetotal posture, disagreed with the friendly societies'
propensity to hold their meetings in public houses, the combined presence of
these two institutions forged the creation of a 'respectful' society.

The prudence displayed by the Cornish miner in his attachment to a plot
of land was also reflected in the popularity of benefit societies. In fact the
early promotion of friendly societies, in the last quarter of the eighteenth
century, came from the agricultural community. Encouraged by the prospect
of a possible reduction in the poor rate, agricultural societies and farmers
endorsed the creation of local friendly societies.[33] The Cornish labourer
appears to have enthusiastically adopted the concept, for in 1803 9 per cent
of the 1801 enumerated population were members of a friendly society.[34] By
1815 48 per cent of Cornish families held a friendly society membership, with
33 per cent of men over 15 years old being members.[35] In the early part of
the nineteenth century Cornwall was placed twelfth among 42 counties in its
density of friendly society membership, and in 1831 Cornwall was in a small
group of counties where the total society membership was in excess of 10 per
cent of the population.[36]The consensus must be that, although these statistics
have to be interpreted with care, the friendly society movement made an
early and significant contribution to collateral support to the structure of
community life in Cornwall.

The members of the early friendly societies saw in them the possibility of avoiding applying to the poor law, at least in the case of temporary loss of income. Although few societies insured their members against unemployment, some societies explicitly declared in their rules that their purpose was to avoid dependence upon poor relief.[37] According to Lord Beaumont, speaking in defence of the independence of friendly societies, it meant, 'placing within the power of the labouring classes the means of making themselves independent in their old age by means of sacrifices during the earlier portion of their lives' so that they could 'look to coming years without the prospect of the workhouse'.[38] Later, in addition to its contribution to financial security, the membership of a friendly society became a mark of acceptance and eventually respectability. The fact that a weekly surplus was available to pay for membership was in itself a step towards an enhanced status. In this regard the early advancement of the friendly societies paralleled the growth of Methodism in Cornwall; both organizations held strong views on the social standing of their members.

Respectability was 'the great Victorian shibboleth and criterion, a means by which to judge strangers on the basis of their appearance and behaviour. Provided a person was sober, conventionally dressed, he could attain respectability.'[39] Kirk, cited in Cordery, moves away from this emphasis on appearance and behaviour to stress other avenues by which respectability might be attained. He proposes that the institutional vehicles for working class respectability were friendly societies, temperance societies and religious institutions.[40] As a further refinement, religion was seen 'as the glue which held communities and society in one piece ... a means of discouraging aberrant behaviour, which included all forms of able-bodied poverty and indebtedness as well as criminality'.[41] In Cornwall, where the Methodist Church was a significant influence on community life, particularly in the mining areas of the west, the countrywide trend to respectability was reflected and enhanced. The combined presence of Methodism and friendly societies forged the creation of a 'respectful' society; a community bound by certain conventions and disciplines of appearance and actions. Such 'respectability brought with it ... a growing concern for public reputation. Many workers rejected relief because it had come to be seen as stigmatising.'[42] Thus the combination of an old established make-do economy, based on collateral support from land use, and the development of the traditionally independent class of Cornish miners, into a new respectability-based community, ensured that the demands placed upon the local Board of Guardians, even in times of great economic stress, were kept to a low level.

Unlike the farm labourer, the Cornish miner's engagement with poor law relief was governed by a spirit of independence. As early as 1841 miners were described as possessing 'that independence of feeling, and have reluctance to have recourse to the poor-rate, which characterise the class to which they belong'.[43] However, with the developing capitalization of the mining industry during the nineteenth century, mine owners were increasingly sensitive to the need for a consistent and dependable workforce and the freedom previously enjoyed by miners was curtailed. Rule considers that from the early nineteenth century miners' plots, 'are better considered as pursuing a supplementary activity'.[44] But, despite this partial loss of employment autonomy, those associated with the mining industry maintained an independence and with the advent of Methodism, which they enthusiastically accepted, moved seamlessly into Victorian respectability. F.M.L. Thompson, cited in Hollen Lees states, 'Resort to poor relief ... came to be equated with the loss of respectability'.[45] These two elements, the early autonomous employment pattern and the later evolution of the 'respectable society', form the basis of the distinctive pattern of poor relief found in Cornwall in the nineteenth century.

Conclusion

King, in his comprehensive work on the historical geography of the poor law, writes, 'while broad spatial divisions ... might adequately pick up variations in the scale of poverty, they would not necessarily pick up variation in the character and role of the communal welfare system or in the composition of the economy of makeshifts'.[46] This statement is fully confirmed by the micro-level data revealed in this study. The motivation for further research at that level was greatly encouraged by Burke's work on the relief of distress in West Cornwall. Her assertion that the poverty stricken of that area received 'minimal provision of both indoor, outdoor and (later) charitable relief'[47] provided a challenging starting point. This, together with Probert's suggestion that, 'in some senses there is no Cornwall, as it includes such a diversity of regions',[48] validates Deacon's stimulating article on the opportunities for micro-level studies within Cornish Studies.[49] These propositions led comfortably to a study of the spatial comparisons of the expenditure on poor relief in Cornwall for the period under review.

The subsequent disclosure of an emphatic and persistent disparity of poor law expenditure per inhabitant both vindicates Probert's assertion and poses questions about the underlying causes. While the introduction of the Poor Law Amendment Act of 1834 led to fundamental change, this was not the prime cause of the pattern of nineteenth century poor law expenditure. A relationship between poor law costs and the occupational structure pre-existed the Act. The data from 1784 onwards confirm the early presence of a distinction between the east and west of Cornwall, a difference which rested not upon the higher per capita rates in the agricultural areas of the east, where the wages remained comparable with those in other western counties, but with the consistently lower cost per inhabitant in the mining districts of the west. This enduring pattern raises the possibility of a deeply seated underlying cause, entirely divorced from the superficial and transient factors of economic circumstances; a characteristic profoundly engrained in the social structure of the area. By the late eighteenth and the first half of the nineteenth centuries subsistence aids, which for some generations had been the practice of the mining community, had minimized their need for relief from the poor law. Examining the occupations of the agricultural labourer and the miner reveals differences in the type and character of the collateral support available to each. The singular attitude adopted by the mining community, of an independence grounded in their long history of a multi-sourced income, isolated them from many of the aspects of poverty and of recourse to poor law relief, and contributed to the disparity of expenditure exhibited in eighteenth-century Cornwall. Rowse, commenting on the attitudes of the Cornish, writes, 'It is instinctive among the Cornish to be fairly independent, to make themselves so, by taking another part-time occupation on, if necessary. This goes back to the dominant social pattern in Cornwall for centuries: a small holding of one's own, with tin-streaming or tin-mining on the side. A man might be poor, but he had an essential independence of spirit.'[50] Later, especially during the period of the economic crisis of the closing decades of the nineteenth century, although the effect of the traditional subsistence support had diminished, it was replaced by the equally powerful factor of 'respectability', providing a cultural continuity that outlasted its material production.

In the nineteenth century, this stance, converted as it was with the advent of a nationwide Victorian propriety and enhanced by local Methodism and friendly societies, emerged as respectability. Even in the face of great distress during the collapse of a major industry, there was a reticence to apply for assistance thereby placing themselves, as Hollen Lees observes, 'in a social category to which they refused to belong'.[51] Locally, in 1878, at the time of a desperate situation for miners in the St Just district, the relieving Officer for the Western District of the Union reported that, 'many miners are doing badly and earn scanty wages, yet they are reluctant to apply to the Relieving Officer'.[52] The significance of the unquantifiable factor of 'respectability' has perhaps been understated by historians. Burke, in her work on the poor in West Cornwall in the 1870s blamed their parlous state on the Board of Guardians, who, she suggests, were concerned to protect the well being of the majority of rate-payers of the Union. That would imply that a large number of applications for relief were rejected, but there is little evidence to support this. She concludes with the assertion that, 'in these circumstances permanent emigration became the only option for many unemployed miners and their families'.[53] This claim, at least in part, is seemingly supported by Deacon in his detailed examination of nineteenth-century migration patterns in Cornwall. Here he shows that during the 1870s the St Just in Penwith sub Registration District experienced 'a gross out-migration of young men' (15–34 years),' well over 60 per cent in that decade, a major migration flow by any standards'.[54] However, these bald data mask a situation reported by Brayshay, who records that in St Just the number of households headed by women had risen from 15 per cent in 1851 to 26 per cent in 1871. Many of the entries in the Census Enumerators' books were accompanied by phrases such as 'husband abroad' and 'annuity from husband',[55] intimating that men had left to seek work elsewhere as a temporary expedient. It is suggested that far from being driven from the district by the minimum relief policy of the Board of Guardians many miners had already taken the option of emigration; not on a permanent basis, but planned as a makeshift to maintain family income, to avoid pauperism and the loss of social standing.

This study began by examining the comparative expenditures of the Cornish Poor Law Unions in the nineteenth century. The micro-level examination, disaggregating Cornwall, led to an interpretation which identified community characteristics. The early emergence of industrial activity in Cornwall, allied with 'relatively autonomous work relations' enabled 'the emergence of equally autonomous village communities'.[56] The dense networks of mutual support, and the available collateral aids present in Cornish mining communities formed the foundation of an 'independence' upon which the advent of friendly societies and Methodism built a new cultural dimension. Whetter, cited in Deacon, writing of the seventeenth century, refers to an economic division of Cornwall, suggesting a line from Padstow to Fowey.[57] Deacon expands on this proposal by drawing a parallel with the similar linguistic 'boundary' of sixteenth-century Cornwall, submitting that the economic division 'tended to mirror and perhaps reinforce cultural ones'.[58] The long-standing east–west divide of dispositions revealed in this study confirms and emphasizes these assertions. In the eighteenth century, to this notional economic division was added the considerable influence of Methodism, creating, 'the Cornish culture region ... dominated by mining and Methodism'.[59] From this renascent culture emerged a potent manifestation of respectability, which became a persuasive motivational element in nineteenth century Cornish society. The previous assumption that the comparatively low expenditure on poor relief in the western part of Cornwall was attributable to the diligence of the dispensers of aid and their protection of the ratepayer needs to be reviewed. The attitude of resolute independence, displayed by members of Cornwall's uniquely constructed mining communities, must be given due prominence. Cultural identity is neither a readily identifiable nor quantifiable quality, for it leaves few footprints for the enlightenment of historians. For the present we are left with the intriguing prospect of a possible 'Cornish' dimension still evident in the western part of Cornwall in the late nineteenth century, one with long roots back into the early modern period.

Acknowledgment

I should like to thank Bernard Deacon for his invaluable advice, encouragement and assistance in the production of this article.

Notes and references

1. Bernard Deacon, 'The Spatial Dimension and Cornish Studies', in Philip Payton (ed.), *Cornish Studies: Eight* (Exeter, 2000), p. 214.
2. Steve King, *Poverty and Welfare in England 1700–1850: A Regional Perspective* (Manchester, 2000), p. 264.
3. Gill Burke, 'The Poor Law and the Relief of Distress: West Cornwall 1870–1880', *Journal of the Royal Institution of Cornwall* VIII Part 2 (1979), pp. 148–59.
4. Gill Burke, 'The Poor Law', p. 159.
5. B. Wellington, 'Public Opinion and the Introduction of the New Poor Law in Cornwall', *Old Cornwall*, IX, No. 1 (1980), p. 69.
6. Steve King, *Poverty and Welfare*, p. 52.
7. Polanyi cited in George R. Boyer, 'The Old Poor Law and the Agricultural Labor Market in Southern England: An Empirical Analysis', *Journal of Economic History* vol. XLVI 1 (1986), p. 116.
8. Digby cited in George R. Boyer, 'The Old Poor Law', p. 117.
9. Damaris Rose, 'Home Ownership, subsistence and historical change: The mining district of West Cornwall in the late nineteenth century', in Nigel Thrift and Peter Williams (eds), *Class and Space: the making of an urban society* (1987).
10. E.H. Hunt, 'Industrial and Regional Inequality: Wages in Britain 1760–1914', *Journal of Economic History* vol. 46 4 (1986), p. 965.
11. J.V. Mosley, 'Poor Law Administration in England and Wales, 1834–1850, with special reference to the problem of able bodied pauperism', unpub. Ph.D. thesis (London University, 1975), p. 177.
12. Abstract of Answers and Returns under Act for procuring Returns relative to Expense and Maintenance of Poor in England. British Parliamentary Paper, 1803–04 (175), 717.
13. B.R. Mitchell, *British Historical Statistics* (Cambridge, 1988), p. 35.
14. Peter Higginbotham, '1834 Poor Law Amendment Act – An Act for the Amendment and better Administration of the Laws relating to the Poor in England and Wales', http://users.ox.ac.uk?-peter/workhouse/poor laws/1834intro. html, 2004.
15. Royal Commission on Labour, Report by C.M. Chapman. British Parliamentary Paper, 1893–94 [C.6894–11], 113.

16. S.G. & E.O.A. Checkland, *The Poor Law Report of 1834* (Harmondsworth, 1974), p. 287.
17. Rose, 'Home Ownership', p. 137.
18. Royal Commission on Labour, Report by C.M. Chapman. British Parliamentary Paper, 1893–94 [C.6894–11], 113.
19. Royal Commission of Inquiry into Administration and Practical Operation of Poor Laws. British Parliamentary Paper 1834 (44).
20. Rose, 'Home Ownership', p. 120.
21. John Rule, 'The Labouring Miner in Cornwall c.1740–1840: A study in Social History', unpub. Ph.D. thesis (Warwick University, 1971), pp. 97, 99.
22. Ibid.
23. Royal Commission on Labour, Report by C.M. Chapman. British Parliamentary Paper, 1893–94 [C.6894–11], 113.
24. Michael Tangye, *Tehidy and the Bassets* (Redruth, 1984), p. 48.
25. Rose, 'Home Ownership', p. 117.
26. Royal Commission on Childhood Employment in Mines and Manufactories. First Report (Mines and Collieries) Appendix. British Parliamentary Paper 1842[380][381][382], 754.
27. Bernard Deacon, 'The Reformulation of territorial identity: Cornwall in the late eighteenth and nineteenth Centuries', unpub. Ph.D. thesis (Open University, 2001,) p. 256.
28. Rose, 'Home Ownership', p. 119.
29. Royal Commission of Inquiry into Administration and Practical Operation of Poor Laws. British Parliamentary Paper 1834 (44), 210.
30. Poor Law Commission: Appendices to Twelfth Annual Report. British Parliamentary Paper 1846 (745), 93.
31. Cynthia Lane, 'Too Rarely Visited and Too Little Known: Travellers' Imaginings of Industrial Cornwall', in Philip Payton (ed.), *Cornish Studies: Thirteen* (Exeter, 2000), p. 186.
32. Thomas Shaw, *A History of Cornish Methodism* (Truro, 1967), p. 100.
33. Margaret Fuller, *West Country Friendly Societies – an account of village benefit clubs and their brass pole heads* (Lingfield, 1964,) p. 6.
34. M. Gorsky, 'The growth and distribution of English friendly societies in the early nineteenth century', *Economic History Review* 51 (1992), p. 493.
35. Ibid.
36. Gorsky, 'English friendly societies', p. 493. John Rule, 'The Misfortunes of the Mine: coping with life and death in nineteenth-century Cornwall', in Philip Payton (ed.), *Cornish Studies: Nine* (Exeter 2001), p. 136.
37. Fuller, *West Country Friendly Societies*, p. 9.
38. S. Cordery, 'Friendly Societies and the discourse of Respectability 1825–1875', *Journal of British Studies* 34 (DATE), p. 53.
39. Kirk cited in S. Cordery, 'Friendly Societies', pp. 37–39.
40. Ibid.
41. Lee Davison, Tim Hitchcock, Robert Shoemaker (eds), *Stilling the Grumbling Hive – The response to Social and Economic Problems in England, 1689–1750* (Stroud, 1992), p. 152.
42. L. Hollen-Lees, *The Solidarities of Strangers: The English Poor Laws and the People 1700–1948* (Cambridge, 1998), p. 298.

43. Deacon, 'The Spatial Dimension', p. 246.
44. Rule, 'The Misfortunes of the Mine', p. 131.
45. Thompson cited in Hollen-Lees, *The Solidarities of Strangers*, p. 298.
46. King, *Poverty and Welfare*, p. 5.
47. Burke, 'The Poor Law', p. 159.
48. Kayleigh Milden, 'Are You Church or Chapel? Perceptions of Spatial and Spiritual Identity within Cornish Methodism', in Philip Payton (ed.), *Cornish Studies: Twelve* (Exeter, 2004), p. 146.
49. Deacon, 'The Spatial Dimension'.
50. A.L. Rowse, *The Cornish in America* (London, 1967), p. 17.
51. Hollen-Lees, *The Solidarities of Strangers*, p. 305.
52. Ibid.
53. Burke, 'The Poor Law', p. 155, 159.
54. Bernard Deacon, 'We don't travel much, only to South Africa: Reconstructing Nineteenth-century Cornish Migration Patterns', in Philip Payton (ed.), *Cornish Studies: Fifteen* (Exeter, 2007), p. 100.
55. W.M. Brayshay, 'The Demography of Three West Cornwall mining Communities: A Society in Decline', unpub. Ph.D thesis (University of Exeter, 1977), p. 34.
56. Deacon, 'The Spatial Dimension', pp. 216–22.
57. Ibid.
58. Ibid.
59. Ibid.

5

'A Cornish Voice in the Celtic Orchestra'

Robert Morton Nance and the Celtic Congress of 1926

Derek R. Williams

Introduction

In the Winter 1932 issue of the journal *Old Cornwall*, Robert Morton Nance, National Secretary for Cornwall of the Celtic Congress, reported on the 'complete success from beginning to end' of the first Congress that Cornwall had just hosted. He summarized, too, the address of Henry Jenner who, as President of the Congress that year, spoke of 'the vastly improved conditions to-day, when thanks to the Old Cornwall Movement no intelligent Cornish person can remain utterly ignorant of his or her Celtic nationality, and thousands take a real pride in it'.[1] A decade earlier things were very different indeed and over the first six years of the 1920s, what was by British standards a very minor drama was staged in certain homes in west Cornwall, Wales and, to an even lesser extent, in Scotland, Ireland and Brittany.

The subject of the drama was where the fledgling Celtic Congress should be held each year – and, more specifically, the venue for the proposed 1926 Congress. Using the extensive correspondence housed in the National Library of Wales, between such Celtic luminaries as Edward T. John, D. Rhys Phillips, Robert Morton Nance, Agnes O'Farrelly and a number of lesser players, this article examines how, inspired by Henry Jenner's early efforts to gain recognition for Cornwall as a Celtic nation,[2] Nance was largely responsible for bringing her once again into the fold after the decline of Pan-Celticism during the war years of 1914–18. His efforts reflected the continuing deep-seated concern among Cornish revivalists that Cornwall be accepted by its sister nations as a *bona fide* Celtic country, one of the great preoccupations of the Cornish movement in the twentieth century. The staging of the Celtic Congress in Cornwall would be the outward and visible sign of Cornish Celticity and its acknowledgment by the other Celtic nations. Nance's aim, therefore, was to bring the Congress to Cornwall.

Celtic congresses and conferences

There had been 'Inter-Celtic' or Pan-Celtic gatherings from the early years of the twentieth century onwards – and, indeed, occasionally before that.[3] Nance himself, for instance, recalled in 'The Spirit of the Celtic Movement' how he had met his former French teacher Paul Barbier at a Celtic gathering of 1899.[4] The most celebrated gathering as far as Cornwall was concerned was, of course, the Caernarfon Conference of 1904 when Jenner's speech in Cornish gained the acceptance of the land as 'Celtic'. Although there were subsequent Pan-Celtic 'congresses' (Dublin in 1907[5] – or was it Edinburgh, where Jenner represented Cornwall?[6] – and Namur, Belgium in 1910), there was no central organization, and that is what E.T. John had in mind when he issued an invitation to all the Welsh societies to send delegates to a meeting of the Celts at Birkenhead between 3 and 5 September 1917, during the Welsh National Eisteddfod. Having been elected President of the Conference, he outlined in his address a proposal for a provisional and tentative organisation to facilitate, 'when the appropriate hour came', the prompt formation of a permanent organisation to bring the Celtic peoples together.[7] Although, for now, their discussions would be limited to matters of Celtic culture, 'The time for Celtic re-union and re-assertion of their primal power and prominence was surely at hand'.[8] This was pure rhetoric on John's part and, as Peter Berresford Ellis asserts, after 1917 the Congress lost the political impetus of its first decade and a half when 'most of the scholars supported, to varying degrees, the concept of political independence for each of the Celtic countries'.[9] There were no representatives from Cornwall at the Birkenhead Conference of 1917, but Jenner and Reginald Reynolds of Penzance both sent telegrams which were read to the assembly on the afternoon of Tuesday 4 September. Jenner's bore 'Heartiest greetings from the RCPS [Royal Cornwall Polytechnic Society] and RIC [Royal Institution of Cornwall]', while Reynolds wished 'for revival of interest in all things Celtic, especially in their reference to the Duchy of Cornwall'.[10]

Jenner also submitted a paper entitled 'The Present Position & Prospects of Celtic-Cornish Studies in Cornwall' which E.T. John summarized for the Conference. Although he was rather pessimistic about the revival of the Cornish language and the prospect of a literature in it, he drew his readers' attention to papers on the subject that had appeared in the *Journal of the Royal Institution of Cornwall* and the Annual Reports of the Royal Cornwall Polytechnic Society and apologized for seeming 'to be rather egotistic', but the fact of the matter was that very little had been done of late by anyone else. He continued: 'I do not think that this will be the case much longer, for a good many people are beginning the study, and at any rate I have found it very easy to get intelligent and interested audiences'. A few sentences later he added: 'Besides those to whose papers I have alluded [these were Thurstan Peter, who had died just prior to the writing of Jenner's paper, Revd Thomas Taylor and W.J. Stephens], there are several others who will do good work in the future, and some of them, I am happy to say, are quite young people.'[11] Jenner was then 69 years of age, while Nance was a relatively youthful 44.

On the morning of the last day of the Conference, a resolution was passed that there should be an Executive Committee which would endeavour to form a provisional General Council representing all the organizations engaged in the promotion of Celtic culture. There would be ten representatives each from Brittany, Ireland, Scotland and Wales and five each from Cornwall and the Isle of Man. (There would also be representatives from Celtic societies in England and from overseas.) The names approved as representing Cornwall on the Provisional Committee were Jenner (Convenor), Maj. J. Penberthy, Dr J. Hambley Rowe and Mr Morton Nance. (It should be pointed out here that it was not until the 2nd Conference at Neath in 1918 that the title 'Celtic Congress' was adopted for the 1919 meeting at Corwen, North Wales, where E.T. John was elected Congress President and Jenner Vice-President for Cornwall).[12]

Dramatis personae

The drama that absorbed the energy of a small number of individuals in the Celtic territories was played out courtesy of the Royal Mail which delivered the letters – and the occasional telegram – in which the events unfolded. The principal members of the cast and the main settings were as follows. In Cornwall there was Robert Morton Nance[13] (sometimes referred to as 'Dr' Nance), at 'Chylason', his Carbis Bay home, and Henry Jenner[14] (Bard *Gwaz Mikael* of the Breton Gorsedd, who was often referred to as Dr Jenner), at 'Bospowes', his Hayle home. Other, bit parts were played by Cornish exile Reginald T. Reynolds (bard *Gwas Piran* of the Welsh Gorsedd) who was at the time living in South Kensington; Joseph Hambley Rowe;[15] W.H. Lane, Mayor of Penzance in 1926; J. Howard Preston, also of

Penzance, temporary convenor of meetings and possibly Nance's right-hand man; and finally, Olive Wesley, who in June 1926 was appointed Local Secretary for the Congress at Penzance. In Wales the main players were David Rhys Phillips[16] (Bard *Beili Glas* of the Welsh Gorsedd), Welsh and Celtic Librarian at Swansea Public Library, Celtic Secretary of the Union of Welsh Societies, Secretary of the 1917 Birkenhead Conference and Secretary of the Celtic Congress until 1925; Edward Thomas John,[17] Liberal, then Labour and Welsh Nationalist politician, home-rule advocate, President of the Union of Welsh Societies and, as we have seen, President of the Birkenhead Conference; (he actually lived in London most of the time); the third Welsh player was May Roberts, John's private secretary from 1917 until his death in 1931. Bit parts were played by Illtyd Morgan; Alfred Percival Graves of Harlech, writer and lecturer on Celtic themes; W.J. Gruffydd, a writer who in 1921 was Professor of Celtic at University College, Cardiff; and finally, there was another Welsh exile, the Rev. G. Hartwell Jones, who was rector of Nutfield in Surrey and a writer. The one Irish member of the cast was Agnes O'Farrelly, a lecturer in Irish at University College, Dublin and from c.1925 General Secretary of the Celtic Congress. And in Scotland, Lachlan MacBean, editor of the *Fifeshire Advertizer*, author of *The Celtic Who's Who* and Treasurer of the Celtic Congress, had a walk-on part.

The Cornish claim, 1921–1925

The earliest relevant letter as far as Cornwall is concerned, from E.T. John to D. Rhys Phillips, is dated 1 July 1918, i.e. about a month before the Welsh National Eisteddfod at Neath and the associated Celtic Conference. In it John writes as follows from Llandinam Hall, Llanfair P.G., Anglesey:

> I think it quite delightful that our friends in Cornwall are exerting themselves to promote Celtic studies in their contemplated South Western University. I would warmly approve of some suitable resolution recognising this and supporting it, being passed at Neath. If we can assist in any other way, we shall all, I am sure, be quite prepared to do so.[18]

At the beginning of August Jenner attended the Welsh National Eisteddfod at Neath and, presumably, the associated Celtic Conference. In press reports Cornwall is referred to in passing, its Celts being described as being like those of Wales, in that they were 'mainly Nonconformist'.[19] On 13 September 1919 Phillips wrote to John, suggesting in his almost illegible handwriting that if Reginald Reynolds, whom he described as 'the owner of the Cornish <u>Cornubian</u>', was going up to Edinburgh, the setting for the 1920 Congress, he might – as 'a R.B.A. with a studio in London and another in Cornwall' – join in the art discussion.[20]

The following May, Phillips informed John that he had received an invitation (presumably for the Celtic Congress to be held there) from Cornwall, through Dr Henry Jenner.[21] Two days before Christmas Phillips informed John that Jenner had enquired about the next Congress and that he (Phillips) had asked him (Jenner) to let them know if he *did* propose to attend, so that a place could be found for him on the agenda. He mentioned, too, that the St Ives Old Cornwall Society had a class of fifteen to twenty learning Cornish and that, in Jenner's words, 'there are talks of similar societies in other towns'.[22] Five days later John replied saying that he was very interested to hear of Dr Jenner's [sic] enquiries and hoped that he would make it to the Isle of Man (the 1921 Congress was held at Douglas). He expressed a strong desire to visit both Cornwall and Brittany before his term of office as President of the Celtic Congress expired.[23] The following day, 29 December, Phillips replied, urging John to visit and consult the leading men of Brittany, as a precursor to a 'Celtic Congress in that country'. He continued:

> A similar visit to Cornwall, while Dr Henry Jenner is still hale and hearty would I think also make a wonderful impression and help to ensure the further inspiration of those who support his pro-Celtic work and are likely to carry it on after his day. He wields so much personal influence, by his scholarship and many attainments, over the intellectuals of that Duchy – quite beyond anything known on the literary history of Cornwall – that I feel it incumbent upon present Celtic Congress leaders to do all they possibly can to deepen the impression now, while he is in harness.[24]

The idea of doing things while Jenner was still alive is a recurring theme in the correspondence – as it is in relation to the first Cornish Gorsedd of 1928.

The following June, Phillips sent John his thoughts on the venue for the 1922 Congress. Although Ireland was out of the running, the War of Independence being then in full swing, there were other options:

> The invitation to Cornwall is open, and since I heard from Mr Morton Nance who is fully Celtic like Dr Jenner and many others, I have no doubt the welcome will be most hearty. The existence of Cornish classes is not a bad index, and the country itself is a romance ...

Further ... it would be a fine thing to crown his [Jenner's] great Celtic devotion by giving them the Congress for one year.[25]

Later that month, Reginald Reynolds wrote to Phillips as a 'lay' individual to say that if it was decided to hold the 1922 Congress in Cornwall, he and Mrs. Reynolds would do their utmost to make it a success, although they had no headquarters in the Duchy just then. He recommended Truro as a venue.[26] A year later, in June 1922, Nance sent Phillips a cheque for 10/6 as a subscription to the Celtic Congress for that year and enquired whether the Congress was being held in Dublin, as proposed.[27] In the event, there was no Congress that year.

The following January, Phillips informed John that Nance's report from Cornwall was very encouraging, with a Cornish Dictionary and a Cornish Reading book needed for those who were learning the language. 'To-day,' he continued, 'I rec'd one subscription of 10/6 from Dr J. Hambley Rowe (with promise of more later) who adds: "I hear whispered that the next Congress is to be at Penzance; if so please tell me the date, as I want to be present." Penzance is new to me!'[28] This was the first mention of what we might call the Penzance rumour or jinx. Three days later John replied, underlining the need to come to a quick decision about the 1923 Congress. With Ireland hesitating, he saw the options as follows:

> What then remains open to us is to ask whether Brittany would care to have the Congress this year, whether we should endeavour to hold it in Wales or accept the suggestion that it be held in Cornwall. I am myself inclined to the latter course in order, largely, to secure the participation of Dr Henry Jenner.[29]

In his reply the very next day, Phillips agreed that a decision needed to be made and that a short Congress was needed 'because of the hardness of the times and the difficulty of attendance at any distance'. He continued: 'Even tho' Cornwall is commercially and industrially stricken, we may never see Dr Jenner again and a brief Celtic Congress there (so that Scots and the few Irish and Breton cd travel back and fore within one week) wd therefore be a gallant thing to do'.[30]

Jenner would in fact live for another 11 years, but the earnest correspondents were not to know this! John, though, thought that Cornwall was unlikely to be practicable for the 1923 Congress and favoured Wales, preferably Bangor. Agnes O'Farrelly, on the other hand, was of the opinion that the Congress *should* go to Cornwall that autumn. She, too, favoured a one or two day affair, the publicity helping to keep the event in the public eye. But it was soon too late to do anything. For the second year in a row, there was no

Celtic Congress in 1923, E.T. John being preoccupied with his idea of a Celtic Federal Union, a more political animal altogether.

There was a Congress in 1924, held at Quimper in Brittany and attended by Nance and, possibly, the Reynoldses, the former deciding at the last minute to go as a delegate from the Royal Institution of Cornwall, to whom he reported at its Autumn Meeting. Nance was under no illusions about the degree of suspicion, even hostility, with which Cornish claims were still received in some Celtic quarters, and he knew that their assertion would have to be carefully diplomatic rather than aggressively dogmatic. A month before the event he wrote a long letter to D. Rhys Phillips. 'I think it behoves a Cornish representative at a Celtic Congress,' he stated, 'to be very retiring, for he has no Celtic Nation at the back of him, and very, very few friends at home who take the faintest interest in anything Celtic. Still I think the voice of Cornwall should be heard in the Celtic orchestra or there would be a gap, and, at least in a discussion, I would for the moment be that voice.'[31] At Quimper he discussed with Phillips projects that he was working on, including a folklore paper that broke new ground, 'no-one with a knowledge of Cornish having previously thought of the language as a source of folklore'.[32] On 6 October Phillips wrote to John saying that he had that very morning received from Nance and Jenner 'the official request (which he should have delivered at Quimper) for the Celtic Congress of 1925 to be held in Cornwall. He states that their invitation is supported by the various other Celtic countries and has been formulated since over two years ago, and is now finally repeated.'[33] In the light of future events, this observation is important, reiterating as it does the fact that Cornwall had been trying since the beginning of the decade to get the Celtic Congress there.

The following March Phillips received from John a suggested draft of an Irish Conference and felt obliged to remind the Congress President of Cornwall's claim. 'You will not forget,' he wrote, 'the <u>Document of Invitation</u> sent by Mr Morton Nance on behalf of the Cornish Societies. I have since been rather severely reproved by a group of Cornishmen for allowing the Celtic Congress to lapse in 1922–23 – I cited the poverty of the Duchy at the time and their reply was "That only occurred in one little corner: and we had definitely extended an Invitation in 1921. Ireland has let you down repeatedly and may do so again." So much for spilt milk. I have shown the draft to the group who usually take an interest.'[34] The 'one little corner' – an understatement, if ever there was one – was almost certainly the Camborne/Redruth area, the plight of which was known across Britain, with the Cornish Miners' Choir giving concerts far from home in aid of the Tin Miners' Distress Fund, and relief money coming from London, Cardiff, Ireland and the English Midlands.[35]

The Celtic Congress, 1926: a variety of suggested venues

Stung, perhaps, by the criticism from his Cornish cousins, Phillips was by now obviously keeping Nance fully informed, for on 24 March the latter wrote to him as follows:

I am glad that you are keeping Cornwall's claim forward, though not yet with any definite success. It will strengthen your hand, I hope, to know that yesterday at a very representative gathering at Penzance ... I brought up the question of an invitation to the Congress to come to Penzance in 1926, stating as nearly as I could what it would require in the way of local organisation. The idea was taken up most warmly by those representing the town as well as those representing antiquarian and 'Old Cornwall' work, and I can assure you that our disappointment will be keen if we can not look forward to having you here then. Mr Jenner of course supports me [and] adds to his several previous invitations this renewed one. All the Cornish societies are ready to do their best to make the event a memorable one in the history of Cornwall ... All this I am authorised to send you as expressing the voice of the meeting.

A few lines later, Nance drove home Cornwall's claim:

I hope, in speaking next to Mr E.T. John of the Cornish invitation, that you will put it to him that no Celtic country needs the help that would be given by the holding of the Congress in it as Cornwall does. Celtic things here are literally gasping for the vital breath that you people in lands more happily placed can bring us. That and the natural and historic attractions of the country ought to be strong reasons for accepting our invitation.[36]

Three days later he wrote to the Congress President himself, reiterating what he had written to Phillips and giving four strong reasons for the Congress meeting in Cornwall:

1. There is no Celtic country that so badly needs help from outside in its efforts to keep its individuality.
2. There is no other Celtic country that has not yet had a pan-Celtic congress held in it.
3. The invitation is a very long-standing one, and Mr Jenner, who first gave it, is not a young man, though his age as yet has not

caused him to give up his Celtic studies. His services to such studies deserve such a recognition.

4.   At Quimper, although I did not actually invite the Congress formally at the business meeting which closed it, I had already done so in a Cornish speech which I expected to be understood as well as I found myself able to understand the Breton speeches; and having mentioned the subject in conversation with representatives of all Celtia I found them full of interest in Cornwall's small efforts and quite in favour of a Cornish visit. Had I understood that the business meeting was, as I now realize, my best opportunity for getting this question of a visit to Cornwall settled, I should certainly not have missed it, as in my extreme modesty, as a novice and as representing a nation heb iaeth ['without language', in Welsh], I unfortunately did.

Besides all these reasons, the Cornish had a beautiful country that they wanted to show him. '[I]n our place-names,' continued Nance, 'and in the voices of our people if not in their words here in West Cornwall we are Celtic still. All is going fast, though, unless we can save it quickly, and nothing would help us more than the strong support of the Celtic-speaking peoples and their interest in our Celtic things.'[37] Nance was clearly adept at 'playing the field' and that same day he wrote again to Phillips, informing him that he'd written to John, who would therefore know that the invitation to Cornwall was 'a genuine thing'. His letter is one of the most interesting in the collection, revealing Nance's thoughts on politics and religion. He advocated Cornwall as a moderating influence on the Congress's more militant members, in particular the Bretons, and saw 'Anti-industrialism, or rather propaganda in favour of Celtic culture versus big business' as enough to keep the Congress busy.[38] On 15 April John replied to Nance's letter of 27 March:

With regard to the locale of the Congress for 1926 this will be decided in Dublin. Personally I very fully appreciate all that you urge so cogently and eloquently. Wales will undoubtedly make an application as it has not been visited since the new series was initiated at Edinburgh in 1920. I hear some suggestion that London may also apply and possibly the United States. We will, however, see that your application is fully considered and you will undoubtedly with some of your friends be present to press the claim of Cornwall.[39]

Nance replied almost immediately, expressing his pleasure that Cornwall's claim was still on the table and regretting that he would not be in Dublin for that year's Congress.[40] Four days later he again wrote to Phillips, expressing the view that he did not think the Congress President was quite converted by his (Nance's) arguments for Cornwall. He wished he could go and 'be cogent and eloquent' in Dublin, but the cost of an already planned long holiday in Brittany ruled that out. He reiterated Cornwall's strong points:

> 1) No pan Celtic conference of any kind has been held there, and our fellow Celts hardly realize that Cornwall exists except as a tripper resort. 2) Celtic feeling and Celtic nationality are being, except for a few recent efforts, allowed to die in their sleep here and outside stimulus is urgently needed. 3) Mr Jenner, our grand old man, is likely to be less and less equal to the strain of a Congress and he personally deserves the recognition that the coming of the Congress to Cornwall would mean. There are the attractiveness of Cornwall and heaps of other reasons, but I think these three are the <u>best</u>.[41]

On 3 July – ahead of the Dublin Congress – Phillips once again reminded E.T. John of the Cornish claim, trusting that 'For the sake of unity, … the Cornish plea of Mr Morton Nance to you and myself will be given favourable consideration'.[42] Despite the sense of urgency that now surrounded the matter in Cornwall, no decision was arrived at in Dublin and on Christmas Eve John informed Congress member and speaker Augusta Lamont of Edinburgh that the decision had still to be made, adding, in a comment that revealed something of his true feelings about Cornish Celticity, that personally he was of the opinion that they had 'to be content with Cornwall'.[43]

Early in 1926 the sense of muddle and indecision that would bedevil the whole affair was confirmed by Alfred Percival Graves of Harlech, who on 6 February wrote the following to E.T. John: 'When we parted at Holyhead you told me you did not think the next Celtic Congress would be held in Cornwall. A letter from Henry Jenner rather confirms this as he supposes it will be held in North Wales.'[44] Taking Graves to task for misunderstanding what he had said, John insisted that he favoured holding the Congress in Cornwall during the week preceding the August Eisteddfod and informed him that they were communicating with 'our friends in Cornwall' to this effect.[45] That same day, 15 February, rather belatedly he wrote to Nance to do just that:

> I hear from Mr A.P. Graves that Dr Jenner is under the impression that this year's Celtic Congress will not be held in Cornwall. I can understand this impression arising, but our desires are precisely to the contrary. When we met at Dublin there was unhappily nobody over from Cornwall to urge its claim. I however throughout favour the

holding of the Congress in Cornwall this year and in Wales 1927. We were rather embarrassed by the enthusiasm of our Irish friends who pressed a suggestion that the Congress on a still wider scale should be held in Ireland again this coming summer. We felt that it would at the moment be somewhat ungracious to turn down the invitation absolutely, and deferred it to a Meeting we then hoped to hold in Dublin in November. It proved, however, impractical to convene the contemplated Meeting, but towards Christmas time Miss O'Farrelly happened to be in London and after some discussion we came to the conclusion that Cornwall was the proper venue for 1926. I arranged with Miss O'Farrelly that she should forthwith communicate this decision to our friends in Cornwall. I am not very sure whether this or not has been done or not. In any case, I hope that yourself and your colleagues will find it practicable, even with the short notice you have, to receive the Congress this year. The dates we suggest are Monday July 26th to Saturday 31st, the week immediately preceding the Swansea Eisteddfod. This will facilitate Celts from all parts combining the Congress and the National Eisteddfod … We are inclined to limit the Congress this year to one week as it is possible some of our friends will desire to proceed to Philadelphia for the Exhibition in September, where it is quite possible some representation of the Celtic areas at home may be desired. If it will at all help matters I should be glad to run down to Cornwall early in March.[46]

1926 and all that!

Nance replied immediately, stating that they had certainly been under the impression that the Congress would not be held in Cornwall that year, no one, to his knowledge, having heard from Miss O'Farrelly:

Of course I am delighted to hear of your decision and we will get together as quickly as possible to decide how best we can make the Congress a success on our part. Meanwhile it would be a great help if you could tell Mr Jenner or myself a little as to the sort of local organisation that will be required, and it probably would help us a great deal if you could spare time to run down a little later on, when things will at least have arrived at the first stage of organisation with us, I hope.

The list of subjects for papers looked very promising, and he believed that, given respectable weather, the Congress was bound to please everyone if held on Cornish soil.[47] Two days later, on 22 February, he wrote to *Beili Glas*. Among the things he mentioned was their desire to see a special gathering of the [Welsh] Gorsedd at the stone circle of Boscawen-Un. 'Poor old Cornwall,' he continued, 'is in a sad condition of poverty amongst the Celtic nations, but if this might help her to take the role of peace maker among her richer sisters, this would be a good thing after all.'[48]

Did July seem a long way off? It would seem so, for although the wheels began to turn, they did so very, very slowly. Two weeks later, in a letter to Edward John, Nance blamed the lack of any ready-made organization for the delay in making any first steps towards organising the Congress. However, he hoped soon to be able to report on the establishment of a committee and the recent formation of an Old Cornwall Society at Penzance was viewed as a useful development. Accommodation was seen as a potential problem and Nance asked for some idea of the number of people (minimum and maximum) who might be expected to attend.[49] On the very last day of March, Nance reported to John that preparations seemed to be getting on well, with the Federation of Old Cornwall Societies undertaking the initial work, a county committee of supporters on the point of being formed, and local committees at Penzance, to do the actual work, in the offing. Mona Douglas of the Isle of Man had made useful suggestions. Nance felt that there was still plenty of time, but accommodation and the booking of halls were major concerns for, in his words, 'the week chosen comes right up against the Bank Holiday let of the hotels, when a week's booking is very apt to clash with someone else's fortnight or three weeks bid; and this being actually in the season at Penzance, though not in the height of it, there are other bidders likely to come on for the use of halls'. Charabancs, too, would need to be 'bespoken well beforehand'! Once again, he asked that Congress members be circularized so that some idea of numbers could be ascertained. Obviously feeling the need to put the Welsh right concerning his status, he signed the letter '(not Dr) R. Morton Nance'.[50] Two weeks later, on 15 April, Nance reported to John that the previous evening a committee had been formed at Penzance to carry on the actual work of making preparations and that the Mayor had convened a Public Meeting for the purpose. Once again, accommodation and hospitality were raised, with some in favour of retiming the event to run from the 22nd to the 29th or 30th (in order to avoid the Bank Holiday weekend itself) or even to September. Nance concluded:

I, with Mr Henry Jenner, Secretary of the Old Cornwall Federation, am still acting as organiser until a Secretary has been appointed for the Penzance committee, and of course I shall keep in close touch with what they do there. If Miss Douglas comes down later, as she has promised to do, we should of course put her in charge, meanwhile it makes things difficult to explain when questions are asked as to the latest news that I have had from headquarters, and my last official letter is dated February 20th, when you were just going abroad. We should be very grateful for some statement of the progress already made towards gathering the Congress together and ascertaining its strength.[51]

A letter to May Roberts, John's secretary, four days later concerned the subjects for the papers to be given, with Nance saying that they would certainly like the Cornish language to be allocated some time. Accommodation and the numbers that might be expected to attend were considered to be the main issues.[52] That same day May Roberts replied on Edward John's behalf to Nance's previous letter. She conveyed John's agreement on the dates 22 to 29 July and recommended following the course pursued by the Isle of Man committee. She thought there had been about 120 overseas visitors in Dublin the previous year.[53] Having already received from Mona Douglas an estimate of 200 at the lowest for the fast-approaching Congress, Nance informed May Roberts that the Penzance committee would find out what private hospitality was to be had and reiterated his own position:

> As I really have no official position in the Congress ... I am sure it would be better for the communications to Ireland and Scotland to come from headquarters. I haven't Miss O'Farrelly's address or I should have written asking how many she expected to go from Ireland. Miss Douglas, of course, I am in communication with. But you will see my point – that I am not even Secretary for Cornwall which is Mr Jenner's position, and that something will be expected from the General Secretary of the Congress. If one could be appointed pro. tem. as I suggested to Mr John in my last letter to him, it would meet the case, but at present I feel that too much responsibility for the whole thing is thrown on to those who will have the work to do perhaps, but who are not really officially authorized to call the Congress together.

In a postscript, Nance appeared to lose his cool somewhat: 'I had hoped that it would be possible to circularize all members of the congress asking them to give in their names and sort of accommodation wanted. Is this not done?'[54] Replying the very next day, May Roberts thought that Cornwall could safely put the maximum number of Congress visitors at 100 and indicated that she would circulate members as far as possible over the coming days.[55]

On 24 April Nance informed Roberts that the had managed to provisionally book St John's Hall from 24 to 29 July, and somewhat belatedly raised the question of finance:

> A point that the Penzance Committee want made clear is their own financial position, and as I know so little of the way in which the Congress is worked I should be glad to know in whose name halls are to be booked or arrangements made. The absence of a General Secretary to write to is a lack that they feel very much as it makes the Celtic Congress seem a vague thing with no-one to take responsibility, and knowing only what I can tell them, that it has never been known to let down the local committee as far as I have heard, they rather want to know just what the possible liabilities that they may be letting themselves in for may be.

He concluded his letter on a more optimistic note, indicating how much interest was being shown in the event in Penzance, both the Chamber of Commerce and the Rotary Club, in addition to the Old Cornwall Society, being represented on the local committee. J. Howard Preston was 'acting as Secretary pro. tem.' and would be pleased to hear from her direct on the points mentioned in his [Nance's] letter.[56] In her reply (to Nance) two days later May Roberts pointed out that, with regard to finance, in other areas the local committee was usually responsible for all liabilities, money being raised by the receipts from concerts held and plays performed during Congress week.[57]

A couple of letters from E.T. John, both dated 19 May, are quite revealing as to how Cornwall was viewed in the 1920s, at least by certain of her Welsh 'cousins'. One note to W.J. Gruffydd, Professor of Celtic at University College, Cardiff, for instance, included the following observation:

> I know you regard the area [Cornwall] has too negligible a factor to merit this measure of attention, but we have really been governed by two considerations. We desire to pay this compliment to Dr [sic] Henry Jenner and in addition we require another twelve months in order to prepare for a Congress in Wales on lines complementing adequately, and I hope approaching, if not fulfilling your own ideals and aspirations, which I am sure I very fully share.[58]

And on the very same day, he wrote to the Rev. G. Hartwell Jones that, as he would readily appreciate, the choice of subjects was unusually difficult, seeing that their main interest, the language question, was 'so irrelevant to local conditions' in Cornwall.[59]

'They seem to be going ahead in Cornwall'

Nance was clearly worried about the industrial unrest that was gripping Britain and felt the need to unburden himself. One of his correspondents was Agnes O'Farrelly at Rathgar, Co. Dublin, who on 24 May informed E.T. John that she had received a long letter from him and suggested that it would be good if he could run down and hearten the Cornish up a bit – or write to them. She herself was giving Nance all the information she could about the running of the Congress.[60] Her letter contained the statement 'They seem to be going ahead in Cornwall', and in interpreting her sense of mild surprise we need to remember the turmoil Britain was in at that moment. Although the General Strike lasted officially from only 3 to 12 May 1926, tensions remained high and the economic uncertainty continued, with the coal miners staying out until December and nearly a quarter of the National Union of Railwaymen's members (45,000 men) still waiting to be taken back by the rail companies as late as the autumn. The first mention in this extensive correspondence of the industrial unrest came in a letter from E.T. John to Nance, dated 29 May, in which he revealed that he had 'naturally at times felt some trepidation as to the effect of the continuance of the strike'. They were, nevertheless, proceeding with the work of getting the promised papers,[61] although John revealed in a letter to Agnes O'Farrelly that very same day that he rather begrudged restricting such an authority on economics as Dr George O'Brien to 'a topic of such limited scope as the Tin Mines of Cornwall'![62] Two days later Nance thanked John for the suggested programme and informed him that they, too, had been allowing matters to rest until the coal question was sufficiently settled to indicate whether travelling would be reasonably easy and cheap by July. Once again, accommodation and attendance numbers were raised. It seems that the Cornish had been contemplating postponing the Congress until October and a visit from John during the next week or ten days would encourage the committee. Once again, Nance concluded optimistically:

> Our execution [presumably he meant 'executive'] committee is not in being yet as a separate entity and no programme has yet been arranged, but the idea will be to show The Land's End and Lizard districts, with as many of their antiquities as can be worked in. The Saturday excursion might be made to extend to Tintagel, but that is a far cry and personally I think that we have enough near Penzance without aiming at this famous spot. One day, it has been proposed, should include a visit to the Museum of the Royal Institution of Cornwall at Truro, and a trip on the Fal river, which is much like the Odet at Quimper. This might perhaps be included in the Lizard trip.[63]

On 4 June E.T. John wrote to J. Howard Preston to reassure him about the effects of the miners' strike and offering to come down. 'So far as we are concerned,' he wrote, 'we scarcely regard the situation today as sufficiently disconcerting to make the holding of the Congress at all doubtful. The situation is still most difficult, but the fact that the mine owners have again taken the initiative is much more hopeful.'[64] Four more days elapsed before Preston, very much the committee man and bureaucrat, wrote a singularly unhelpful letter by way of reply, bearing in mind that the planned Congress was now just six weeks away:

I am afraid that up to the receipt of your reply we were all under the impression that such Congress expenses would be met by Congress funds ... we also were seeking guidance as to the requirements usual in the way of sub-committees and their particular duties, so that they might work in conjunction with your Central Body.

Personally, I have strongly felt the desirability of our being made acquainted, at the outset, with the whole method of your usual procedure at these Congresses – this would have enabled us to call our committee together for action. Yesterday I received a visit from Mr Jenner and Mr Nance and subsequently I saw the Mayor and we have decided that the best course will be to call a meeting of the Committee for Monday evening next to discuss the whole matter as it then appears ... also to appoint a Secretary and any other Officers and Sub-Committees to assist in making the Congress a success ... I should, perhaps, explain that at the preliminary public meeting held on April 14th I was requested to undertake to convene the next meeting (pending the appointment of a Secretary) – therefore my official [role] automatically terminates then.[65]

Following the General Committee meeting at the Guildhall on Monday 14 June, Nance wrote a 3-page letter to John in which the continued uncertainty as to the numbers attending was the first item to be mentioned. Press and other notices had resulted in only one request for accommodation and two or three enquiries about private hospitality. Strangely, at this late stage, the bulk of the letter was concerned with the Cornish papers to be read at the Congress, with visits and with the prospect of plays being brought down by delegates for performance during Congress week.[66] The following day, Olive Wesley, who had been appointed Local Secretary at the meeting two days earlier, wrote to John to clarify her own position – just over a month before the beginning of the Congress. 'When are you likely to be in Penzance?' she quizzed him. 'In what way may we obtain assistance from the Central Committee? Who is the Secretary thereof and what function does it fulfil?

Everything at the moment seems very vague and indefinite. We have certain Committees formed, are these to use their own initiative and act to the best of their ability or is there anyone to whom we are to look for further instructions?'[67] One can but sympathize with poor Olive Wesley! The very next day, 17 June, E.T. John threw the struggling Cornish a lifeline:

Dear Mr Nance,

Many thanks for your letter of the 15th.

I quite appreciate the difficulty you are in as to the people likely to come to Penzance for the Congress. They are however not, I fear, likely to be such as to tax your resources at all seriously. In fact the position is very much otherwise. From Scotland, Mrs. Burnley Campbell, Miss Farquaharson and Dr Calder have definitely intimated that they are unable to come and it is now very doubtful whether Mr MacBean, our Treasurer, can be present. These are amongst our most loyal friends, so that I very much fear that Scotland will not be represented at all.

I have a letter from Mons. Mocaer this morning lamenting the latest development of the franc and explaining how impracticable it is for any of our Breton friends to be with us. We probably can count upon the presence of half a dozen of our Irish friends unless they are later deterred by the difficulties of travel. I had counted very much upon a goodly contingent from Wales but the gloomy outlook with regard to the coal trouble is certainly very discouraging. I fear there is little ground for supposing that the trouble will be over within the next four to six weeks. It is even clouding the prospects of the Swansea Eisteddfod itself.

You have waited so long for the Congress to come to Cornwall that I should be very distressed if when it is held it proves to be really but a shadow of what it should and would be in normal times. Although your Committee have very little time left to make the considerable arrangements necessary, I do not doubt that this can be managed, but I should be sorry if your efforts did not receive the recognition of an adequate attendance of members of the Congress.

With regard to other points raised in your letter, the difficulties as to the presentation of Irish, Scots and Welsh Plays will be much accentuated by the present position.

Your suggested programme of excursions would, I am sure, be very delightful but I think I must leave you and the Committee to seriously consider whether we had better persist in the effort to hold the Congress in July or postpone it to some more auspicious date.

I remain,

Yours sincerely,[68]

Nance wasted no time in replying. So anxious had they been as to the effect that the coal stoppage was likely to have on the coming together of Celts from so far afield into 'a place as remote as Penzance', that John's letter suggesting the advisability of postponing it would surely come as a relief to all those who had been working for the event. He continued:

> The feeling that the whole thing was likely to be a fiasco unless this national question was settled soon has been weighing on us all.
>
> I know that I am speaking for Penzance as a whole in saying that late September or even October, when the Congress would come as a short prolongation of the ended season, would find the town in the best possible situation to welcome it. This will also give us time to organize a guarantee fund on a scale adequate, I hope, to the inviting down of some of the promised plays and some specially worth while artistes for the concerts. With the industrial cloud that hangs over every Cornish industry and the apparent prospect of a ruined 'visitor' season, no worse time than the present could be found for raising anything like the amount that we should like to have available.
>
> I am writing this of course simply as giving my impressions, and will give you as soon as the committee comes together whatever proposals may be made for a more auspicious date to be aimed at by us. We of course are in no way less eager to have the Congress here. All that we want is that it should be a good one, and this extra time will I hope be the means of ensuring this.
>
> The plays, attractive as they would be, are not likely to pay their way. Miss Douglas offers a one-act play with four characters, running for about half an hour, and going into costs, we find this runs to about £10 per actor. If we are to have these from each country, most of them bigger plays, it will need more than a mere guarantee fund to provide them. Are there societies who would pay part expenses I wonder? [69]

It would seem that Nance had still not fully grasped the message that John was trying to convey in the vague 'some more auspicious date', and the very next day (19 June) John wrote the following, carefully worded, but less ambiguous, reply:

Dear Mr Nance,

Many thanks for yours of the 18th. I am very pleased that you find yourself so much in agreement with my suggestion. I have been most reluctant to say or do anything to damp the enthusiasm and ardour of our friends in Cornwall, and they have no doubt been equally wishful to demonstrate their desire to proceed with the contemplated arrangement, but I feel that on both sides we would be making a great mistake to attempt to hold the Congress under existing conditions. It would be very much better to postpone it to a time when we can come to Cornwall in force. My own view is that it should be put off until an occasion when we can with the help of Cornish Societies the World over, combine a World Cornish Reunion with the Celtic Congress. I scarcely think that this could be done in September or October, but we can discuss this later. In the meantime I think it would be helpful to all our friends to know that it is not proposed to proceed with the matter at the moment. It is not only your good people at Penzance that are affected, but the economic outcome of the stoppage is really extraordinarily far-reaching.

   With kind regards,
   Yours sincerely,[70]

There was seemingly the need for a formal decision to be made at once, but ten days would elapse before the following telegram was handed in at Carbis Bay at 2.35pm on Thursday 1 July 1926:

John 63 Warwick Square [?] Ldn.
   Comm. Agreed best postpone Congress. Sorry to have left matter at all doubtful.
   Nce.[71]

Although Nance was undoubtedly relieved that a final decision had been made, he was clearly depressed by the whole saga, for on 24 July he wrote to John to say that Jenner had instructed him to submit Cornwall's claim for the 1927 Congress. 'Whether this year's fiasco has deprived us of any right to put in a claim for next year or not,' he continued, 'is a matter for the decision of yourself and your executive committee. It seems evident that no large congress will be attracted to Cornwall, which is only natural seeing how very little Cornwall's part in the Celtic movement can be, but Penzance is still very willing to do its utmost.'[72]

Conclusion

All the indications are that, even without the severe industrial unrest and economic uncertainty that prevailed in 1926, the Celtic Congress would have been something of a damp squib had it taken place in Cornwall that year. The cultural infrastructure was not yet robust enough and the 'Celtic' Cornish were just not ready to shoulder the responsibility for such an event.

Had the event taken place and failed, the worst fears of Cornwall's detractors in the wider Celtic world would have been confirmed, and the project to promote Cornwall's place in this Celtic fraternity would have suffered a severe set-back. As it was, the failure of Cornwall to organize a Congress in 1926, after some years of seeking the privilege, could hardly have impressed those suspicious of or hostile to Cornish claims. Yet, notwithstanding this unpromising debacle, Nance had won many of the arguments and had, despite his own doubts, whetted appetites in Cornwall, fostering new aspirations and expectations. After 1928, the year that saw the all-important inauguration of Gorseth Kernow at Boscawen-Un, Cornwall was in more self-confident mood, with an improved infrastructure ready to tackle the complexity of managing an international event. The stage would be set for a drama that would have a very different outcome: the hugely successful Celtic Congress in Cornwall in 1932.

Notes and references

1. R. Morton Nance, 'Old Cornwall and the Celtic Congress', *Old Cornwall*, vol. 2, no. 4 (Winter 1932), p. 22.

2. See Henry Jenner, 'Cornwall: A Celtic Nation', in Derek R. Williams (ed.), *Henry and Katharine Jenner: A Celebration of Cornwall's Culture, Language and Identity* (London: Boutle, 2004). In '"Gwas Myghal" and the Cornish Revival', *Old Cornwall*, vol. 2, no. 8 (Winter 1934), p. 5, Nance wrote that 'all were inspired by his [Jenner's] ideal of Cornwall as a Celtic Nation'. For the coming together of Jenner and Nance, and the extent to which the latter can be considered the cultural heir of the former, see Peter W. Thomas and Derek R. Williams, 'Introduction', pp. 23–4, and Ann Trevenen Jenkin, 'Reawakening Cornwall's Celtic consciousness', in Thomas and Williams (eds), *Setting Cornwall on its Feet: Robert Morton Nance, 1873–1959* (London, 2007).

3. Mari Ellis's 'A short history of the Celtic Congress', *Proceedings of the Celtic Congress* (Aberystwyth, 1983) and http://www.evertype.com/celtcong/cc-hist-mellis.html (accessed 21 November 2007), is a useful introduction to the subject, as is Peter Berresford Ellis, *The Celtic Dawn* (London, 1993), pp. 73–86. See also R. Morton Nance, 'The Spirit of the Celtic Movement', in Thomas and Williams (eds), *Setting Cornwall on its Feet: Robert Morton Nance, 1873–1959* (London, 2007), pp. 273–4.

4. R. Morton Nance ' "Gwas Myghal" and the Cornish Revival', p. 5.

5. The website of the International Celtic Congress, http://www.evertype.com/celtcong/cc-res.html (accessed 21 November 2007).

6. Henry Jenner, 'The Present Position and Prospects of Celtic-Cornish Studies in Cornwall', in D. Rhys Phillips (comp), *The Celtic Conference 1917: Report ...*, Perth: Milne, Tannahill, and Methven (1918), pp. 113–14.

7. Phillips, *The Celtic Conference 1917*, p. 13.

8. Ibid.

9. Ellis 'Celtic Congress', p. 79. Jenner, of course, was opposed to any political expression of Celtic nationalism, while Nance, though outwardly more amenable to the idea, nevertheless often saw Cornwall's role within the Congress as a moderating one.

10. Phillips, *The Celtic Conference 1917*, p. 58.

11. Jenner 'The Present Position ... in Cornwall', pp. 112–13.

12. 'The National Eisteddfod', in *Oswestry and Border Counties Advertizer*, 7 August 1918.

13. See Thomas and Williams, *Setting Cornwall on its Feet*.

14. See Williams, *Henry and Katharine Jenner*.

15. Hugh Miners and Treve Crago, *Tolzethan: The Life and Times of Joseph Hambley Rowe* (Cornwall, 2002).

16. See *The Dictionary of Welsh Biography 1941–1970* (2001), p. 206; E. Ernest Hughes, 'In Memoriam D. Rhys Phillips, F.L.A., F.R.S.L., F.S.A. (Scot)', in *The Journal of the Welsh Bibliographical Society*, vol. 7, no. 3 (July 1952), pp. 119–21.

17. See *The Dictionary of Welsh Biography down to 1940* (1959), London, p. 440; Alan Jobbins, 'E.T. John and the Second Home Rule Campaign', in *Ein Gwlad*, vol. 3, no. 2 (May 2006), pp. 41–5.

18. National Library of Wales, E.T. John Papers (GB0210ETJOHN), ETJ 1936.

19. *Oswestry and Border Counties Advertizer*, 7 August 1918.

20. NLW, John Papers, ETJ 2307.

21. Ibid, ETJ 2535, 10 May 1920.

22. Ibid, ETJ 2777, 23 December 1920.

23. Ibid, ETJ 2779, 28 December 1920.

24. Ibid, ETJ 2782.

25. Ibid, ETJ 2871, 6 June 1921.

26. Ibid, ETJ 2895, 25 June 1921.

27. National Library of Wales, Papers of David Rhys Phillips 2 (Correspondence), letter 3588, 5 June 1922.

28. Ibid, John Papers, ETJ 3773, 29 January 1923.

29. Ibid, ETJ 3774, 1 February 1923.

30. Ibid, ETJ 3777, 2 February 1923.

31. Ibid, Phillips Papers 2, letter 3590, 9 August 1924.

32. Ibid, letter 3591, 22 January 1925.

33. Ibid, John Papers, ETJ 4240.

34. Ibid, ETJ 4345, 21 March 1925.

35. See 'Cornish Choir at Salop. Help for the Tin Miners', in *Oswestry and Border Counties Advertizer*, 9 August 1922; 'Want in Cornwall. Tin miners faced with starvation', in *Times*, 7 October 1921.

36. NLW, Phillips Papers 2, letter 3593, 24 March 1925.

37. Ibid, John Papers, ETJ 4352, 27 March 1925.

38. Ibid, Phillips Papers 2, letter 3594, 27 March 1925.

39. Ibid, John Papers, ETJ 4362.

40. Ibid, ETJ 4366, 17 April 1925.

41. Ibid, Phillips Papers 2, letter 3595, 21 April 1925.

42. Ibid, John Papers, ETJ 4486.

43. Ibid, ETJ 4541.

44. Ibid, ETJ 4558.

45. Ibid, ETJ 4563, 15 February 1926.
46. Ibid, ETJ 4566.
47. Ibid, ETJ 4569, 17 February 1926.
48. Ibid, Phillips Papers 2, letter 3596.
49. Ibid, John Papers, ETJ 4576, 10 March 1926.
50. Ibid, ETJ 4585, 31 March 1926.
51. Ibid, ETJ 4588.
52. Ibid, ETJ 4589, 19 April 1926.
53. Ibid, ETJ 4590.
54. Ibid, ETJ 4592, 21 April 1926.
55. Ibid, ETJ 4593, 22 April 1926.
56. Ibid, ETJ 4594, 24 April 1926.
57. Ibid, ETJ 4596, 26 April 1926.
58. Ibid, ETJ 4607, 19 May 1926.
59. Ibid, ETJ 4608, 19 May 1926.
60. Ibid, ETJ 4614.
61. Ibid, ETJ 4622.
62. Ibid, ETJ 4623.
63. Ibid, ETJ 4628, 31 May 1926.
64. Ibid, ETJ 4632.
65. Ibid, ETJ 4638, 8 June 1926.
66. Ibid, ETJ 4644, 15 June 1926.
67. Ibid, ETJ 4645, 16 June 1926.
68. Ibid, ETJ 4647.
69. Ibid, ETJ 4648, 18 June 1926.
70. Ibid, ETJ 4649, 19 June 1926.
71. Ibid, ETJ 4655.
72. Ibid, ETJ 4662.

6

A Preference for Doing Nothing or a Misplaced Focus on Men?

Problematic Starting Points for Early Twentieth-Century Public Health Reform in Cornwall

Catherine Mills and Pamela Dale

Introduction

Historically there have been very few published studies on health in Cornwall. This dearth of secondary literature applies equally to assessments of the health of the population and to any evaluation of services provided by the statutory or voluntary sectors. The few authors who have addressed these important questions have been quick to draw attention to the limited primary sources addressing Cornish health topics.[1] This unfortunate situation may usefully be contrasted with the voluminous and readily accessible material for comparable areas such as Devon, Somerset, and Dorset. Even routine Cornish paperwork such as the Annual Reports of the Medical Officer of Health (MOH) are difficult to read locally, although London libraries have incomplete sets available.[2]

This lack of direct knowledge of Cornish health problems and health provisions has led to speculation about the alleged 'backwardness' of Cornwall rather than full discussion of any distinctive patterns in the demand for, as well as supply of, health care. Sheaff has started to correct this one-sided view of the problem,[3] but work in the field is still under-developed compared to extensive literature that has, for example, identified unique Cornish work cultures, community practices and migration patterns.[4] These factors all undoubtedly had an impact on health, but full analysis of their respective influences is beyond the scope of this article. Instead, we simply suggest that in Cornwall certain long-standing concerns and traditions may have served to prioritize male health at a time when central government was turning its attention to the welfare of women and children.[5]

It was Deborah Dwork who first suggested that war is good for babies and other young children.[6] She demonstrated that specialist services were developed in response to the social, economic and political problems that were identified retrospectively after the Boer war and re-emphasized during the First World War. These services, formalized and encouraged by the 1918 Maternity and Child Welfare Act, became a major public health project for the new Ministry of Health after 1919. For some commentators, such as Jane Lewis, this was an unhelpful direction for the public health services to take,[7] but they certainly provided new criteria against which central government officials were increasingly keen to measure local performance. Cornwall, as a late and reluctant promoter of maternity and infant welfare services, looked increasingly weak in top–down assessments of health care, and this may have distorted views of the quality and quantity of inter-war provision.

Historians exploring the origins of the welfare state, and especially the campaign for a National Health Service,[8] have identified the interwar period as an important moment; at least in the negative sense of revealing the inadequacy of local arrangements and the need for fundamental reforms.[9] The years between 1919 and 1939 thus emerge as a period of conflict; where major debates about the powers and duties of the local and national state were conducted inside and outside of government and given particular urgency by the crisis created by the great depression.[10] The 1929 Local Government Act and the transfer of many Poor Law functions to local councils emerged as a defining moment in British welfare policy. Such a significant realignment of services also encouraged a new interest in the performance of the responsible local authorities, and section 104 of the Act empowered the Ministry of Health to conduct detailed public health surveys of all the county and county borough councils in England and Wales. These were duly undertaken by a team of inspectors who wrote a series of survey and re-survey reports in the 1930s.

The voluminous paperwork created represents a potentially useful source for uncovering what was going on in particular regions and some clues as to why certain developments were being encouraged or discouraged. For a territory like Cornwall, where other sources are limited, the survey report offers potentially unique insights into these questions. The Cornish services explored in this article do not provide a comprehensive overview of what was on offer, but the detail of provision helps to fill in some important gaps in existing knowledge and the critical edge provided by the Ministry inspection draws the case study into wider debates about health and healthcare at this time. Analysis falls into four parts. First there is an attempt to assess the value of the survey as a source; since it has its limitations. Consideration is then given to the Cornish context outlined in the survey document, and this is followed by discussion about the services that featured in the report. In the final section the results of the survey are compared to other accounts of health and health services in Cornwall and attention is given to factors that the inspectors appear to have either overlooked or omitted when framing their comments.

The scope and limitations of the survey

The public health surveys conducted under section 104 of the 1929 Local Government Act served a variety of purposes for contemporary actors. This perhaps explains the cautious use that later historians have made of them. However, the surveys represent a potentially useful source of information, as their content can be as interesting and illuminating as attempts to uncover the motivation for compiling them, and the hidden central government agendas they might reveal. Levene, Powell and Stewart note the need for care with the surveys, but their work on hospital provision develops an interesting comparative analysis of services in different areas based on the detailed information contained in the reports.[11] This approach works well because the statistical evidence presented in the surveys was checked and rechecked by several different people against local knowledge, statistical information and reports periodically returned to the Ministry of Health and the results of previous central government inspections. Whatever bias there may in accompanying commentary, the statistics themselves may be taken to be fairly robust. If a survey report says there was a fifty-bed local voluntary hospital with an occupancy rate of eighty percent on the date of inspection this can be accepted as correct, and any breakdown of patients by age, sex or condition should also be understood to be accurate. This is important for an area such as Cornwall, where such information may not otherwise be readily available due to the paucity of surviving local sources.

One of the agendas that lay behind the survey exercise was an attempt to assess local services against national criteria determined by the Ministry of Health. The comparative approach adopted, with councils explicitly assessed against similar local authorities as well as national averages, was apparently designed to reveal differences and encourage standardization with preferred Ministry of Health schemes.[12] Local actors appear to have found the inspection regime intrusive, but in most cases not without value. The survey exercise provided a useful opportunity to make a detailed local assessment of what was wanted and required in terms of future public health services. This enabled interested actors to make new demands on the Ministry and/or gain the support of Ministry of Health officials in local battles over the future direction of, and funding for, different services.[13]

The modern mixed economy of care in health is closely associated with ideas about the value of local autonomy and the importance of imposing national targets and benchmarks to raise standards across the board.[14] Supporters of this approach point to the benefits of sharing best practice and identifying and remedying weaknesses, while detractors oppose the burden of inspection and point to the distorting effects of artificial targets. It was ever thus, but inspection regimes which generate data for national league tables provide a valuable historical source, despite their well known limitations. Some of the survey data has certainly been put to good use, with Peretz using the Oxford and Oxfordshire data to develop a comparative analysis of infant welfare services. The data presented are supplemented by quotations from the accompanying commentary to highlight the limitations of what was offered; Peretz sharing the Ministry view that such prosperous areas could and should have been doing more to help poor women and their children.[15]

Comparative analysis at a regional level along the lines developed by Peretz is still quite rare in historical assessments of health services. While local variations in the quality and quantity of provision are a recurrent theme in any study of health care, and have special resonance in work that looks at the emergence of the National Health Service [NHS], the way the historiography is organized can lead to somewhat unhelpful generalizations. Thus a particular council may be identified as 'progressive', or not, or it is acknowledged that across the country some groups (e.g. children) or services (such as acute care) received more resources than what became known in the NHS era as the Cinderella services (for the elderly, chronic sick and disabled and the mentally ill). These conclusions are important, but there are other points that may be illuminating. Thus a 'progressive' council may have gained such a reputation for significant innovation in a limited number of fields, and it is helpful to understand what was being neglected and why.[16] Likewise an apparently 'backward' area may have offered some services that met or even exceeded national standards, or simply imaginatively coped with unusual circumstances in a way that other disadvantaged regions could benefit from adopting even if the level of service achieved was only average.

The Cornish context

The surveying team from the Ministry of Health explicitly identified Cornwall as a 'backward' area, and one that faced unusual problems. Contemporary commentators in the 1930s were heavily influenced by this view even before beginning their investigations. The Ministry of Health had long been frustrated by the apparent determination of Cornwall County Council to do as little as possible in the field of public health. When Dr Allan C. Parsons comprehensively surveyed the administrative county in 1931 he was angered that progress had been even slower than previously suspected.[17] His criticism was particularly damning as it drew on his own comparative assessments of public health services in neighbouring counties, such as Devon and Somerset, which faced problems not totally dissimilar to those in Cornwall.[18]

The inspection team led by Parsons was, however, prepared to consider Cornwall as a special case suffering under unusual disadvantages. Adverse factors identified in the survey report included remoteness from London and geographical features that 'unhelpfully' dispersed the population and made transport and communications difficult.[19] This was, it was considered, a problem compounded by the complexity of local administration in a county structure that had no towns of county borough status but maintained twelve non-county boroughs, sixteen urban districts, fourteen rural districts and 227 civil parishes.[20] Population decline (from 328,098 in 1911 to 317,951 in 1931) was linked in the report to major difficulties experienced by all the major local industries (mining, agriculture and fishing) and identified as a problem in its own right.[21] Although the number of people receiving indoor and outdoor relief in 1930 was not viewed as excessive, unemployment was above average compared to rural parts of England and Cornwall as a whole was regarded as 'poor'.[22] This limited the amount that could be raised by the rates, which inhibited any public health schemes that the county council might seek to instigate.

The survey report makes it clear, however, that Parsons and his team were not very impressed by the Cornwall County Council, or its public health record. Although economic difficulties were understood to restrain progress, Parsons also identified a worrying preference for other forms of public expenditure. Highways and schools accounted for unusually large proportions of the available budget and council borrowings.[23] Parsons thought it doubtful 'whether the health department gets its fair share', and used the low salary offered to the Cornwall Medical Officer of Health [MOH] to support this conclusion.[24] He returned to this theme later in the report, arguing that the low salary of the MOH reduced his status among the council's senior officers and restricted his ability to represent his department's interests.[25] This was a problem made worse by the lack of prestige attached to service on the council's public health and housing committee.

The main criticism of the health department, and by implication the responsible committee, fell into two main areas. First, there was evidence that Cornish vital statistics were deteriorating as other areas of Britain made greater inroads into key death rates. Cornwall had a lower than average birth rate, and the crude death rate had showed no decline over the 1920s. Maternal mortality rates and deaths from tuberculosis, cancer and heart disease were consistently above the average for English counties.[26] Parsons found no evidence of official concern in Cornwall about this; instead it appeared that other indicators (lower than average infant mortality and deaths from infectious disease other than enteric fever) were encouraging complacency. There was also recourse to an argument that insisted that population trends (a rapid ageing of the population as young adults left in search of work) were to blame. Parsons expressed some sympathy with this view, noting 'to some extent ... Cornwall is a county for the retirement of elderly people', but drew a direct correlation between the high maternal mortality rate and the unsatisfactory state of Cornish maternity and child welfare services, and linked excessive deaths from enteric fever to inadequate sanitation .[27]

Secondly, the poor state of local services was a consistent theme in Parsons' report. He blamed a serious lack of ambition among the officials and councillors who did not seem to grasp the importance of public health improvement or appreciate the need for urgent reform. The public health and housing committee was tasked with a number of duties under various pieces of legislation and maintained three sub-committees to deal with blind persons, maternity and child welfare and tuberculosis.[28] Parsons thought that this committee took a minimalist approach to its work, inappropriately delegating responsibilities to the other local authorities in Cornwall or ignoring them altogether.[29] The committee tended not to attract the more ambitious councillors, and had to share responsibilities for health services with other (more powerful) committees.[30]

This fragmentation of responsibilities for medical and health services (shared and split with the education, public assistance, mental hospital and mental deficiency committees) could have been less damaging if the officials in the health department had been able to adopt an effective coordinating role. Parsons was, however, unimpressed by the quantity and quality of the available personnel and their performance. The department was badly understaffed, even compared to neighbouring rural counties not known for lavish public health provision, but for Parsons this was made more serious by the way the department was organized which reduced flexibility to a minimum.[31] This made pre-war staffing levels even less effective in the interwar period as the school medical work was bolstered at the expense of other services.

Another major problem was the poor qualifications of the medical staff employed, which Parsons linked to the low salary policy in Cornwall. The whole-time medical staff of seven included four school medical officers, two of them female, none of whom had public health qualifications. They did the school medical inspections but this left important areas of work uncovered as, apart from Dr Clarke the county MOH whose job was largely administrative, the other staff concentrated exclusively on tuberculosis. Part-time medical officers covered venereal disease and orthopaedics, to a degree, but there was no special provision for routine maternity and child welfare work or mental health.

These tasks were, in a limited way, delegated to a team of health visitors who conducted domiciliary visiting (for the school, maternity and child welfare, and tuberculosis services and under the Children Act), and did a certain amount of clinic work under the tuberculosis scheme. With just eight full-time and two part-time health visitors the service they could offer a population of more than 300,000 was obviously limited. Apart from a separate school dental department (employing two dentists and two dental nurses) there was just an orthopaedic sister. Parsons noted, with more than a hint of irritation, that there were no 'municipal nurses and no sanitary inspectors'.[32] The clerical staff of six clerks also seemed inadequate to Parsons, especially when he noted in other parts of his report that some of the clerks and even caretakers undertook clinical duties to keep essential services going. Parsons made a strong case for appointing more staff, and then re-organizing the staffing system. He used Dorset as a possible model that made economic use of limited resources in a predominantly rural area.[33] The point was to get staff out of the office and into the field where they could achieve more themselves and also encourage other actors in the statutory and voluntary sectors to be more visible and dynamic.

Parsons was concerned that a 'spirit of defeatism' infected the health department in Cornwall.[34] Key officials seemed ill at ease and disinclined to put forward any schemes that cost money. One suggested that the only way forward was to combine with Devon to develop public health provision. Parsons was infuriated, not least because of his own reservations about the state of public health administration in Devon, and the detailed remarks he makes about different services he inspected do reflect his obvious frustration.[35] Yet while Parsons found much that concerned him there was also evidence of some good practice, or at least better-than-expected services being offered in near-impossible circumstances. Specialist provision for women and children in Cornwall was undeniably weak but in other areas of provision the picture was not universally so gloomy. This is an important point to consider today, when it is noteworthy that ongoing difficulties with the provision of health care in Cornwall continue to be blamed on a shortage of resources and a lack of understanding of the special needs of Cornwall within a centralized and relatively monolithic NHS.[36] The detailed picture that emerges from the case studies below is that in the past local control imparted strengths and weaknesses. Under this model there was potential for innovation and flexible working but localism also created its own difficulties in terms of organization and finance.

The services

The first service dealt with in the voluminous Cornwall survey report was mental welfare.[37] Parsons noted that mental health and mental deficiency were only of limited concern to his work, and further made it plain that as a non-expert in these subjects he was reliant on reports from the Board of Control and offering something of a layman's opinion. This is interesting, because although there were concerns about some aspects of provision Parsons also found much that was praiseworthy. The 'county asylum' at Bodmin appeared to be running smoothly and patients detained at various public assistance institutions under the Lunacy Act appeared to be housed appropriately.

The council had no dedicated accommodation for mental deficiency cases and a recent plan to purchase a mansion for this purpose had come to nothing. While Parsons identified a need to provide more accommodation he was impressed by the quality of care offered at local workhouses, which were increasingly being used as specialist centres in Cornwall. Parsons recorded; 'I thought that the circumstances of the mental defectives in the institutions at Bodmin, St Columb and Falmouth were very satisfactory and the quarters for imbeciles at St Austell were very good'.[38]

The survey report advocated protecting and expanding these services, making the case that they were effectively meeting client needs: 'I was impressed, too, not only by the cheerfulness of the men [patients] I saw at work but by their keenness and application. There seems to be a good tradition behind this side of the work at the Falmouth institution and as far as I could judge the accommodation was suitable.'[39]

At the Bodmin institution there were also positive signs: 'For the men there is plenty of scope for exercise and occupation in the garden and in the care of pigs and poultry; the women are healthily and usefully employed in household duties and laundry work; their yard is not particularly attractive but the adjoining children's yard which is asphalted is generally available.'[40] The conclusion appeared to be that, with limited further investment, these facilities could provide the core of a very effective service that would negate the need for costly specialist provision. This was good for county council finances, but also good for patients involved, as the alternative scheme preferred by the Board of Control was for Cornwall to invest in the Starcross asylum in Devon – which would require Cornish patients to be sent a long distance from their families and communities.[41]

The idea that ingenuity and goodwill could overcome distinctly Cornish problems and actually meet the real (rather than assumed) needs of the people of Cornwall is a definite theme in Parsons' analysis. The tuberculosis scheme offers a good example of his thinking on these points. The scheme shared the common Cornish problem of being severely understaffed, with just one clinical tuberculosis officer, but Parsons thought Dr Day seemed competent and committed.[42] He was dealing with a large case load but was getting appropriate referrals from other medical practitioners and was running four dispensaries and a clinic (at Tuckingmill, Truro, Penzance, St Austell and Liskeard) successfully.[43] Dr Day was imaginatively using domiciliary visits as an alternative to dispensaries in sparsely populated areas and was credited with organizing the health visitors into a particularly effective team of tuberculosis visitors.

Community care for tuberculosis patients, and suspected cases, was assessed by Parsons to be generally good and improving, with a tentative correlation drawn to declining numbers of diagnoses and deaths. Institutional care under the tuberculosis scheme was also viewed as surprisingly good, although meeting Cornish needs and circumstances rather than an ideal model. In an area where the council maintained minimal institutional provision the Tehidy sanatorium was somewhat unusual. Its origins lay in voluntary sector effort, being the gift of the Cornish War Memorial Committee, but it was well managed by the council.[44] Parsons thought the resident medical officer, Dr Chown, had admirable personal qualities as well as professional qualifications, and his own prior history as a tuberculosis sufferer encouraged a good relationship with patients.

The Tehidy institution had originally been planned as a proper sanatorium but to meet local needs had been adapted to also serve as an observation centre, a treatment facility for advanced cases and what might be termed a hospice for terminal cases. Parsons feared this mixing might depress patients, reporting that while Chown thought patients were philosophical about the inevitable deaths, an un-named health visitor believed the work was hindered by a perception that 'to go to Tehidy was to die'.[45] Nonetheless, Parsons was impressed by the facilities on offer and the support the institution enjoyed from the local medical community. Parsons also thought provision was generous; certainly Tehidy provided more beds than the Astor scale suggested Cornwall needed.[46] The institution also supported other schemes by doing all the dispensary x-rays (with the help of a clerk) and offering artificial light treatment to patients suffering from a variety of illnesses. There were aspects of the tuberculosis scheme that Parsons thought would benefit from development but generally things were 'sufficient for the present'.[47]

One point that Parsons did find remarkable was the lack of voluntary after-care committees in Cornwall. He mentioned to staff that Somerset had a comprehensive scheme involving twenty such groups but there seemed no enthusiasm for such work in Cornwall, amongst the officials or the public. Dr Clarke, the MOH, was reported to be 'of opinion that such voluntary care associations do not flourish on Cornish soil where any movement associated with the collecting of money is ill-regarded. He is inclined to think that they are not really necessary.'[48]

Local factors also featured strongly in Parsons' assessment of the scheme for venereal disease, although this service combined a county council clinic with recourse to the larger in and out patient facilities available to Cornish patients in Plymouth. The clinics at the South Devon and East Cornwall Hospital were staffed by the Plymouth health department and the costs were shared with Cornwall and Devon. The separate Cornwall clinic was somewhat unusual, and so Parsons described it in some detail.[49] The clinic was based in an adapted private house at Tuckingmill that also served as a tuberculosis dispensary. Rooms in the house were also allocated to in-patient care for patients suffering from venereal disease and certain maternity cases.

The Ministry of Health had approved the arrangements in 1928 and 1929 but Parsons was keen to see how they operated in practice. He praised the location of the property, which was sufficiently private to encourage use but was also easily accessible from the most populous parts of Cornwall. Parsons was concerned that the lease was due to expire and made a strong case for extending it. Inside the house, however, Parsons found less to be pleased about. Staffing the clinic was difficult, as the local health visitor refused to live in. She had officially complained about the accommodation but may have been unwilling to take responsibility for the wards as the resident nurse. Parsons found a rather unsatisfactory arrangement where the county VD officer attended some clinic sessions but intermediate out-patient treatment was offered to men by the caretaker and to women by the health visitor. The wards were not really used for treatment but simply accommodated patients who were unable to attend as outpatients. This made Parsons wonder what would happen if the maternity beds were in use. He noted that so far no such cases had been admitted, and the health visitor explained that she thought no woman would consent to being treated in a known VD centre in any circumstances. Parsons tended to agree, but dwelt on the benefits of a unified centre where some good work was being done despite necessary economies that gave the equipment a 'Heath Robinson' appearance.[50] Parsons praised the work of Dr Rivers, the part-time medical officer and local GP, noting the training he had given to the clinic staff and the good liaison work done with other statutory and voluntary sector organizations.

The schemes for venereal disease and tuberculosis were not without problems but they were fairly long established and were attracting a growing number of patients. The Cornish orthopaedic scheme was, however, relatively new and Parsons was keen to investigate its key features.[51] In this case, unlike the VD service, the Royal Cornwall Infirmary was central to the scheme, though a number of other clinics also operated alongside arrangements for in-patient care and domiciliary visiting. Patients were referred from the maternity and child welfare, school and other services, though oddly the tuberculosis scheme was organized separately and Parsons thought this tended to reduce the effectiveness of the orthopaedic work. This was also hampered by transport difficulties that made it difficult for patients in some parts of Cornwall to attend clinics and a general shortage of treatment facilities. Parsons, who was keen to avoid wasteful duplication of effort, tied the future of the Cornish scheme to the development of a new orthopaedic hospital in Plymouth but despite his critical remarks it seems that there was quite a bit of enthusiasm for the work, including voluntary sector support, and the scheme had developed significantly during its short period of operation.

Following quite lengthy discussions of the different services that were offered by Cornwall, Parsons turned his attention to the obvious gaps in provision. While the inspection team had found much to commend in the foregoing analysis, and certainly did not find the limitations of the Cornish schemes unique, there is a sense that it could not quite believe that Cornwall County Council was neglecting certain key areas. Parsons noted that Cornwall completed significantly lower than average amounts of sampling work, with the implication that the population was left dangerously exposed to the sale of unfit and/or adulterated food supplies and contaminated milk. Since these problems went largely un-investigated it was impossible to even begin to gauge the extent of the problem in Cornwall; a situation made more problematic by a lack of laboratory facilities and reliance on a London-based expert for analysis.[52]

Health topics that were attracting national attention, and even seemed to affect the Cornish population disproportionately, received virtually no attention from the county council. There was no particular effort to educate the local population about cancer prevention despite above average death rates and a series of Ministry of Health circulars on the subject.[53] Local voluntary hospitals were not averse to offering cancer treatments but without any clear leadership from the council were waiting on developments in Devon (including Exeter and Plymouth), where cancer services were recognized as a priority. This reliance on other centres certainly reduced the infrastructure for cancer care in Cornwall. Parsons acknowledged that this was a threat to Cornish pride but considered that local patients did not necessarily suffer as both the health and public assistance committees had well-tried arrangements to send Cornish cases to regional and even national cancer facilities.

One area that Parsons was keen to develop was health propaganda. He was very surprised that the health department made no special effort in this regard. In Somerset a vigorous outreach campaign, led by a full-time woman health propaganda officer, was understood to be usefully filling in the inevitable gaps in a scattered rural service. Yet in Cornwall even the clinics were devoid of the usual posters and leaflets routinely displayed elsewhere. Parsons credited individual health visitors with developing a role 'as missionaries in the cause of better health' but thought instruction in the clinics could be established on a more systematic basis and extended to wider health initiatives.[54]

For Parsons, a particularly disappointing aspect of the Cornwall County Council's work was the limited response made to the opportunities presented by the 1929 Local Government Act. A few tasks, such as infant life protection work, had been allocated to the health visitors but there was no plan to make immediate or comprehensive changes. The only declaration made by the council on the provision of relief other than by means of the Poor Law, expressed the hope of doing something 'as soon as circumstances permit'.[55] This was a very conservative response, as other local authorities not only committed to definite dates but made considerable progress towards achieving them. Cornwall had reorganized its twelve Poor Law unions into five guardian committee areas but despite unusually cordial relations between the MOH and the public assistance committee, virtually nothing had been done about transferring poor law medical facilities to the control of the health committee.

The County Council had inherited 13 workhouses and 11 children's homes from the guardians.[56] Three of the former were made available to the mental deficiency committee but no other plans had materialized. Parsons thought the 512 available sick beds were probably more than was required (216 being empty at the time of inspection) but the scattered population made it difficult to concentrate provision in fewer centres and none of the institutions approximated 'a thoroughly modern hospital'.[57] Parsons thought there was potential to develop the facilities at St Austell, which uniquely had an operating theatre, albeit an unsatisfactory one, and Liskeard and Redruth where maternity provision was rated as 'fair'.[58]

The situation was perhaps not as bad as Parsons suggests. In fact, he himself noted that the beds in the public assistance infirmaries were particularly suitable for the elderly and chronic patients who at the time of the survey slept in them at night but vacated them during the day. What the county council lacked, however, and was not going to acquire from the former workhouses, was comprehensive provision for its maternity cases, surgical patients and cases of infectious disease. Two possibilities existed. Cornwall would either have to develop its own hospital facilities or enter into negotiations with local voluntary hospitals to see what they could provide and how they might best co-ordinate with council services. Parsons was concerned to find that neither option was being properly considered let alone taken up, although pre-existing schemes with the Royal Cornwall Infirmary and the West Cornwall Miners' and Women's Hospital were continuing.[59]

On the other hand, arrangements with the County Nursing Association were working well with all but fifteen parishes covered by an affiliated or unaffiliated district nursing association.[60] The county council made grants totalling £2,794 in 1929 to support the work, with dedicated funds made available for school nursing as well as health visits. The council also made a training budget available for midwives. This concern with midwifery in Cornwall was in marked contrast to the general neglect of infant welfare. Parsons noted that the council made no grants to any of the eighteen voluntary sector clinics and as a result the county medical officer 'exercises no supervision over ... [their] organisation or work'.[61] This was part of a wider and worrying trend that Parsons identified operating in Cornwall: 'There is a good deal of dependence in Cornwall upon voluntary assistance in health work, but there is not always as much coordination and cooperation on the part of the council as one might expect. The virtual independence of the voluntary committees conducting infant welfare centres may be noted as an example'.[62]

Parsons returned to these themes in his concluding remarks and attributed the problem, and other deficiencies that he had discussed, to the inadequate staffing arrangements he had already identified, a shortcoming that exacerbated the unique disadvantages Cornwall was understood to suffer from. He further argued:

> Essentially, I think, the poor progress, for which Cornwall has long been notorious in this department [of the Ministry of Health], is due not so much to the natural circumstances of the county but in great measure to human causes. Chief among these causes is the fact that in those responsible for carrying out local government, as well as those they represent, the public health conscience is undeveloped.[63]

Discussion

In the background to his survey Parsons rehearses some familiar arguments that help explain why the Ministry expected to find problems in Cornwall. He mentioned the 'adverse' geographical features that dispersed the population, making it impossible to provide centralized services. It was generally accepted in public health circles that rural provision would always be more expensive and less comprehensive, simply on the grounds of distance and population density.[64] Yet Parsons was quick to state that other predominantly rural counties still managed to significantly outperform Cornwall in terms of the quantity and quality of services provided.

This led Parsons to develop an economic argument. He drew particular attention to significant problems in all the major industries, noting the ongoing decline of mining, and short-term difficulties in both agriculture and fishing. Cornwall was experiencing particularly severe social and economic problems in the 1930s but had limited resources to address them. Yet this difficulty was itself understood to be symptomatic of an historical resistance to investing in services, even when economic conditions were better. Parsons concluded that where agricultural interests dominated the local political landscape, as they did in Cornwall, there would always be a reluctance to spend money and a lack of appreciation of the long term health and wealth benefits derived from investment in public services.

This was also a factor in Devon, as Parsons had clearly noted in his Devonshire Survey, but there were other factors that applied to an unusual extent in Cornwall.[65] The problems of migration were emphasized in the Cornish case, with Parsons noting the exodus of both skilled miners and young people. These phenomena were linked in the survey to economic dislocations but were also correlated with the 'isolation' of Cornwall and the apparent desire of people to move away to be closer to the centre of affairs. Distance from London was singled out by Parsons as a factor explaining both a local lack of interest in new developments in public health and an inability to attract the services of the more ambitious public health officials.

The emphasis placed on the damaging lack of leadership offered by key officials and councillors is explained by the orientation of the Ministry of Health inspectors and the political and professional agendas that underpinned the whole survey exercise. What Parsons may have missed in his top-down analysis of Cornwall's public health problems were the alternative traditions of independence and self-help, strongly embedded in local work cultures, that Sheaff, among others, has argued gave rise to distinctive patterns of demand for, as well as supply of, Cornish health services.

While Parsons was critical of the standards achieved overall, the lack of imagination shown in grappling with problems encountered, a tendency to evade responsibility, and a general lack of enthusiasm (on the part of service-users as well as service-providers) for the type of public health work that was being institutionalized elsewhere, he nonetheless found some beacons of excellence and some areas of special concern. The main weaknesses were found in the field of maternity and child welfare services, where a qualitative assessment of apparent shortcomings was backed by a comparative analysis of statistics that suggested that Cornwall should have been doing better. There were four areas where Parsons identified much better performance.

One of these, mental welfare, was somewhat anomalous and at the periphery of Parsons' concerns but the other three deserve further consideration. The services that Parsons identified as having the most potential, as well as achieving the highest level of current performance were the schemes addressing tuberculosis, venereal disease and orthopaedics.

In the survey report Parsons drew a close correlation between the success of the first three schemes and the personal commitment and professional expertise of their responsible medical officers. This was in marked contrast to his analysis of the failures of the infant welfare and other schemes which were attributed to weaknesses in organization and management; problems blamed on a lack of local interest as much as a lack of local resources. The different schemes were discussed in more detail above, but while we might agree with Parsons that some of the successes were due to individual officers doing excellent work in challenging circumstances, and some of the failures began and ended in the woefully mismanaged health department, there are other factors to consider.

What Parsons, who was tasked with examining responses to the 1929 Local Government Act, would have missed was the historical importance of occupational rather than public health in developing Cornish services. An area dominated by mining industries needed its health services to be able to respond to the distinctive medical problems faced by miners.[66] The emergence of support for tuberculosis and orthopaedic schemes probably went beyond the personal interventions of the medical officers singled out for praise by Parsons to a long-standing requirement to make some provision for chest conditions and the repair of bone and joint injuries. In a similar way the migration, and return, of the male miners provided an obvious risk of the importation of infectious disease. The perceived risks of imported infection within distinct migrating communities (sailors as well as miners) provide a better context for understanding the commitment made to developing venereal disease surveillance and treatment services.

The vital though often over-looked connection to work, and also work cultures, also helps to explain other policy developments and the identification of specific health problems as urgent priorities. Although the Ministry of Health was enamoured with a theory of 'backwardness', a preoccupation that helps to explain the unenthusiastic reception its preferred models of public health reform received in the 1930s, a dialogue between local elites and other parts of Whitehall had previously served to advance health agendas and make Cornwall a national focus of concern and innovation. To take just one unusual example, the campaign to control debilitating hookworm infection amongst the miners in the late nineteenth and early twentieth centuries drew on, and served to re-enforce, many of the late-Victorian and Edwardian pre-occupations with national efficiency and racial deterioration, concerns that other historians have placed at the centre of movements to improve maternity and child welfare.[67] In Cornwall these services for women and children were noticeably under-developed, in both the statutory and voluntary sectors. It may be argued that the concern with underground labour had led to a situation where the attention and interests of health reformers were fixed on men and not women or children.[68] Even at the mines, their gendered work-place health concerns were traditionally marginalized, and problematically misrepresented in the few sources that examine the health of the Cornish bal maidens.[69] The emphasis on work and working conditions arguably had the further damaging effect of linking the health of the community to the state of its main industry, which allowed the terminal decline of the latter to overshadow attempts to promote the former. A situation further complicated by the fact the institutional memory of the sustained effort to promote mine, and thereby community and public, health was located within the Home Office through the records of the Mines Inspectorate, and not within the Ministry of Health.

Conclusion

Many of the above points remain speculative as available sources do not allow for their full evaluation. However, they provide a counterpoint to the sometimes unduly critical analysis of personal failings and local difficulties that can be found in the 1931 Cornish public health survey. None of the surveys (and each county council and county borough council in England was surveyed) was written from an entirely objective perspective, and collectively they say as much about the pre-occupations of Ministry of Health officials as they do about the quality of local health services. Yet the Cornish survey is an important one, not least because it offers a uniquely detailed external assessment and critique of services that are not easy to study because of the limited range of primary and secondary sources available.[70] Significantly, some of the themes identified and comments made by Parsons and discussed in this article also continue to have resonance with current debates about the future of health care in Cornwall.

Notes and references

1. See for example R. Sheaff, 'A Century of Centralization: Cornish Health and Healthcare', in P. Payton (ed.), *Cornish Studies: Four* (Exeter,1996) pp. 128–46.
2. The Wellcome Library catalogue lists available reports and gives a brief background to the evolution of public health authorities in the county. The series of County

Medical Officer of Health reports held in the Cornwall County Records Office begins in 1926.
3. Sheaff, 'A Century of Centralization'.
4. For example see G. Burke, 'The Cornish Diaspora of the Nineteenth Century', in S. Marks and P. Richardson (eds), *International Labour Migration: Historical Perspectives* (London, 1984), pp. 57–73; J. Rule, 'A Configuration of Quietism: Attitudes Towards Trade Unionism and Chartism Amongst Cornish Miners', *Tijdschrift Voor Sociale Geschiedenis*, xviii, 2/3 (1992), pp. 248–62; J. Rule, 'A Risky Business, Death, Injury and Religion in Cornish Mining 1780–1870', in B. Knapp, V. Pigott and E. Herbert (eds), *Social Approaches to an Industrial Past, The Archaeology and Anthropology of Mining* (London 1998), pp. 155–73; C. Mills, A Hazardous Bargain: Occupational Risk in Cornish Mining 1875–1914', *Labour History Review*, 70, 1 (2005), pp. 53–71, R. Burt, 'Industrial Relations in the British Non-ferrous Mining Industry in the Nineteenth Century', *Labour History Review*, 70, 1 (2006), pp. 57–79; S. Swartz, 'Bridging "The Great Divide": The Evolution and Impact of Cornish Translocation in Britain and the USA', *Journal of American Ethnic History*, 25 (2006) and S. Schwartz and B. Deacon, 'Cornish Identities and migration: A Multi Scalar Approach', *Global Networks: A Journal of Transnational Affairs*, 7, 3 (2007), pp. 289–306.
5. Recent work by Lara Marks confirms the centrality of maternity and child welfare services in the development of municipal medicine and state welfare. L. Marks, *Metropolitan Maternity: Maternal and Infant Welfare Services in Early Twentieth Century London* (Amsterdam, 1996). In a comparative study of urban environments Marjaana Niemi argues tuberculosis services could serve similar agendas, that embraced patient care but also extended to policing the community and reinforcing social norms relating to work, gender roles and family life. M. Niemi, *Public Health and Municipal Policy Making: Britain and Sweden, 1900–1940* (Aldershot, 2007), pp. 1–24.
6. D. Dwork, *War is Good for Babies and Other Young Children: A History of the Infant and Child Welfare Movement in England 1898–1918* (London, 1987).
7. J. Lewis, *What Price Community Medicine? The Philosophy, Practice and Politics of Public Health Since 1919* (Brighton, 1986).
8. B. Harris, *The Origins of the British Welfare State: Social Welfare in England and Wales, 1800–1945* (Basingstoke, 2004).
9. C. Webster, *The Health Services Since the War. Volume 1. Problems of Health Care. The National Health Service before 1957* (London, 1988).
10. This point has been explored with relation to health policies, but a new dimension to the debate is added by A. Digby, 'Changing Welfare Cultures in Region and State', *Twentieth-Century British History*, 17, 3 (2006), pp. 297–322.
11. A. Levene, M. Powell and J. Stewart, 'The Development of Municipal General Hospitals in English County Boroughs in the 1930s', *Medical History*, 50, 1 (2006), pp. 2–28, pp. 5–6.
12. This agenda could serve to accelerate or retard the adoption of particular schemes. Niemi sees central government opposition to BCG vaccinations as a major reason why they were not adopted by progressive local authorities in Britain. Niemi, *Public Health*, p. 145.
13. Ministry of Health inspectors explicitly used the survey report for Halifax to help the MOH there resolve a long-standing dispute about the allocation of

duties between the health and education departments and in the West Riding of Yorkshire there was an attempt to use the report to bolster the position of a newly appointed MOH who was struggling to assert his preferred model of institutional care. National Archives (hereafter NA), MH 66/1071, paragraphs 91–104 and 527–41; NA, MH 66/289 West Riding of Yorkshire Public Health Survey, Dr C.J. Donelan, 1933, paragraphs 794–8.

14. Saving Lives: Our Healthier Nation Department of Health, British Parliamentary Papers, July 1999, (Cm 4386).

15. E. Peretz, 'Infant Welfare in Inter-War Oxford', *International History of Nursing Journal*, 1 (1995–96), pp. 5–18.

16. International comparisons are also illuminating, See Niemi, *Public Health* for detailed comparative study of Birmingham and Gothenburg.

17. NA, MH66/30, Administrative County of Cornwall, Report on a Survey of Health Services (hereafter Cornwall Survey) by A.C. Parsons. (Survey conducted 25 September to 15 October 1931).

18. See for example Cornwall Survey, p. 13.

19. Cornwall Survey, p. 2.

20. Cornwall Survey, p. 4.

21. Cornwall Survey, p. 2 and p. 6.

22. Cornwall Survey, pp. 3–4 and p. 6.

23. Cornwall Survey, p. 6 and pp. 90–1.

24. Cornwall Survey, pp. 6–7.

25. Cornwall Survey, pp. 13–16.

26. Cornwall Survey, p. 8.

27. Cornwall Survey, p. 9.

28. Cornwall Survey, p. 10.

29. Parsons found it odd the public health and housing committee did nothing under the Housing (Rural Workers) Act, 1926 and was not swayed by their arguments for this inactivity. Cornwall Survey, p. 22.

30. This was by no means unique to Cornwall and has been used by many authors to explain how service on the less popular committees like health allowed elected and co-opted women to gain footholds in local government.

31. Cornwall Survey, pp. 13–14.

32. Cornwall Survey, p. 12.

33. Cornwall Survey, pp. 15–16.

34. Cornwall Survey, pp. 16–17.

35. NA, MH 66/58, Administrative County of Devon, Survey Report (hereafter Devon Survey) by Allan C Parsons, January–February 1931, p. 1 and pp. 73–4.

36. Sheaff, 'A Century of Centralization', pp. 135–40.

37. Cornwall Survey, pp. 18–22.

38. Cornwall Survey, pp. 19–20.

39. Cornwall Survey, pp. 20–1.

40. Cornwall Survey, p. 21.

41. For discussion re this policy and its impact on other councils in the region see G. Chester and P. Dale, 'Institutional Care for the Mentally Defective, 1914–1948: Diversity as a Response to Individual Needs and an Indication of Lack of Policy Coherence', *Medical History*, 51, 1 (2007), pp. 59–78, pp. 60–1.

42. This did not however mean his expertise was fully appreciated by other medical

practitioners. Cornwall Survey, p. 27. Niemi, *Public Health*, pp. 140–2, discusses the lack of prestige attaching to tuberculosis officers and the problems this created.

43. Cornwall Survey, pp. 27–8.
44. Cornwall Survey, pp. 32–3.
45. Cornwall Survey, p. 33.
46. Cornwall Survey, p. 34.
47. Cornwall Survey, p. 36.
48. Cornwall Survey, p. 36.
49. Cornwall Survey, pp. 39–42.
50. Cornwall Survey, pp. 40–1.
51. Cornwall Survey, pp. 47–8.
52. Cornwall Survey, pp. 51–4.
53. Cornwall Survey, p. 58.
54. Cornwall Survey, p. 60.
55. Cornwall Survey, p. 61.
56. Cornwall Survey, pp. 62–3.
57. Cornwall Survey, pp. 63–4 and pp. 68–9.
58. Cornwall Survey, pp. 70–2.
59. Cornwall Survey, p. 86.
60. Cornwall Survey, p. 84.
61. Cornwall Survey, p. 85.
62. Cornwall Survey, p. 89.
63. Cornwall Survey, p. 89.
64. Peretz, 'Infant Welfare in Inter-War Oxford', pp. 14–15, shows higher costs involved with doing less in Oxfordshire than Oxford.
65. Devon Survey, p. 7.
66. This concern had been a factor behind nineteenth-century research, often carried out under the auspices of the Royal Cornish Polytechnic Society and the Royal Institute of Cornwall, which drew a clear distinction between the health of miners (or mining areas) and the rest of the population in Cornwall. An early example of this is R. Blee, 'An Inquiry into the comparative Longevity of Mining and other Districts of the County of Cornwall', *Annual Report of the Royal Cornwall Polytechnic Society*, 1838, pp. 68–80. A focus on mining also provided a national forum to discuss the health of underground workers and others. In 1914 Telfur Thomas argued women and non-mining men in the county were relatively free from tubercular disease. Testimony of J. Telfur Thomas, MOH for Camborne, *Second Report of the Royal Commission on Metalliferous Mines and Quarries*, British Parliamentary Papers, 1914, Evidence and Appendices, Vol. II, Cd. 7477 (15,997), p. 185.
67. C. Mills, 'The Emergence of Statutory Hygiene Precautions in the British Mining Industries 1890–1914', *Historical Journal*, 51, 1 (forthcoming 2008), pp. 1–24; A. Davin, 'Imperialism and Motherhood', *History Workshop Journal*, 5 (1978), pp. 9–65.
68. Efforts to redress this imbalance have tended to concentrate on women at work. Burke, G., 'The Decline of the Independent Bâl Maiden: The Impact of Change in the Cornish Mining Industry', in A.V. John (ed.), *Unequal Opportunities: Women's Employment in England 1800–1918* (Oxford, Basil Blackwell, 1986),

pp. 179–206, and S. Schwartz, 'In Defence of Customary Rights: Labouring Women's Experience of Industrialisation in Cornwall c.1750–1870', *Cornish Studies*, 7 (1999), pp. 8–31, and S.P. Schwartz, '"No Place for a Women": Gender at work in Cornwall's Metalliferous Mining Industry', in P. Payton (ed.), *Cornish Studies: Eight* (Exeter, 2000), pp. 68–96.

69. For example Mayers, *Bâl Maidens*, pp. 131–51, extrapolates an 1842 survey to represent health concerns across the entire nineteenth century.

70. The main report runs to 95 pages and is accompanied by several lengthy appendices and special reports.

7

Cultural Capital in Cornwall
Heritage and the Visitor

Graham Busby & Kevin Meethan

Introduction

'Cultural capital', broadly understood, has two forms: 'personal' and 'destination-based'. The term itself appears to have been first used by Bourdieu and Passeron in 1973,[1] although it did not become familiar to a wide audience until the publication in 1979 of Bourdieu's seminal work *Distinction* (English translation 1984). Bourdieu[2] and Richards[3] suggest that the concept refers to an individual's ability to 'understand' what they are looking at, based largely on their level of education, which will predispose them to value and interpret certain forms of culture above others. This is 'personal' cultural capital. In recent years, 'cultural capital' has also been employed as a term to refer to the potential economic value which may be derived from the inventory of cultural 'assets' at a given destination.[4] This is 'destination-based' cultural capital. In this article we addresses the particular case of Cornwall, presenting examples of both 'destination-based' and 'personal' forms of cultural capital, and then consider where the nexus between the two might exist.

Cornwall has been popular with both domestic and international visitors for more than a century,[5] possessing a cultural heritage often considered distinct from that of England.[6] Nineteenth-century folklore compilations saw 'Cornishness' as emblematic of a 'primitive', dark and wild 'Celtic' culture.[7] The 1893 Ethnographic Survey of the British Isles decided that there existed in Cornwall a 'remarkably uncorrupted race of "primitive" people'.[8] Perceived by visitors as an exotic 'other', the Cornish were said sometimes to receive 'gazey-money' for permitting tourists to stare at them,[9] an estimation echoed today perhaps in films such as *Saving Grace* (1999) and the recent television series *Doc Martin*.[10] As Gareth Shaw and Alan Williams have observed, 'folkloric practices are attractions in their own rights'.[11] Yet beneath these folkloric attractions, packaged for and consumed by the visitors, was a genuinely distinctive Cornish culture which was also 'different'. This was reflected (for example) in the rich literary repertoire of medieval Cornish-language miracle plays[12] – as Fukuyama has observed, language is 'the most important tool for creating and transmitting culture'[13] – and subsequently in Cornu-English dialect, which became an important badge of linguistic 'difference' during Cornwall's industrial age.[14] To these and other indigenous expressions of 'difference' was added, during the nineteenth century and into the twentieth, the artists' and writers' 'gaze', one which incorporated dramatic landscapes into portrayals of 'Cornishness' and offered yet further enticements for the visitor.[15] During the course of the twentieth century, all this was further overlaid by the 're-invented' Celticity of the Cornish Celtic Revival.

Taken together, these cultural constructions have allowed multiple representations of Cornwall and the Cornish, from the popularly held stereotypical images of 'guide book culture'[16] to the full-blown romance of 'pirates, piskies and sweeping landscapes filled with exotic Celts'.[17] As Busby and Laviolette have argued, so prevalent are such ideas that it is frequently taken for granted that Cornwall is worthy of a visit just because it is 'different'.[18] As Shaw and Williams have also observed: 'tourists have very distinctive perceptions of Cornwall'.[19] And as McGettigan and Burns have shown in relation to Ireland, even for those visitors drawn to particular destinations by attractions other than heritage sites, considerations of indigenous culture are almost always implicit in their perceptions of place.[20] As in Cornwall, so in Ireland constructions of the 'Celtic other' are never far away.[21] Especially 'Celtic' are religious sites – holy wells, ancient crosses and so on – and within Cornwall the two hundred plus medieval churches are often seen by visitors as being a key component of Cornish 'Celtic heritage'.[22]

Heritage tourism

The term 'heritage' evokes notions of continuity between the past and the present, and is also linked to the concept of common ownership by some collectivity (e.g. 'English Heritage' is 'owned' by the English nation, 'Cornwall Heritage' by the Cornish)). As Williams has suggested,[23] heritage relates typically to places and the built environment; in other words, to selected material elements of culture. As such, heritage will reflect and encapsulate popular imaginings of place, history and culture, ranging in the UK (for example) from the industrial heritage of the South Wales valleys to the stately homes of England. Growing out of a popular critique of urban development in the latter decades of the 20th century, this 'heritage' – as Tunbridge[24] argues – has become entwined in a number of contemporary issues such as place promotion, lifestyle diversity and environmental amenity, all encapsulated in an emphasis on the creation of distinctive local identities, often with an explicit economic and touristic aim.[25] This is what Inglis and Holmes refer to as a 'heritagization' process, where cultural resources are converted into products for tourist consumption.[26] The 'natural' environment may not at first glance appear to be such a 'cultural' resource,[27] although, once a landscape is 'valued' and a social construction is placed upon it, it becomes a 'cultural landscape' and is likewise turned into a product for visitor consumption.[28]

A central issue here is that of commodification,[29] which lies at the core of Silberberg's definition of 'heritage' and the way it is packaged for the tourist industry.[30] As Lowenthal reminds us, heritage as a form of consumption is not a 'testable' account of a particular past. Rather, it is 'a *declaration of faith* in that past'.[31] This echoes Harvey, who considers that heritage involves a 'subjective interpretation of selective material', one which emphasizes particular aspects of an imagined past and discards or ignores others.[32] Thus the value of heritage sites rests is in the experiences of place and history they routinely evoke in the mind of the observer, rather than in any intrinsic quality of the place or artefact itself.[33] This evocation of the past also bridges the divide between the individual and social memory, reflecting the popular collective values that are encapsulated in particular places or things.[34]

For the purposes of this article, it is considered that the many ecclesiastical sites in Cornwall constitute a 'Cornish church heritage', and that this heritage attracts a broad range of visitors, many of whom can thus be described as 'heritage tourists'. The locations visited incorporate numerous features from widely different historical periods, although most are routinely considered 'Celtic' by visitors. 'Celtic' is a notoriously controversial label that has been subject to periodic re-negotiation and dispute, not least in academic circles, yet it still enjoys enormous popular currency among the visiting public, especially those seeking evidence of a 'Celtic Christianity' among the artefacts of the Cornish church heritage.[35] For these visitors, the sites provide a tangible link with the 'Celtic' past and so permit 'society to make sense of the present'.[36] Yet while some prior research exists regarding these sites and their tourist attraction potential,[37] there has been no consideration thus far of the relationship between the level of education of visitors and individual perceptions of the heritage. In other words, there has been almost no discussion of the role of 'personal cultural capital' in the relationship between individuals and the Cornish church heritage they seek to experience. At the same time, it is increasingly evident that the 'religious heritage' embodied in these Cornish sites has become a significant resource within a wider tourist destination portfolio in Cornwall, a clear example of Richard's and Wilson's[38] model of creative tourism development where 'destination-based cultural capital' is deployed for economic ends.

Combining both quantitative and qualitative approaches, the research reported in this article adopted two data collection methods; namely, content analysis of church Visitors' Books, and a substantive empirical study conducted over forty-eight days which resulted in 725 respondents. These methods have been discussed in previous volumes of *Cornish Studies*[39] and so are described only briefly here.

As Holsti has observed, words represent 'the author's inner feelings ... there are constant, though probabilistic, relationships between the content of communication and underlying motives of their authors'.[40] Thus when such 'words' are provided in textual format, as in the Visitors' Books in Cornish churches, they can often provide telling insights into an individual's possession of personal cultural capital: not only the level of literacy and the ability to articulate ideas and aspirations but also the general level of education exhibited in historical allusion or displays of other knowledge. In this way, the visitors' books provided important qualitative material for this study. The face-to-face, interviewer-completion survey comprised the quantitative dimension of the research. The method adopted permitted a high degree of random sampling – non-probability sampling, in this context[41] – and enabled the researchers to address a range of concepts besides the construction of a visitor profile.[42] Sixteen questions were posed, designed to illuminate the relationship between visitors and cultural capital.

Destination-based cultural capital

'Destination-based' cultural capital exhibits features, both tangible and intangible, which are readily discerned by observers and can often be deployed for touristic purposes. Karlsson has argued that 'cultural capital refers to the influence of culture and tradition for the development of tourism',[43] and has suggested that all potential destinations can commodify their inherent resources for tourism promotion. Alzua *et al.*[44] refer to this process as the 'construction of cultural capital', and Boissevain suggests that such construction has occurred in Malta with regard to the mobilization of the island's religious resources for touristic purposes.[45] Generally, such resources may be site-specific or destination-wide, and a cursory review of Prentice's proposed twenty-three types of 'heritage attraction' shows that some aspects of cultural capital need not be site-specific. For example, for visiting motorists from England, Welsh-language road-signs encountered in Wales 'can be a significant part of an area's attractiveness to tourists.'[46] In this context, it is interesting to note that Penwith District Council in west Cornwall approved similar bilingual road signs in 1997.[47]

A destination's resources are either 'latent' (almost always tangible elements) or 'potential' cultural capital. Urry's commentary on Lancaster illustrates the nature of latent cultural capital:

> Three conditions are necessary ... there would have to be a number of attractive and reasonably well-preserved buildings from a range of historical periods. In Lancaster's case these were medieval (a castle), Georgian (the customs house and many town-houses) and Victorian (old mills) ... such buildings would have to be used for activities in some ways consistent with the tourist gaze ... the buildings should in some sense have been significant historically, that they stand for or signify important historical events, people or processes.[48]

Potential cultural capital, by contrast, may exhibit less tangible heritage elements, such as the connections between authors and particular localities, many of which have been deployed for tourism promotional purposes.[49] Connections between an author and a locale can also be juxtaposed with other heritage – for example, at one of the three survey churches (Lanteglos-by-Fowey) novelist Daphne du Maurier was married on 19 July 1932. Thus the church has become one element of a wider 'du Maurier Country', which is itself celebrated in the eponymous annual festival, an event which attracts many in international visitors. Some of these visitors these are drawn to the church. Here are two examples of comments in the Visitors' Book in 2000:

'Can see where Daphne du Maurier gained some of her inspiration'
– Visitor from Ruthin, Wales, 26 April

'Felt Daphne's spirit'
– German visitor, 8 July.

The nationality of the latter visitor emphasizes the global–local nexus of 'du Maurier Country'. In this context, du Maurier's key volume *Vanishing Cornwall*[50] and her repertoire of 'Cornish fiction' act as 'the marker'[51] for the locality, serving to attract what Munt has the termed 'the new middle classes':[52] those with the time and money as well as the inclination to seek out such heritage destinations.

In establishing the annual Daphne du Maurier Festival in 1997, Restormel Borough Council commodified this latent cultural capital,[53] the deployment of the famous author adding 'a measure of cultural capital to the projected images'[54] of mid-Cornwall. The conversion of literature to the 'big screen' can also unlock cultural capital,[55] and it is no accident that several Hollywood versions of du Maurier 'classics' – notably *Rebecca* – are still widely available on DVD, their locations interpreted by viewers as quintessentially Cornish. Of course, the du Maurier effect is but one instance of a wider discourse of the influence of literature upon Cornwall[56] – note, for example, an equivalent 'Betjemanland' in North Cornwall – and sometimes destination-based cultural capital can be unlocked in unlikely ways: as in the impact on South Wales tourism of the new *Dr Who* television serialization.[57]

It is only once it has been commodified that 'destination-based' cultural capital can reach a wide audience. A good example of deliberate commodi-fication was the introduction by Cornwall County Council Trading Standards Service in 1991 of the 'Made in Cornwall' scheme. This provided a clearly identifiable logo (a mine engine house) for genuinely Cornish products. According to the Cornwall Trading Standards Officer:

> the description 'Cornish' is generally associated with quality. Unfortunately, like so many good things, someone always tries to copy or impersonate the Cornish identity, and descriptions such as 'Cornish Ice Cream', 'Cornish Pasty' and 'Cornish Cream Fudge', which are in use daily by companies throughout the country, are examples of this. The range of products registered with the ['Made in Cornwall'] scheme continues to grow as more and more manufacturers join. The scheme has attracted over 500 small and large producers looking to sell good quality, locally made goods.[58]

This well-intentioned initiative has not created in the minds of visitors a new association of Cornwall with pasties and other products. Clearly, such an association long pre-dates the 1990s. What the scheme has done is to commodify these products for consumption (often in a very literal sense) by visitors: in other words, they have become vehicles for a particular reading of Cornish culture. As such, they demarcate 'Cornishness' in a way that sets it apart from the perceived dominance of the wider culture of the UK. In the same way, visitors to Cornwall are likewise encouraged by such commodi-fication to purchase pewter brooches and other jewellery depicting Celtic crosses, engine house and other recognisably 'Cornish' icons as 'souvenir gifts'.[59] Thus 'Celtic Cornwall' is both created and sold in the marketplace,[60] a commodification that may not be destructive but which certainly reinforces popularly held stereotypes of place.[61]

Turning to another form of 'destination-based' cultural capital, the establishment of the National Churches Tourism Group (now the Church Tourism Association) in the late 1990s recognized the need for dissemination of good practice between members, now that 'more people visit churches than attend'.[62] In many cases, local authorities have become involved in active promotion of churches as tourism resources, developing what is in effect another example of latent cultural capital. West Lindsey District Council, for example, holds an annual Churches Festival, involving 65 participating properties,[63] and South Somerset and East Devon District Councils each produce promotional literature for local churches. Keeling has discussed the components of five such initiatives: Hereford & Worcester's 'Through the Church Door', Lincolnshire's 'Church Tourism Network', 'The Christian Heritage of Northumbria', 'Signposting Herefordshire Churches', and 'Ely Church Trails', all of which involved either the regional tourist board or local authorities.[64]

Before considering the Cornish church heritage, mention must be made of the nature of the church heritage experience. Despite the attempts at promotion noted above, the experience itself is neither packaged nor controlled, and as such is a matter of individual interpretation,[65] only rarely filtered through the presence of interpreters or cultural intermediaries.[66] This contrasts strongly with Richards' analysis of the development of visitor attractions such as shops and malls, where an ever-greater level of product awareness and experience is demanded.[67] Indeed, some tourist attractions deliberately use the term *experience*, and those that do imply that there is a 'story' to be told and around which the attraction is constructed:[68] 'The Oxford Story', 'A Day at the Wells', 'The Canterbury Tales', and so on. This is in marked contrast to the individual interpretation of the church heritage experience. Ritzer has claimed that the malls, department stores and other retail outlet settings are the 'cathedrals of consumption ... [possessing] sometimes even sacred, religious character for many people'.[69] Even if this is true (and he provides little evidence to support his view), it is a misplaced metaphor, for the church heritage experience is fundamentally different.

Hamilton Jenkin[70] identified 220 parish churches in Cornwall; these are the classic examples of what Kennedy and Kingcome term 'serious heritage'.[71] The current estimate of listed church buildings, based on the 2001 Truro Diocesan Directory, suggests that there are 224 Anglican churches in Cornwall, of which 130 are listed grade I and 66 are II*, representing 58 per cent and 29 per cent of the total respectively. Yet they are not actively promoted as tourist destinations – although they attract visitors for a plethora of reasons[72] – and to that extent represent excellent examples of latent cultural capital.

That said, there has been some attempt – assisted mainly by the growth of the World Wide Web – to publicize certain Cornish churches, not so much in the interest of attracting tourists but rather as celebrating the role of churches in Cornish history and culture. The web-site Cornish Light (www.cornishlight.freeserve.co.uk) depicts a number of examples of churches, while some parishes have created web-sites for their own churches. St Just-in-Roseland, one of the top two most visited churches in Cornwall, has an extensive range of views of the property (www.stjustinroseland.org.uk), and the Diocesan web-site (www.truro.anglican.org) features a Parish of the Month link. Virtual tours of some of these properties are complemented by virtual Visitors' Books. Another form of web-site is provided by the Lynher Valley marketing consortium (www.lynhervalley.co.uk), where details of the twelve churches along the length of the river are provided. This web-site juxtaposes notions of Cornish diaspora with the Lynher Valley, providing a family history page. Of the three messages viewable on 23 August 2005, two provided place of origin (of poster): one was Ontario, the other New Zealand.

The concept of personal cultural capital

Does the possession of graduate qualifications confer 'personal' cultural capital on an individual? The answer is almost certainly, yes, although the attribute can also be acquired in other ways. 'Uncertificated' education can sometimes be of equal importance. Consider, for example, John Harris' rise to eminence at the Royal Institute of British Architects, following spells working with Nikolaus Pevsner (celebrated author of *The Buildings of England* series), Howard Colvin and James Lees-Milne.[73] Few would doubt that Harris possessed a significant stock of personal cultural capital, despite leaving school at a young age. More prosaically, personal cultural capital may be accumulated via membership of learned societies or bodies such as the National Trust. In the Cornish survey, 43 per cent of respondents were members of the National Trust; 5 per cent belonged to English Heritage, and 3 per cent belonged to a further thirteen different heritage organizations. It is argued that membership of such bodies provides both contextualised and subliminal learning.

However, despite this potential flexibility in the acquisition of personal cultural capital, it is also the case that an individual's socio-economic profile remains the most reliable indicator of his/her ability to develop the capacity for personal cultural capital. Table 1 illustrates such data for the visitors to the three survey churches. 35.8 per cent of the sample was male and 64.2 per cent female, reflecting the estimated gender ratio of visitors observed over a number of days. As might be expected, the age profile was predominantly middle-aged. The 14.8 per cent of respondents aged 35–44 corresponded closely to the 2001 UK national population figure of 14.9 per cent.[74] However, in the 45–54 age band, the respondents represented 23.4 per cent of the sample compared to a national figure of just 13.2 per cent. The next age band, 55–64, showed greater differentiation still: 30 per cent of respondents were in this category compared to the national figure of 10.6 per cent. The figures for 65–74 were 20.5 per cent for the respondents and 8.4 per cent for the total population. Finally, 5.1 per cent of respondents were aged over 75 compared to the national figure of 7.5 per cent. It may be that older people have a greater appreciation of history but it is also clear that the passage of the years increases an individuals stock of personal cultural capital.[75] But, as might also be expected, a significant association (p=<.001) was found to exist between education qualification and social class in this survey.

Table 1.   Church survey respondent features

Respondent data	Gunwalloe	St Just-in-Roseland	Lanteglos-by-Fowey
n =	286	294	145
British	266 (93 per cent)	266 (90 per cent)	131 (90 per cent)
Overseas	20 (7 per cent)	28 (10 per cent)	14 (10 per cent)
Day visitor	29 (10 per cent)	18 (6 per cent)	24 (17 per cent)
First visit to Cornwall	17 (6 per cent)	31 (11 per cent)	11 (8 per cent)
Three or more visits	217 (76 per cent)	208 (71 per cent)	95 (66 per cent)
Under 25	2 (1 per cent)	5 (2 per cent)	0
25–34	17 (6 per cent)	12 (4 per cent)	8 (6 per cent)
35–44	42 (15 per cent)	43 (15 per cent)	22 (15 per cent)
45–54	73 (26 per cent)	52 (18 per cent)	44 (31 per cent)
55–64	82 (29 per cent)	99 (34 per cent)	35 (24 per cent)
65–74	51 (18 per cent)	67 (23 per cent)	30 (21 per cent)
Over 75	18 (6 per cent)	15 (5 per cent)	4 (3 per cent)
Retired (E)	123 (43 per cent)	123 (42 per cent)	53 (37 per cent)
Socio-economic type A,B	82 (29 per cent)	100 (34 per cent)	63 (44 per cent)
Graduate qualifications	80 (30 per cent)	107 (39 per cent)	68 (50 per cent)
Household income –			
Under £7,499 p.a.	15 (7 per cent)	9 (4 per cent)	0
£7,500 – £9,999	12 (5 per cent)	3 (1 per cent)	2 (2 per cent)
£10,000 – £14,999	28 (12 per cent)	27 (12 per cent)	9 (10 per cent)
£15,000 – £19,999	26 (12 per cent)	33 (15 per cent)	9 (10 per cent)
£20,000 – £24,999	24 (11 per cent)	29 (13 per cent)	9 (10 per cent)
£25,000 – £29,999	21 (9 per cent)	30 (13 per cent)	12 (13 per cent)

£30,000 – £39,999	40 (18 per cent)	24 (11 per cent)	15 (16 per cent)
£40,000 – £49,999	26 (12 per cent)	26 (12 per cent)	6 (7 per cent)
£50,000 – £59,999	14 (6 per cent)	18 (8 per cent)	9 (10 per cent)
£60,000 – £69,999	8 (4 per cent)	10 (4 per cent)	6 (7 per cent)
Above £70,000 p.a.	12 (5 per cent)	17 (8 per cent)	15 (16 per cent)

Notes:
1 Missing values predominate within the household income variable (n = 544).
2 Percentages rounded.
Source: Busby, 2004.

While there are 'inherent fallacies' in attempting to assign particular newspaper or magazine readership to social or political groupings,[76] there is nonetheless a symbiotic link between educational attainment (in the broad sense used above) and an individual's reading habits. In this way, so-called 'gratuitous knowledge' may be acquired from reading habits, the better-educated correspondingly acquiring the greatest knowledge. An important component of this knowledge is the ability or propensity to remember cultural or stylistic traits; for example, 'It's a Rembrandt' and 'It's Impressionist'.[77] Bourdieu asserts that the likelihood of an individual reading a national newspaper increases strongly with 'educational capital', with the likelihood of reading a local newspaper 'varying in the opposite way'.[78] The visitor survey confirms this, with the association between type of newspaper and sub H.E./H.E. qualification being significant at the 99.9 per cent significance level (Pearson chi-square=88.812, df=3, p=.000).

It is argued that possessors of personal cultural capital are also likely to utilize specific publications – such as Pevsner's (1951) *Buildings of England* series or Simon Jenkins' (1999) *England's Thousand Best Churches* (Pevsner's 1970 second edition is still in print with Yale University Press and not difficult to acquire). Here, for example, is comment about Jenkins' book, taken from a visitors' book entry:

'Visiting the 1,000 best'
    2 August 2000 Lanteglos-by-Fowey church

From a quantitative stance, the data presented in Table 2 are particularly illuminating, with an indication that those possessing higher level qualifications are more likely to use Pevsner's or Jenkins' guides. There is a resonance with MacCannell's concept of the 'marker', 'a piece of information about a site'[79] and, of course, the wider concept of cultural capital.

Table 2.   Name of guide book * Fewer qualification categories
cross-tabulation

			Fewer categories		Total
			Sub H.E. qualification	H.E. qualification	
Name of guide book	Simon Jenkins'	Count	2	20	22
		Expected Count	10.8	11.2	22.0
	Other	Count	2	2	4
		Expected Count	2.0	2.0	4.0
	Pevsner	Count	1	3	4
		Expected Count	2.0	2.0	4.0
	No guide book used	Count	322	318	640
		Expected Count	312.8	327.2	640.0
	Missing	Count	1	0	1
		Expected Count	0.5	0.5	1.0
Total		Count	328	343	671
		Expected Count	328.0	343.0	671.0

As suggested above, content analysis of Cornish church visitors' books is a useful tool and provides other indicators of the possession of cultural capital – in varying degrees – among visitors. Here are a few telling examples of visitor comments:

'Is the stained glass by Kemp, or perhaps his pupil??'
4 October 2000, Gunwalloe church.

'the patterns on the pews were (*sic*) very artistic and were (*sic*) intricately carved'
21 February 2002, St Just-in-Roseland church.

'Incredible to find remains of original rood screen in a Cornish church'
27th March 2000, Gunwalloe church.

Besides observing a clear relationship between cultural practices and educational capital (defined by qualifications), Bourdieu also considered social origin to be of key significance.[80] The proportions of socio-economic types A and B, in the table above, are pertinent for they indicate possible origins, despite mobility, and are relevant to any children in the group. Of those visitors with children in their group (n = 87), 90 per cent considered the visit to be an educational experience – an early development of personal cultural capital.

Utilization of Likert scores for perception of 'Celticity' in the church appearance is illuminating: a statistical association exists, at the 99.5 per cent level, between whether the survey church is perceived as 'Celtic' and highest level of qualification (Pearson chi-square = 11.108, df = 2). In the light of Richards' substantial survey, which indicated 'those with professional occupations and higher incomes … [are] significantly more likely to be interested in local culture and history' than others,[81] it is argued that perception of the survey church by such individuals is less likely to be part of a hegemonic discourse and more likely to be a 'rational' perspective. Others, who eye the church with a 'romantic gaze', do not possess the requisite cultural capital to appreciate the temporal development of what is being viewed. But, as Harvey has shown,[82] the nexus may also be environmental, the 'gaze' moulded by familiarity and association: 'places [have] become humanised, with feelings of belonging, rootedness, and familiarity [repeat visitation], through the recognition of symbolic qualities in the "natural" environment "by association with current use, past social actions or actions of a mythological character" (Tilley 1994: 24)'[83]

Visitors recognize the extant church heritage through a range of stories, some mythological. This links closely to the church setting within the Cornish landscape. Moffat's recent re-assertion of the traditional view that Cornwall is the 'Land of the Saints'[84] can be tested statistically from the survey data, where there is an association at the 99.9 per cent level between knowledge of the Cornish Saints and religiosity, operationalized as frequency of worship (Pearson chi-square = 23.737, df = 3). This has a particular resonance with Bradley's observation that currently there is a 'booming interest in Celtic Christianity'.[85] However, from another perspective, there is no association between perceptions of Celticity and religiosity. As Bourdieu reminds us 'it is vital not to operationalize cultural practices as a discrete set of variables but as a carefully constructed space of lifestyles',[86] and some of those with a passionate interest in Cornish Saints may not be practising Christians – 'Celtic' or otherwise.

The nexus between personal and destination-based cultural capital

Engagement with those attractions created from destination-based cultural capital is predicated on a range of factors, including levels of education, prior awareness of the site (repeat visitation), interest in the site, its meaning, availability of time, and the presence of competing activities.[87] As McKercher observes: 'An independent tourist who spends four hours at a cultural site probably will have a qualitatively different experience than a coach-trip tourist who spends only five minutes at the same site, simply by virtue of the amount of time invested ... people travelling for similar motives may have fundamentally different experiences.'[88]

The individual spending four hours will, almost axiomatically, 'connect' more with a specific site. Timothy believes it is the level of connectivity with a site which is significant, and suggests that local sites (such as a Cornish church) will foster a greater sense of personal connectivity than national or global ones (such as the Tower of London).[89] Connectivity and depth of experience are, then, closely related. Yet, as McKercher recognizes, the level of personal cultural capital is also critical here: two individuals spending four hours each at the same site may still have widely different levels of experience.[90] Multi-dimensional scaling[91] would permit varying levels of personal cultural capital to be mapped. The possession of personal cultural capital certainly permits the visitor to obtain a qualitatively better experience when visiting a church site. But, concomitantly, the visitor also acquires a certain social distinction through the consumption of such experiences and the deployment of his/her personal cultural capital, claiming common cause and affinity with the likes of Pevsner and Jenkins.[92] Distinction is also created by the ability to seek out the places to be experienced, and here travel as well as disposable income is a key component in the search for the elusive 'other'.[93]

Furthermore, engagement with attractions created from destination-based cultural capital carries within it the seeds of contestation. Gvili and Poria[94] argue that any given 'heritage site is a complex construct' – for heritage and culture are not value-neutral – and that such sites may have widely different meanings for different people.[95] A central question here, of course, is 'whose heritage is it anyway'? Edson[96] suggests that individuals believe in heritage because they need to, 'what they believe in has minimal inherent value'. An 'up-country' visitor to a remote Cornish church may feel that he/she has discovered a unique window to the elusive Celtic 'other'; a Cornish visitor might consider that he/she is merely communing with his/her personal inheritance. There are, as Deacon has observed, multiple constructions of Cornwall, and so perceptions and interpretations of individual Cornish sites may vary widely.[97] Ideology and cultural politics are never far beneath the surface in such situations. For example, Graham has studied the Ulster Folk and Transport Museum in Northern Ireland to show how such attractions can be perceived as sectarian and class-based.[98] The profile of visitors to the Ulster Museum inclined towards the middle-aged, Protestant middle-class, revealing a high level of connectivity between the attraction and Protestant culture. At the same time, Catholics also tended to see the Museum as a Unionist establishment, a view reinforced by its geographical location in the heart of a Protestant area. Here the cultural capital of heritage had become 'a symbolic resource with a capacity for power',[99] an important reminder that power relationships and ideological predispositions often underlie the creation of heritage sites and the deployment of cultural capital

As suggested above, the issue of contestation is manifest in Cornish churches. Some visitors, for example, may be enthusiastic 'church-crawlers' but others might be determined members of the 'Cornish diaspora',[100] visitors from Australia, the United States, New Zealand, Canada, or South Africa[101] anxious to discover the Cornish roots of their nineteenth-century emigrant forbears. Increasingly, these latter-day 'transnational Cornish' are seen as an important component of Cornwall's tourist market.[102] And well they might. It has been estimated, for example, that as many as 240,000 Cornish had gone overseas in the years 1840–1900, while in 1900 something like a quarter of the white miners on the South African Rand were from Cornwall.[103] It is also worth noting Payton's reporting of Price's estimate: 'in 1992 between 245,000 and 290,000 Australians were of significant Cornish descent, with perhaps as many as 850,000 with some Cornish connections in their family trees'.[104] Payton has also emphasized the strength of identification with Cornwall for many of these descendants living in the United States, Australia, Canada and elsewhere.[105]

In these days of relatively low cost international travel, the behaviour of this contemporary 'Cornish diaspora' is yet another illustration of the global-local nexus.[106] As recently as 1969 Clive James found it necessary to spend thirty days on a ship to journey from Australia to Europe as a result of the prohibitively expensive 'stratospheric air fares'.[107] Yet in less than four decades, this has changed completely. The journey time has been transformed from thirty days to less than twenty-four hours, at significantly lower cost in real terms. This can only serve to stimulate identity-forming exercises, for 'diasporic travel and tourism shape an individual's self-perception'.[108] Such 'diasporic' visitors are also likely to possess a high degree of gratuitous knowledge in their personal cultural capital, not least by dint of their extensive reading and research in pursuit of their fascination with genealogy.

Conclusion

The literature indicates that 'cultural capital' is a ubiquitous term, used interchangeably to refer to either an individual's attributes or to those of particular destinations. This article has used Cornwall as a case study to illustrate both forms of the term. Possession of personal cultural capital is, as shown above, linked closely to levels of education, both 'certified' and otherwise obtained. Possessors of personal cultural capital are generally those who come armed with more comprehensive, specialist, guide books; they also tend to read 'quality' national daily newspapers. Destination-based cultural capital consists of both tangible and intangible elements; tangible elements are said to provide latent cultural capital while potential cultural capital is intangible – illustrated, for example, in the relationship between particular authors and certain areas.

In Cornwall, the tangible heritage is manifest in the plethora of megaliths, castles, churches and other sites – including the UNESCO 'World Heritage Site' mining landscape. The intangible heritage is also strong – for many visitors Cornwall has an aesthetic, mystical, almost spiritual quality – and there is an intimate relationship between particular localities and writers such as Daphne du Maurier and John Betjeman. Although the identity of a place may alter as a result of tourism activity,[109] with critics pointing to exploitation and even 'enkitschment',[110] churches have remained a relatively unchanging and consistent component in the destination mix in Cornwall, seen by many as 'timeless' and therefore seminal in the creation of local distinctiveness.[111] Many visitors view these churches through the lens of a wider cultural reproduction of Cornwall; according to Payton: 'Cornish churches slip easily into constructions of "Celtic Cornwall"'.[112] The proportion of the total of Cornish churches listed as grade I hints at more than just architectural importance. The churches of Cornwall form a significant component of the extant heritage, and for the 'diasporic' visitor contribute importantly to notions of Cornish identity.

The nexus between personal and destination-based cultural capital is observed in the level of engagement with particular visitor attractions. In the case of Cornish churches, the level is high, with visitors on the whole exhibiting strongly developed personal cultural capital, and the sites themselves possessing equally powerful destination-based cultural capital. Ancient rood screens, carved bench ends, chevrons, memorials, holy wells and churchyard crosses are irresistible attractions for those who, armed with their Pevner and Jenkins guides or their du Maurier novels and Betjeman poems, seek the hidden sanctuaries of the Celtic 'Saints of Cornwall' about which they have read so much.

Acknowledgement

An earlier version of this article was presented at the 18th Biennial International Tourism and Hospitality Congress, Opatija, Croatia, 3–5 May 2006.

Notes and references

1. P. Bourdieu and J.-C. Passeron, *Cultural Reproduction and Social Reproduction* (1973), cited at http://en.wikipedia.org/wiki/Cultural_capital, accessed on 18 April 2006.
2. P. Bourdieu, *Distinction – a social critique of the judgement of taste* (London, 1986).
3. G. Richards, 'Demand Evolution in Cultural Tourism', *ATLAS News*, Number 24 (May 2001a), pp. 21–29.
4. A. Alzua, J.T. O'Leary and A. Morrison, 'Cultural and Heritage Tourism: identifying niches for international travellers', *Journal of Tourism Studies* 9 (1998), pp. 2–13; K. Meethan, 'Selling the difference: tourism marketing in Devon and Cornwall, South-West England', in R. Voase (ed.), *Tourism in Western Europe* (Wallingford, 2002), pp. 23–42; G. Richards and J. Wilson, 'Developing creativity in tourist experiences: a solution to the serial reproduction of culture?' *Tourism Management*, 27 (6) (2006), pp. 1209–23.
5. B.P. Andrew, 'Tourism and the Economic Development of Cornwall', *Annals of Tourism Research*, 24 (3) (1997), pp. 721–35; H. Gilligan, 'Visitors, Tourists and Outsiders in a Cornish town', in M. Bouquet and M. Winter (eds), *Who from their Labours Rest? Conflict and Practice in Rural Tourism* (Aldershot, Avebury, 1987), pp. 65–82; A.M. Williams and G. Shaw, 'The Age of Mass Tourism', in P. Payton (ed.), *Cornwall Since The War* (Redruth, 1993), pp. 84–97.
6. Andrew, 'Tourism'; D.C. Harvey, 'Landscape Organization, Identity and Change: Territoriality and Hagiography in Medieval west Cornwall', *Landscape Research*, 25 (2) (2000), pp. 201–12.
7. J. Vernon, 'Border Crossings: Cornwall and the English (imagi)nation', in G. Cubitt (ed.), *Imagining Nations* (Manchester, 1998), pp. 153–72 (p. 157).
8. Vernon, 'Border Crossings', p. 159.
9. C. Brace, 'Cornish Identity and Landscape in the work of Arthur Caddick', in P. Payton, (ed.), *Cornish Studies: Seven* (Exeter, 1999), pp. 130–46 (p. 134).
10. A.M. Kent, 'Screening Kernow: Authenticity, Heritage and the Representation of Cornwall in Film and Television 1913–2003', in P. Payton (ed.), *Cornish Studies: Eleven* (Exeter, 2003), pp. 110–41.
11. G. Shaw and A. Williams, *Tourism and Tourism Spaces* (London, 2004), p. 12.
12. N. Orme, *The Saints of Cornwall* (Oxford, 2000).
13. F. Fukuyama, *The Great Disruption – Human Nature and the Reconstitution of Social Order* (London, 1999), p. 165.
14. A.M. Kent, 'Scatting it t'lerrups: Provisional Notes towards Alternative Methodologies in Language and Literary Studies in Cornwall', in P. Payton (ed.), *Cornish Studies: Thirteen* (Exeter, 2005), pp. 23–52 (p. 27).

15. P. Laviolette, 'An Iconography of Landscape Images in Cornish Art and Prose', in P. Payton (ed.), *Cornish Studies: Seven* (Exeter, 1999), pp. 107–29 (p. 125).
16. B. Deacon, 'Cornish Culture or the Culture of the Cornish?' *Cornish Scene* NS1 (1988), pp. 58–60, cited in A. Hale, 'Representing the Cornish', *Tourist Studies*, 1 (2) (2001), pp. 185–96.
17. A. Hale, 'Representing the Cornish', *Tourist Studies*, 1 (2) (2001), pp. 185–96 (p. 187).
18. G. Busby and P. Laviolette, 'Narratives in the Net: Fiction and Cornish Tourism', in P. Payton (ed.), *Cornish Studies: Fourteen* (Exeter, 2006), pp. 142–63.
19. Williams and Shaw, 'Mass Tourism', p. 92.
20. F. McGettigan and K. Burns, 'Clonmacnoise: A Monastic Site, Burial Ground and Tourist Attraction', in G. Richards (ed.), *Cultural Attractions and European Tourism* (Wallingford, 2001), pp. 135–58.
21. P. Laviolette, 'Landscaping Death: Resting Places for Cornish Identity', *Journal of Material Culture*, 8 (2) (2003), pp. 215–40.
22. S. Jenkins, *England's Thousand Best Churches* (London, 1999).
23. S. Williams, *Tourism Geography* (London, 1998).
24. J. Tunbridge, 'The Question of Heritage in European Cultural Conflict', in B. Graham (ed.), *Modern Europe – Place, Culture and Identity* (London, 1998), pp. 236–59.
25. See, for example, D. Bell and M. Jayne (eds), *City of Quarters: Urban Villages in the Contemporary City* (Aldershot, 2004); D.R. Judd and S. Fainstein (eds), *The Tourist City* (New Haven, CT, 1999).
26. D. Inglis and M. Holmes, 'Highland and Other Haunts', *Annals of Tourism Research*, 30 (1) (2003), pp. 50–63.
27. A. Honkanen, 'Churches and Statues: Cultural Tourism in Finland', *Tourism and Hospitality Research*, 3 (4) (2002), pp. 371–9.
28. B. Bender and M. Winer (eds), *Contested Landscapes* (London, 2001).
29. K. Meethan, *Tourism in Global Society: Place, Culture and Consumption* (Basingstoke, 2001).
30. T. Silberberg, 'Cultural tourism and Business Opportunities for Museums and Heritage Sites', *Tourism Management*, 16 (5) (1995), pp. 361–5.
31. D. Lowenthal, *The Heritage Crusade and the Spoils of History* (London, 1996), p. 121.
32. D.C. Harvey, 'Heritage Pasts and Heritage Presents: Temporality, Meaning and the Scope of Heritage Studies', *International Journal of Heritage Studies*, 7 (4) (2001), pp. 319–38 (p. 327).
33. G. Edson, 'Heritage: Pride or Passion, Product or Service?' *International Journal of Heritage Studies*, 10 (4) (2004), pp. 333–48.
34. J.J. Climo and M.G. Cattell, *Social Memory and History: Anthropological perspectives* (Walnut Creek, CA, 2002).
35. B. Deacon and P. Payton, 'Re-inventing Cornwall: Culture Change on the European Periphery', in P. Payton (ed.), *Cornish Studies: One* (Exeter, 1993), pp. 62–79.
36. H. du Cros, A New Model to Assist in Planning for Sustainable Cultural Heritage Tourism, *International Journal of Tourism Research*, 3 (2) (2001), pp. 165–70 (p. 166).
37. G. Busby, 'The Cornish Church Heritage as Destination Component', *Tourism*, 50

(4) (2002), pp. 371–81; G. Busby, '"A True Cornish Treasure": Gunwalloe and the Cornish Church as Visitor Attraction', in P. Payton (ed.), *Cornish Studies: Eleven* (Exeter, 2003), pp. 168–91; G. Busby, 'The Contested Cornish Church Heritage', in P. Payton (ed.), *Cornish Studies: Twelve* (Exeter, 2004), pp. 166–83.

38. Richards and Wilson, 2006.

39. Busby, '"A True Cornish Treasure"' and Busby, 'The Contested Cornish Church Heritage'.

40. O.R. Holsti, *Content analysis for the social sciences and humanities*, (Reading, MA, 1969), p. 32.

41. D. Wheeler, G. Shaw and S. Barr, *Statistical Techniques in Geographical Analysis*, 3rd edition (London, 2004).

42. Busby, 'The Contested Cornish Church Heritage'.

43. S.-E. Karlsson, 'The Social and the Cultural Capital of a Place and their Influence on the Production of Tourism – A Theoretical Reflection based on an Illustrative Case Study', *Scandinavian Journal of Hospitality and Tourism*, 5 (2005), pp. 102–15 (p. 107).

44. Alzua *et al.*, 'Tourism'.

45. J. Boissevain, 'Ritual, Tourism and Cultural Commoditization in Malta: Culture by the Pound', in T. Selwyn (ed.), *The Tourist Image: Myths and Myth Making in Tourism* (Chichester, 1996), pp. 105–20.

46. R. Prentice, *Tourism and Heritage Attractions* (London, 1993), p. 40.

47. J.G. Robb, 'A Geography of Celtic Appropriations', in D.C. Harvey, R. Jones, N. McInroy and C. Milligan (eds), *Celtic Geographies: Old Culture, New Times* (London, 2002), pp. 229–42.

48. J. Urry, *The Tourist Gaze* (London, 1990), p. 117.

49. G. Busby and Z. Hambly, 'Literary Tourism and the Daphne du Maurier Festival', in P. Payton (ed.), *Cornish Studies: Eight* (Exeter, 2000), pp. 197–212; G. Busby, P. Brunt and J. Lund, 'In Agatha Christie Country: Resident Perception of Special Interest Tourism', *Tourism*, 51 (3) (2003), pp. 287–300.

50. D. du Maurier, *Vanishing Cornwall* (London, 1967).

51. D. MacCannell, *The Tourist: a New Theory of the Leisure Class* (New York, 1976).

52. I. Munt, 'The "other" Postmodern Tourism: Culture, Travel and the New Middle Classes', *Theory, Culture and Society*, 11 (3) (1994), pp. 101–23.

53. Busby and Hambly, 'Literary Tourism'.

54. Meethan, 'Selling the Difference', p. 36.

55. G. Busby and J. Klug, 'Movie-induced tourism: The Challenge of Measurement and other Issues', *Journal of Vacation Marketing*, 7 (4) (2001), pp. 316–32.

56. Busby and Laviolette, 'Narratives in the Net'.

57. J. Copping, 'Doctor Who's latest service to mankind ... saving Wales' tourist industry', *The Daily Telegraph*, 16 April 2006, viewed at http://www.telegraph.co.uk/news/main.jhtml?xml=/news/2006/04/16/nwho16.xml&sSheet=/news/2006/04/16/ixhome.html

58. E. Carveth, Trading Standards Officer, Cornwall County Council, personal communication, 11 May 2001 (e-mail).

59. Laviolette, 'Landscaping Death', p. 230.

60. A. Hale, 'Selling Celtic Cornwall: Changing Markets and Meanings?' in K. Meethan, A. Anderson and S. Miles (eds), *Tourism, Consumption and Representation: Narratives of place and self* (Wallingford, 2006), pp. 272–83.

61. Boissevain, 'Malta'; Laviolette, 'Landscaping Death'; Meethan, 'Selling the difference'.

62. G. Evans, 'Glyn Evans new NCTG chairman', *Faith In Tourism* (Spring 2001), p. 4.

63. W. Osgodby, 'West Lindsey, Lincs. Churches Festival', *Faith In Tourism* (Spring 2001), p. 3.

64. A. Keeling, 'Church Tourism – Providing a Ministry of Welcome to Visitors', *Insights* (2000), pp. A13–A22.

65. M. Gold, 'From Preservation to Interpretation: Presenting the Sacred in a Secular Age', unpublished MA dissertation (London, 2000).

66. See, for example, T. Winter, 'Ruining the Dream? The Challenge of Tourism at Angkor, Cambodia' in K. Meethan, A. Anderson and S. Miles (eds), *Tourism, Consumption and Representation: Narratives of place and self* (Wallingford, 2006), pp. 46–66.

67. G. Richards, 'The Experience Industry and the Creation of Attractions', in G. Richards (ed.), *Cultural Attractions and European Tourism*, Wallingford, 2001, pp. 55–69.

68. Richards, *Cultural Attractions*, p. 57.

69. G. Ritzer, *Enchanting a Disenchanted World: Revolutionizing the Means of Consumption*, Thousand Oaks, California, 1999, cited in G. Richards, 'The experience industry and the creation of attractions', in G. Richards (ed.), *Cultural Attractions and European Tourism* (Wallingford, 2001), pp. 55–69 (p. 58).

70. A.K.H. Jenkin, *The Story of Cornwall* (London, 1934).

71. N. Kennedy and N. Kingcome, 'Disneyfication of Cornwall – Developing a Poldark Heritage Complex', *International Journal of Heritage Studies*, 4 (1) (1998), pp. 45–59 (p. 57).

72. Busby, 'The Contested Cornish Church Heritage'.

73. J. Harris, *No Voice From The Hall – Early Memories of a Country House Snooper* (London, 1998); J. Harris, *Echoing Voices – More Memories of a Country House Snooper* (London, 2002).

74. National Statistics *Social Trends No. 33* (London, 2003).

75. P. Gruffudd, D.T. Herbert and A. Piccini ' "Good to think": social constructions of Celtic heritage in Wales', *Environment and Planning D: Society and Space*, 17 (6) (1999), pp. 705–21.

76. Bourdieu, *Distinction*, p. 440.

77. Bourdieu, *Distinction*, p. 26.

78. Bourdieu, *Distinction*, p. 444.

79. MacCannell, *The Tourist*, p. 41.

80. Bourdieu, *Distinction*.

81. G. Richards, 'Tourism Attraction Systems – Exploring Cultural Behaviour', *Annals of Tourism Research*, 29 (4) (2002), pp. 1048–64 (p. 1055).

82. D.C. Harvey, 'Constructed Landscapes and Social Memory: Tales of St Samson in Early Medieval Cornwall', *Environment and Planning D: Society and Space*, 20 (2) (2002), pp. 231–48 (p. 233).

83. C. Tilley, *A Phenomenology of Landscape: Places, Paths and Monuments* (Oxford, 1994), cited in D.C. Harvey, 'Constructed Landscapes and Social memory: tales of St Samson in Early Medieval Cornwall', *Environment and Planning D: Society and Space*, 20 (2) (2002), pp. 231–48 (p. 233).

84. A. Moffat, *Kernow: Part Seen, Part Imagined*, Episode 2, Carlton Television, 20 April 2001.
85. I. Bradley, Face to Faith, *The Guardian*, 4 March 2006, p. 37.
86. M. Savage, M. Gayo-Cal, A. Warde and G. Tampubolon, *Cultural Capital in the UK: A Preliminary Report using Correspondence Analysis*, Research on Socio-Cultural Change Working Paper No. 4 (Manchester, 2005), p. 12.
87. B. McKercher, 'Towards a Classification of Cultural Tourists', *International Journal of Tourism Research*, 4 (1) (2002), pp. 29–38.
88. McKercher, 'Towards a Classification', p. 31.
89. D. Timothy, 'Tourism and the Personal Heritage Experience', *Annals of Tourism Research*, 23 (4), 1997, pp. 948–50.
90. McKercher, 'Towards a Classification'.
91. S. Dutton and G. Busby, 'Antiques-based Tourism: Our Common Heritage?' *Acta Turistica*, 14 (2) (2002), pp. 97–119; P.L. Pearce, *The Ulysses Factor – evaluating visitors in tourist settings* (New York, 1988).
92. Munt, 'The "other" postmodern tourism'.
93. Shaw and Williams, *Tourism*.
94. Y. Gvili and Y. Poria, 'Online Mass Customisation: The Case of Promoting Heritage Tourist Websites', Conference Proceedings, *Perspectives in Tourism Marketing*, Mugla, Turkey, 20–22 May 2005, pp. 61–8 (p. 65).
95. K. Burnett, 'Heritage, Authenticity and History', in S. Drummond and I. Yeoman (eds), *Quality Issues in Heritage Visitor Attractions* (Oxford, 2001), pp. 39–53; Tunbridge, 'The Question of Heritage'.
96. Edson, 'Heritage', p. 336.
97. B. Deacon, 'From "Cornish Studies" to "Critical Cornish Studies": Reflections on Methodology', in P. Payton (ed.), *Cornish Studies: Twelve* (Exeter, 2004), pp. 13–29.
98. B. Graham, 'The Contested Interpretation of Heritage Landscapes in Northern Ireland', *International Journal of Heritage Studies*, 2 (1 & 2) (1996), pp. 10–22.
99. D. McCrone, A. Morris and R. Kiely, *Scotland – The Brand: the making of Scottish Heritage* (Edinburgh, 1995), p. 20.
100. A.L. Rowse, *The Cornish in America* (London, 1969), p. viii.
101. P. Payton, *The Cornish Overseas* (Fowey, 1999); A.L. Rowse, *A Cornishman at Oxford* (London, 1965).
102. Hale, 'Representing the Cornish'.
103. Payton, *The Cornish Overseas*, p. 42.
104. Payton, *The Cornish Overseas*, p. 393.
105. Payton, *The Cornish Overseas*.
106. T. Coles, D.T. Duval and C.M. Hall, 'Tourism, Mobility and Global Communities: New Approaches to Theorising Tourism and Tourist Spaces', in W.F. Theobald (ed.), *Global Tourism* (3rd edition, Amsterdam, 2005), pp. 463–81.
107. J. Baxter, *A Pound of Paper – Confessions of a Book Addict* (London, 2002), p. 134.
108. Coles *et al.*, 'Tourism', p. 474.
109. M. Kneafsey, 'Tourism, Place Identities and Social Relations in the European Rural Periphery', *European Urban and Regional Studies*, 7 (1) (2000), pp. 35–50.
110. J. Howlett, 'Putting the Kitsch into Kernow', in P. Payton (ed.), *Cornish Studies: Twelve* (Exeter, 2004), pp. 30–60 (p. 44).

111. Busby, 'The Cornish Church Heritage as Destination Component'.
112. P. Payton, 'Introduction', in P. Payton (ed.), *Cornish Studies: Twelve* (Exeter, 2004), pp. 1–12 (p. 5).

8

Changing Landscapes of Difference

Representations of Cornwall in Travel Writing, 1949–2007

Robert Dickinson

Introduction

Mobility is a characteristic feature of contemporary life. And with 'travel and tourism' now the world's largest industry it is not surprising that the tourist has become a metaphor of our postmodern times.[1] For Zygmunt Bauman tourists move to 'immerse themselves in a strange and bizarre element',[2] while paying 'for their freedom; the right to disregard native concerns and feelings, the right to spin their own web of meanings'.[3] According to Lash and Urry, places, which were once contemplated as sites of 'high culture', are now consumed as if part of the 'high street'.[4] Indeed, it has been claimed that the tourist's world has 'become one large department store of countrysides and cities'.[5]

It can hardly be a coincidence, then, that at the same time, as Duncan and Gregory observe, we have 'witnessed a double explosion of interest in travel writing'. While bookstore shelves have been filling up with travellers' accounts of their journeys, scholars have increasingly turned their attention to analyzing how such works 'spin webs of colonizing power'[6] and to considering the problematic relationship between representations and reality. If what we consume in postmodernity is increasingly signs or images, as Lash and Urry argue, 'there is no simple "reality" separate from such modes of representation'.[7]

Cornwall has featured in many of these recent accounts. As a major tourist destination, it is for contemporary travel writers in search of an understanding of life in postmodern Britain as essential as it was for the nineteenth century

Romantic writers and artists who sought to contemplate the sublime in its natural landscapes.

This article examines representations of Cornwall in a body of travel writing published from 1949 onwards and argues that these illustrate the processes and features outlined above. During this period a shift occurs from the contemplation of Cornwall as a Romantic landscape to its consumption through signs. At the same time travellers in search of new sensations no longer seek out the exotic and foreign but immerse themselves in the strange and the bizarre. While the works continue to spin webs of colonizing power, representations of the Cornish shift from conquered, and subdued Other to conquered, but hostile Other. Organizationally, the article considers the generic characteristics of travel writing before situating the works in their literary and historical context through a brief discussion of intertextuality and a rapid overview of social, economic and political change in Cornwall in the period concerned. It then proceeds to a detailed textual analysis of recurrent sets of representations and analyses how the dominant representational paradigm is gradually displaced. But first we reflect on what tools might be appropriate for this analysis.

Representation: semiotic and discursive approaches

Representations are the products of a process – *representation*.[8] Although broadly defined as the process by which something is made to stand for something else, such a definition, while telling us *what* it is, says nothing about *how* the process works or anything about its *effects*. Consequently, in order to address both the question of 'poetics', or how meaning is produced, and that of 'politics', or the effects of representation we will draw on two theoretical approaches.[9] While the semiotic approach will provide us with a model for understanding the production of meaning through language, the discursive approach will enable us to analyse the way in which representations are deployed in specific historical circumstances.[10]

Semiotics is concerned with explaining how meaning is produced through language, a system of signs. For Saussure, meaning was essentially relational rather than referential. The meaning of signs lies in their relations with other signs in the system and is not derived from reference to the material world. Relations are of two kinds: contrast or opposition between signs (paradigmatic) and possibilities of combination of signs to create larger units or texts (syntagmatic). These paradigmatic and syntagmatic relations provide a structural context in which signs make sense and are organized into codes. An analysis of these relations can reveal 'meaningful contrasts and permitted or forbidden combinations'.[11]

The discursive approach is concerned with the production of knowledge through discourse as a system of representation. For Foucault, discourse is a set of statements or assumptions belonging to a single formation which structures what can be said about a particular subject and makes claims to knowledge about it. Knowledge applied through a set of institutional practices not only assumes the authority of 'truth' but is able to create the reality it purports to describe. An intimate relationship is thus established between knowledge and power. Knowledge reflects a relation of power between the subject, or knower, and the object, or that which the knower knows or studies. It is a way of categorizing and defining others. As discourses are located in wider social and historical contexts, they are culturally and historically specific.

The works in their context[12]

The popularity of travel writing in our hybrid age is possibly a function of its own generic hybridity. Combining elements of the autobiography, the novel and the ethnography, to name but a few, those very qualities that contribute to its popular appeal also render a precise definition of the genre complex. In view of this, the working definition loosely adopted here is that offered by Tavares and Brosseau, namely that 'most works of travel writing are centred on a narrative that tells the story of a true journey conducted by the autobiographical subject of the text'.[13] Using this definition, a body of five works was selected for analysis. While such a relatively small corpus will restrict our ability to draw any widely generalizable conclusions, it is hoped that the focus on depth rather than breadth will allow us to cross-reference the works in some detail.[14]

The works analysed were published between 1949 and 2007, a period of rapid socio-economic change in Cornwall. Cornwall saw a tourist explosion in the 1950s, a boom in employment in the manufacturing sector in the 1960s and early 1970s, both of which were to bring large-scale inward migration in their wake.[15] But subsequent oil crises and increased global competition turned boom into bust, which, coupled with an increasing population, led to chronic unemployment. Meanwhile, issues of identity began to push their way onto the political agenda and the symbols of a new Cornish national consciousness and cultural renaissance were becoming more visible.[16]

The texts in the study were written by British or American authors, none of whom identified themselves as Cornish. In each work Cornwall was but one stage on a longer journey, either regional or national. *The West of England* (1949) by Ruth Manning-Sanders is the composite account of journeys from Land's End to Bristol. John Hillaby also begins his *Journey Through Britain* (1968) at Land's End as he begins the classic walk to John o'Groats. After living in London for eleven years, American writer Paul Theroux goes in search of the real Britain by travelling around its coast by train, a journey recorded in *The Kingdom by the Sea* (1983). Two more writers who forsake London to find the 'real' country beyond are Ian Aitch, whose *A Fete Worse Than Death* (2004) recounts a summer watching the English at play, and Paul Gogarty, who, in *The Coast Road* (2007), narrates a three thousand mile trip round the edge of England.

These writers are not exploring virgin territory but following a well-beaten literary path. Edward Said contends that earlier works position writers vis-à-vis their subject and structure their choice of narrative themes, modes of address and representations. Just as 'every writer on the Orient assumes ... some previous knowledge of the Orient, to which he refers and on which he relies',[17] every writer on Cornwall arrives laden with a heavy cultural baggage. With the status of 'authorship' problematized by intertextuality, Barthes has declared that '[a] text is ... a multi-dimensional space in which a variety of writings, none of them original blend and clash'.[18] Theroux acknowledges as much when he concedes that 'No British journey could be original'.[19] A dense citationary structure bears witness in the texts to more than diffuse influences by such writers as Celia Fiennes, Daniel Defoe, W.H. Hudson and Daphne du Maurier. Since the late eighteenth century Cornwall has been a site of contested representations as outsiders and insiders have portrayed it as a place of difference with labels like West Barbary, Industrial Civilization, Celtic Other and Delectable Duchy.[20] As we shall see, 'discursive echoes of the past'[21] continue to resonate in contemporary accounts.

A land(scape) of difference

Across the texts studied, Cornwall continues to be characterized by its difference but the mapping of this difference reveals an indeterminate space, whose shifting borders do not coincide with the territory of Cornwall. This results from the ambivalent status of the signs 'Cornish' and 'Cornwall'. 'Cornish' is used in a paradigm set which might be termed 'nationality' and 'Cornwall' in another which could be labelled 'counties'. Far from representing 'some kind of conceptual order ruling perceptual chaos'[22] these signs suggest conceptual confusion. The blurring of boundaries is anathema to social order and leads social groups 'to close ranks, shore up culture and to stigmatize and expel anything which is defined as impure, abnormal'.[23] Consequently, the Cornish in these texts are represented as inferior, racially impure and strange, while Cornwall is remapped as partly Cornish and partly English.

The border of 'Cornwall', the 'county', is the Tamar but 'Cornwall, not-England', is entered further west. The writers locate the 'not-England' spaces differently. For Manning-Sanders the 'essential Cornwall' lies west of a line drawn from Hayle to Marazion, while England begins as roads widen east of Liskeard.[24] Theroux, citing D.H. Lawrence, locates the non-English part on the wild northern Atlantic coast, while the softer south coast is English territory.[25] By 2007, however, Gogarty identifies enclaves of difference such as the Lizard peninsula, while other formerly 'Cornish' sites like Land's End have become familiarized through the '21st-century tawdriness' of the tourist industry. In each case, however, the discursive spaces of difference that are opened frame and validate the representations found in the texts.

Manning-Sanders and Hillaby continue to represent Cornwall within the discursive space created by nineteenth century Romanticism. Peripheral areas of the British Isles such as Wales and Ireland were represented by writers and artists from England as exotic, sublime and picturesque spaces which were inhabited by culturally distinct races whose foreignness was grounded in an archaeological landscape.[26] However, as we have seen, Cornwall is seen as ambiguous, a place where English and non-English spaces are coterminous. In this respect it exhibits parallels with the Lake District, whose hybrid nature, according to Urry, combines a threatening wildness reminiscent of Scotland and an inviting prettiness redolent of the home counties. Consequently, this foreign Cornwall must be located well away from the English areas.

It is on the most extreme tip of that space she terms 'essential Cornwall' that Manning-Sanders chooses to start her narrative. Land's End at dusk, set against the vast expanse of the Atlantic Ocean and the oncoming darkness of night, is the perfect setting for her to evoke Cornwall's threatening wildness. Through a series of binary oppositions clustering around Nature and Wilderness on the one hand and Culture and Civilization on the other, Cornwall is represented as being in an untamed, natural, and thus uncivilized state. This is a place where time has stood still and to which civilization has not been introduced: 'the sense of the primordial, the strange and the savage, the unknown, the *very long ago*, fills the dusk with something that is akin to dread.'[27] The key to understanding 'the very long ago' is an archaeological exploration of the landscape and an anatomical/biological examination of its inhabitants. Archaeology is said to confirm that the menhirs and megaliths which are characteristic of this part of Cornwall date from the Neolithic period and were placed there by an 'ancient sea-borne culture', whose exact origins are not specified but which spread to Cornwall from the Iberian peninsula by way of Brittany. The foreignness which the landscape reveals is matched by that to be read in its inhabitants' facial features, which bear witness to an infusion of blood from several sources. The first person Manning-Sanders meets, who is initially taken to be some kind of monster emerging from the oceanic depths, turns out to be a little old woman with 'a tiny flat Mongolian face'.[28] The Cornish gene pool has apparently not only been added to by Mongolian blood but has received contributions from the Phoenicians, responsible for the 'lean, long-nosed' Cornish type[29] and the Spanish whose passage in the area is to be read on other Cornish faces. In like manner Hillaby deploys an archaeological discourse to map out a terrain from which he can read off foreign influences. He too attributes the megalithic monuments of the Penwith peninsula to the presence of culture that had spread to Cornwall via Spain from its home near Crete. But it is not only the built landscape which bears the imprint of the eastern Mediterranean but the natural one too: 'Cornwall looks like southern Greece. In appearance at least, it might be the Peloponnese.'[30] This 'strange likeness' echoes tropes of familiar exoticism linking Greece and Ireland.[31] Hillaby does not see foreignness in the faces of the Cornish people but he hears it in their speech: 'it might have been a foreign language punctuated with only a few familiar words. It sounds rather Russian.'[32] As we shall see, while in these works Cornwall's difference is marked by a foreign past which shapes the physiognomy of the landscape and its people, in the more recent accounts under study the Cornish are portrayed as living in a strange present, where they do things differently.

In the works published since the 1980s we move from this foreign country of the past into a sort of surreal present-day Cornish alterity, often framed as deviant from an English norm. Entering Cornwall by train Theroux passes through a landscape of rolling hills as far as Redruth after which the land becomes 'peculiarly uneven, with trees growing sideways out of stony ground'.[33] The peculiarity of the natural environment, bathed in a lurid light diffused from a 'granite sky', is mirrored in the ghostliness of the built environment, which consists of abandoned mineworks and solitary cottages. In short, his description confirms Cornwall's reputation for being 'creepy' which the 'oral tradition' circulating in London had led him to expect.[34] The same adjective is used by Aitch to describe Fowey carnival, a description provoked by the presence of young children on the parade's floats, which, for him, gives it 'the appearance of a paedophile car boot sale.'[35] He finds it 'creepy' but it is unsurprising in the light of an earlier walk in the town during which he has already discovered a pony in a pub and children in the street in their nightclothes, leading him to comment: 'This is Cornwall, they can do what they like.'[36] To highlight the distance of this Cornish culture from his own, he adopts an ethnographer's discourse, likening the event he comes to observe in Fowey Regatta Week to 'a cargo cult or some kind of ceremony involving human sacrifice'.[37] Gogarty spends more time in the company of people who have moved down to Cornwall than with the indigenous population and when he does go to meet a local representative he is determined to immerse himself in the eccentric world of a Druid priest, Ed Prynn. The closest Gogarty comes to standing stones in Cornwall are those in Prynn's garden, placed there not by some Neolithic visitors from Crete but by Prynn himself in the previous forty years. As justification for his visit to this bizarre world Gogarty argues that Prynn is simply the contemporary incarnation of a tradition of the surreal in Cornwall which stretches back through the pixies of the Victorian era to medieval saints whose lives and actions passed the boundaries of the normal.

In these works, then, Cornwall continues to be portrayed as a land of difference which provides visitors with new sensations, but the unfamiliar now is more likely to be associated with the strange than the foreign. And, as we shall see now, while there is continuity too across these accounts in the depiction of the Cornish people as conquered Other, there is a move to represent them as increasingly hostile.

The Cornish as 'hostile other'

The assumption that travel writing produces 'a transparent and unproblematic depiction of people and places' has been challenged in recent years.[38] Post-colonial scholars, building on the work of Said, have explored 'the power relations implicit in the production of travel texts' and how these reveal more about their authors' circumstances than the people and places visited.[39] While the inequality of these power relations may be more evident in works produced under colonial regimes, contemporary works have been analysed using the concepts provided by post-colonial critics to '[untangle] the various grids of power and privilege embedded in the representations and intercultural encounters of contemporary travel writers'.[40] We argue here that the travel writing in this study exemplifies what Tavares and Brosseau describe as 'the perpetuation of ethnocentrically superior attitudes towards other peoples and places that often justify practices of control, exploitation and subjugation'.[41]

Manning-Sanders recounts how the Cornish have a reputation of being both good and bad. In both cases, however, the qualities associated with these descriptions position them as inferior. When they are bad, they are duplicitous: superficially friendly but beneath the surface appearance deeply suspicious. When they are good, they are childlike: trusting and guileless. While cautioning against too hasty a characterization of the Cornish, she subscribes simultaneously to both these views.[42] However, it is principally as a conquered people that Manning-Sanders represents the inhabitants of Cornwall. These people are the descendants of waves of 'defeated remnants' who sought refuge by almost literally holing themselves up in 'underground strongholds'.[43] Manning-Sanders' imaginative description of the Cornish as a tribe crammed into underground retreats echoes the trope of a subterranean people already present in representations of Cornwall as West Barbary in the late eighteenth century and still reverberating in Hillaby's chapter titled 'Into West Barbary'. After recounting how the nineteenth-century descendants of prehistoric cave dwellers spent their lives in deep mines, Hillaby's repeated descriptions of Cornish towns as 'deserted' give the impression that their descendants are still lurking underground. This low visibility of the Cornish continues into the 1980s when Theroux, visiting Polruan, can still comment that the inhabitants are 'taking refuge in their small houses and the distant past.'[44]

Another wave of invaders is breaking over Cornwall, but this time it is not warring Saxon kings who are laying siege to the Cornish but tourists. And it is this deeply resented, tourist-led invasion which, Theroux argues, 'had made the Cornish nationalistic'.[45] This national feeling, however, is purely reactive, a product of the tourist influx and, although increasingly commented upon in the works studied, it continues to be interpreted as a reaction against Englishness rather than as an affirmation of a native culture. Theroux dismisses contemporary Cornish culture as consisting merely of 'ghost stories and meat pies'.[46] Aitch is struck by the increased diffusion of Cornish flags since a previous visit but attributes this to the prior re-adoption of the flag of St George elsewhere in England, even though the widespread appearance of St Piran's flag probably predates that of the English flag's by at least a decade.[47] The description of St Piran's flag as a monochrome inversion of the flag of St George suggests that it is the signifier of a society lacking in vibrancy and originality. Later Aitch associates it with technological backwardness through the characterization of the black and white TV set in a B&B as 'patriotically Cornish'.[48] Gogarty employing a colonialist discourse evokes the supposed backwardness of Cornish society in terms reminiscent of those used to describe Native Americans when he refers to the 'dwindling pool of indigenous inhabitants' in seaside resorts who leave their harbourside dwellings for an inland 'reservation'.[49] By their apparent self-removal from the landscape, the Cornish can be construed as legitimizing their near absence from the texts.

This effacement leads to the frequent elision of the Cornish from the accounts, but when they are represented, it is either as a faceless collectivity or as types exhibiting characteristics which call into question their membership of the human community. Such treatment is not uncommon in travel writing. Barthes notes how, in the Blue Guides, through the privileging of depopulated landscapes, individuals disappear, replaced by types who are encountered only in the third-class carriages of trains.[50] Aitch, in classic Blue Guide style, includes an interlude on a bus between St Austell and Fowey so we can overhear 'some local conversation to get a feel for the area.'[51] However, this is merely a pretext to provide a transition to 'Cornwall proper', and he shows no interest in exploring further what the conversation reveals about the problem of drug abuse locally since presumably this is not part of 'Cornwall proper'. Manning-Sanders' only conversation with a Cornish person is with a woman who has more in common with the five types of fairies – who, we are reliably informed, inhabit Cornwall – than the rest of the human race ...[52] Hillaby's encounters with the Cornish are rare, as we have seen, and those he does meet are unremarkable. Having covered seventy miles in over two days of walking he met 'nobody who [came] immediately to mind except an intemperate priest and a very sober publican'.[53] And the priest, it should be noted, was a visitor to Cornwall. Theroux, using a very broad brush, shows no more interest in painting a detailed picture of the local population. For him, the Cornish fall into two types: fishermen and farmers. The former keep to themselves and avoid visitors while the latter have applied the techniques of farming to the holiday trade, 'treat[ing] tourists like livestock – feeding them, fencing them in, and getting them to move to new pastures'. And presumably animal welfare is not high on their list of priorities as 'The loathing for tourists and outsiders in Cornwall was undisguised'.[54] The presence of these visitors is tolerated only on account of the opportunities they provide for financial gain. This 'farmed tourist' trope recurs in Gogarty's account. While it is hard-working incomers who run many of the small businesses in the tourist sector in Cornwall, it is the locals, 'farmers with huge tracts of land', who exploit the visitors: 'Instead of farming sheep, they open their fields to paying cars and fleece the visitors'.[55]

The Cornish then continue to exhibit the duplicity noted by Manning-Sanders but now they welcome the tourists only so that they can rip them off. However, the hostility shown to holidaymakers does not deter visitors but rather reinforces their own sense of superiority, since they are comforted in their belief that the local economy depends on their presence. This then validates the use of a third world discourse in which Cornwall is seen as completely reliant on revenue generated by tourism, which means that however much the Cornish might like to dispense with visitors they are in no position to do since, as one holiday maker confides to Theroux, 'Kick out the tourists and [the Cornish] wouldn't 'ave a penny'.[56]

From contemplation to consumption

Although the view that the Cornish would be penniless without visitors is an exaggeration, tourism undoubtedly makes a significant contribution to the Cornish economy, with around three million visitors to Cornwall annually.[57] What brings so many people to Cornwall? Urry observes, in relation to social spaces wholly or partly dependent on tourists, that 'visitors are attracted by the place myths that surround and constitute such places.'[58] Romanticism provided the place myth and industrialism supplied the means to transport the visitors. At the heart of romantic travel, according to Duncan and Gregory, was 'a passion for the wildness of nature, cultural difference and the desire to be immersed in local colour.'[59] Initially this was a passion reserved for the bourgeoisie but by the twentieth century the development of tourism infrastructure extended the opportunities for travel to the lower middle and working classes who in turn sought a romantic experience but one which was 'well ordered and regimented – a sort of "industrialized" romanticism' ...[60] But while Duncan and Gregory argue that places are still viewed through much the same romantic frame as in the nineteenth century, Lash and Urry emphasise that in the postmodern shift from 'high culture' to 'high street' 'What is consumed in tourism are visual signs and sometimes simulacrum'.[61] It is argued here that the development of Cornish tourism exemplifies these processes and that they are illustrated in the texts analysed.

The romanticized place myth of Cornwall as an ancient and mysterious Celtic land was constructed by writers and artists in the late nineteenth century as the county's mining industry fell into decline.[62] In his *Rambles Beyond Railways*, first published in 1851, Wilkie Collins drew a picture of a remote county, 'still too rarely visited', promising to tell his readers of 'the grand and varied scenery; the mighty Druid relics; the quaint legends; the deep, dark mines; the venerable remains of early Christianity; and the pleasant primitive population of the county of CORNWALL.'[63] The coming of the railway following the opening in 1859 of Brunel's bridge across the Tamar ensured that Cornwall did not remain a rarely visited place. A skilful marketing campaign by the Great Western Railway promoting Cornwall as an exotic, Mediterranean-like destination helped turn the trickle of visitors into a steady stream. In the 1950s and 1960s this stream turned into a flood when the spread of car ownership brought the age of mass tourism to Cornwall.[64] Representations of Cornwall in the works under study reflect these developments. While there is continuity in viewing Cornwall as a picturesque place, mass tourism is associated with an increasing tendency to consume this place through signs and images.

The picturesqueness of Cornwall can be read off from the itineraries which the writers construct. Each destination, selected from a paradigmatic set of possible places to visit, acts as a sign which is combined with others as the journey progresses. The same places recur with regularity: Polperro, Polruan, Fowey, Mevagissey, Lizard, Penzance, Newlyn, Land's End, St Ives, Newquay, Padstow, Tintagel. These towns stand for Cornwall but what meaning do they have? At one level, since meaning is relational, Cornwall is also represented as '*not-*' Camborne, St Austell or Bodmin and so on. But signs are made up of the signifier or form and the signified or concept. What concepts are associated with the places visited and those avoided? For Hillaby,

St Ives is 'picturesque',[65] while Theroux finds its bay 'sublime',[66] and Gogarty is under the spell of 'its charms'.[67] Polperro is commented on for 'its extreme picturesqueness'[68] and described as 'pretty' by both Gogarty and Theroux.[69] Manning-Sanders mentions Camborne, St Austell and Bodmin but hurries on past dismissing them as '[without] claim to beauty', 'uninteresting' and 'drab'[70] while Theroux abandons plans to visit Par because it is 'ugly'.[71] The pattern which emerges is one in which the places considered worthy of a visit are associated with beauty while those shunned are conceptualized as ugly. Cornwall, then, is represented through the itineraries as a picturesque coastline with a hinterland that is not the 'real' Cornwall. This explains how Aitch, who, although alighting from his train in St Austell, can comment that he does not have '[his] first experience of Cornwall proper' until reaching his hotel in Fowey.[72]

These itineraries are not simply texts, however. As Duncan and Gregory remind us, travel writing is produced by 'corporeal subjects moving through material landscapes'.[73] How writers travel through these landscapes is also revealing. In four of the five works studied here the means of transport are explicitly stated: Hillaby walks; Theroux combines walking and trains; Aitch uses trains and buses while Gogarty drives a motorhome. Manning-Sanders' account, which at times tends more to the guidebook, suggests that she moves around in a motor car but makes many excursions on foot to isolated sites. In this respect she and Hillaby are situated closer to their nineteenth century predecessors, for whom walking was seen as an aesthetic choice.[74] Walking, of course, enables the traveller to experience directly the material landscapes of the wild and sublime, which in most cases will be remote from human settlement. Manning-Sanders, lamenting the disfiguring of places like Mevagissey and Looe by the holiday trade, is at a loss to explain why visitors do not take to the footpaths. So, while these writers continue the tradition of rambling beyond railways, Theroux relies mostly on trains to get around, walking only occasionally. His chapter devoted to Cornwall, titled 'The Cornish Explorer', is named after the ticket he buys which allows him 'to go anywhere in Cornwall, on any train.'[75] This, of course, is not quite accurate since it does not allow him to go *anywhere* in Cornwall but only to those places on the rail network. His personal itinerary, then, is very much determined by the infrastructure put in place to develop tourism. Thus he uses the branch lines to visit St Ives and Looe, walking from there to Par only to catch the train to Newquay, where he stays in a B&B. Theroux's experience of Cornwall, then, is that of the industrial romantic. Likewise, Aitch makes use of different forms of public transport: the train to bring him down to Cornwall, buses to move around within Cornwall and the aeroplane from Newquay to return to London. On an excursion to see the Eden Project he takes the bus as far as St Blazey Gate but then decides to walk the rest of the way, but it is a choice motivated by ecological considerations rather than aesthetic ones, for which he is rewarded with a reduction on the entrance fee. Gogarty's motorhome allows him to construct a personal itinerary but one which is constrained by the size of the vehicle, often unsuited to the roads, which 'shrink' as soon as he enters Cornwall, and by the need to stay on caravan parks.[76] There is, then, in the later writers a tendency to move around and experience Cornwall in just the same way as the millions of tourists who come every year.

Cornwall is now primarily experienced through its tourist and heritage industry. The iconic signifiers of Cornwall in the earlier accounts are its ancient stones, redolent of a Celtic past and land beyond time, but by the 1980s the signs representing Cornwall are those with which its 'towns are now festooned'.[77] These market the romantic representations of Cornwall. In St Ives boutiques, carvings are advertised as 'Our Celtic Heritage'[78] while in Mevagissey pasties are sold from 'The Celtic Knot' shop.[79] A sign promoting 'Cornish palms for sale'[80] offers purchasers a transportable signifier of Cornwall's exoticism.

This consumption of signs problematizes the relationship between representation and reality. Manning-Sanders illustrates her account with a photograph of the weighing of fish at St Ives, a scene which, while picturesque in the Newlyn School style, reflects a working environment and not one prepared for tourist consumption. Gogarty, in contrast, illustrates his travelogue with a photograph of Newyln's Pilchard Works. Turning his back on the harbour, which does not correspond to his imaginative geography of Cornwall, he visits the heritage centre in search of 'more edifying fishermen's tales'[81] in the museum's exhibits, which represent for him Cornwall as it should be. And the tale he hears there of how the humble pilchard conquered an up-market niche through its rebranding as the Cornish Sardine exemplifies the process by which it is more the signs which are consumed than the material fish they represent.

The tourist industry not only shapes representations of Cornwall but it also ensures that relationships are mediated in economic terms. The picturesqueness of Cornwall may still engender profound emotions but it comes at a price. Gogarty calculates that the sea vistas fellow campers enjoy at Heligan 'probably cost them £7 or £8.'[82] Pound signs, the new signifiers of Cornwall, are scattered across the texts of Gogary and Aitch like menhirs strewn across Penwith: £2.95 purchases a crab pasty at Rick Stein's, £9.80 an entrance ticket to the Eden Project, £25 buys a surfing session at Newquay, £30 a flight from Stanstead, £480,000 a dream home and £1.2 million a Stanhope Forbes. By 2007 it seems that Cornwall in this age of Industrial Romanticism is essentially a retail experience.

Conclusion

The tourist industry is not only able to shape representations of places but it also positions travellers as mass tourists. Visitors move within both a discourse which is constituted by a certain set of representations and the material infrastructure of the industry which reinforces these representations. It has been argued here that a shift has occurred in the representational regime within which Cornwall is viewed. The aesthetics of high Romanticism have been subverted by the economics of mass consumerism as the tourist industry becomes the dominant influence fashioning representations of Cornwall, commodifying Cornwall for urban consumption. This process, which was set in motion in the early twentieth century, clearly accelerated at the end of the century, as illustrated here in the body of works studied. While in the immediate post-war period Cornwall could still be experienced as if through the contemplation of some canvas created by a Victorian artist, now it is available for purchase as a mass-produced reproduction.

Edward Said has distinguished between what he terms latent and manifest Orientalism. Changes that occur in knowledge of the Orient, he argues, are almost exclusively manifest differences of form and style rather than content. What remains constant is latent Orientalism: the characterization of the Orient as separate, backward, eccentric, degenerate and so forth.[83] We have been arguing here that a similar process is at work in representations of Cornwall. Since romanticism remapped Cornwall as a space of wild nature and cultural difference populated by an inferior people, the map has not been substantially redrawn. We have seen in the works in this study that it is not the characterization of Cornwall as different which changes, but the form it is given: from 'foreign past' to 'strange present'. Likewise the Cornish continue to be represented as a subject people who are created by their neighbours to the East, whether it is the result of war or mass tourism. And while the map of Cornwall still shows the same towns around its coast, the images which illustrate it have changed. Gone are the sea monsters, mermaids and megaliths, replaced by the Rick Stein's restaurants, the Pilchard Works and the Eden Project.

Notes and references

1. See J. Urry, 'Transports of delight', *Leisure Studies*, 20:4 (2001), pp. 237–45.
2. Z. Bauman, 'From Pilgrim to Tourist – or a Short History of Identity', in S. Hall and P. Du Gay, *Questions of Cultural Identity* (London, 1996), p. 30.
3. Bauman cited in Urry, 'Transports of delight', p. 240.
4. S. Lash and J. Urry, *Economies of Space and Time* (London, 1994), p. 272.

5. W. Schivelbush cited in Urry, 'Transports of delight', p. 237.

6. J. Duncan and D. Gregory, 'Introduction' in J. Duncan and D. Gregory, *Writes of Passage: Reading travel writing* (London 1999), pp. 1–13.

7. Lash and Urry, *Economies of Space and Time.*

8. J. Fabian, 'Presence and Representation: The Other and Anthropological Writing', *Critical Inquiry* 16:4 (1990), pp. 753–72.

9. S. Hall, 'Introduction', in S. Hall (ed.), *Representation: Cultural Representations and Signifying Practices* (Sage Publications, 1997), pp. 1–11.

10. The ensuing discussion draws heavily on the following works: Fabian, 'Presence and Representation'; A. Thwaites, L. Davis and W. Mules, *Tools for Cultural Studies: An Introduction* (South Melbourne, 1994); S. Hall, 'The Work of Representation', in S. Hall (ed.), *Representation: Cultural Representations and Signifying Practices* (London, 1997), pp. 13–74; H. Bertens, *Literary Theory: The Basics* (London, 2001); D. Chandler, *Semiotics: The Basics* (London, 2002).

11. Culler, cited in Chandler, *Semiotics*, pp. 79.

12. The works studied are: R. Manning-Sanders, *The West of England* (London, 1949); J. Hillaby, *Journey Through Britain* (London, 1968); P. Theroux, *The Kingdom by the Sea* (London, 1984 (1983)); I. Aitch, *A Fete Worse Than Death* (London, 2004); P. Gogarty, *The Coast Road* (London, 2007).

13. D. Tavares and M. Brosseau, 'The Representation of Mongolia in contemporary travel writing: imaginative geographies of a travellers' frontier', *Social and Cultural Geography*, 7:2 (2006), pp. 299–317.

14. The approach used here is modelled on that employed by Tavares and Brosseau, 'The Representation of Mongolia'.

15. R. Perry, 'The Changing Face of Celtic Tourism in Cornwall, 1875–1975', in P. Payton (ed.), *Cornish Studies: Seven* (Exeter, 1999), pp. 94–106.

16. B. Deacon, *A Concise History of Cornwall* (Cardiff, 2007).

17. E. Said, *Orientalism* (New York, 1979), p. 20.

18. Cited in Chandler, *Semiotics*, p. 196.

19. P. Theroux, *The Kingdom by the Sea* (London, 1984), p. 18.

20. B. Deacon, 'The hollow jarring of the distant steam engines': images of Cornwall between West Barbary and Delectable Duchy' in Ella Westland (ed.), *Cornwall: The Cultural Construction of Place* (Penzance, 1997), pp. 7–24.

21. Tavares and Brosseau, 'The Representation of Mongolia', p. 302.

22. Fabian, 'Presence and Representation', p. 754.

23. Hall, *Representation*, p. 237.

24. Manning-Sanders, *The West of England*, pp. 40, 69.

25. Theroux, *The Kingdom by the Sea*, p. 120.

26. For discussions of representations of Wales and Ireland see P.J. Duffy, 'Writing Ireland: Literature and Art in the Representation of Irish Places' in B. Graham, (ed.), *'In Search of Ireland*, London, 1997, pp. 1–16; P. Gruffudd, D.T. Herbert and A. Piccini, 'In Search of Wales: travel writing and narratives of difference, 1918–50', *Journal of Historical Geography*, 26:4, 2000, pp. 589–604.

27. Manning-Sanders, *The West of England*, p. 39.

28. Manning-Sanders, *The West of England*, p. 39.

29. Manning-Sanders, *The West of England*, p. 42.

30. Hillaby, *Journey Through Britain*, p. 25.

31. See R.S. Peckham, 'The Exoticism of the Familiar and the Familiarity of the

Exotic' in J. Duncan and D. Gregory (eds), *Writes of Passage: Reading travel writing* (London, 1999), pp. 164–84.

32. Hillaby, *Journey Through Britain*, p. 42.
33. Theroux, *The Kingdom by the Sea*, p. 113.
34. Theroux, *The Kingdom by the Sea*, p. 14.
35. Aitch, *A Fete Worse Than Death*, p. 255.
36. Aitch, *A Fete Worse Than Death*, p. 254.
37. Aitch, *A Fete Worse Than Death*, p. 248.
38. Tavares and Brosseau, 'The Representation of Mongolia', p. 300.
39. L. Guelke and J.K. Guelke, 'Imperial eyes on South Africa: reassessing travel narratives', *Journal of Historical Geography*, 30 (2004), pp. 11–31.
40. Tavares and Brosseau, 'The Representation of Mongolia', p. 302.
41. Tavares and Brosseau, 'The Representation of Mongolia', p. 302.
42. Manning-Sanders, *The West of England*, p. 39.
43. Manning-Sanders, *The West of England*, p. 39.
44. Theroux, *The Kingdom by the Sea*, p. 121.
45. Theroux, *The Kingdom by the Sea*, p. 117.
46. Threroux, *The Kingdom by the Sea*, p. 115.
47. See Deacon, *A Concise History of Cornwall*, p. 216.
48. Aitch, *A Fete Worse Than Death*, p. 254.
49. Gogarty, *The Coast Road*, pp. 122, 134.
50. R. Barthes, *Mythologies*. Seuil, 1957, p. 122.
51. Aitch, *A Fete Worse Than Death*, p. 251.
52. Manning-Saanders, *The West of England*, pp. 39–41.
53. Hillaby, *Journey Through Britain*, p. 40.
54. Theroux, *The Kingdom by the Sea*, p. 117.
55. Gogarty, *The Coast Road*, p. 138.
56. Theroux, *The Kingdom by the Sea*, p. 130.
57. See A. Williams and G. Shaw, 'The Age of Mass Tourism' in P. Payton (ed.), *Cornwall Since The War: The Contemporary History of a European Region* (Redruth, 1993), pp. 84–97.
58. J. Urry, *Consuming Places* (London, 1995), p. 194.
59. Duncan and Gregory, 'Introduction', p. 6.
60. Duncan and Gregory, 'Introduction', p. 7.
61. Lash and Urry, *Economies of Space and Time*, p. 272.
62. Deacon, *A Concise History of Cornwall*, pp. 181–2.
63. W. Collins, *Rambles Beyond Railways* London, 1982 [1851], p. 2.
64. Williams and Shaw, 'The Age of Mass Tourism', p. 87.
65. Hillaby, *Journey Through Britain*, p. 25.
66. Theroux, *The Kingdom by the Sea*, p. 115.
67. Gogarty, *The Coast Road*, p. 127.
68. Manning-Sanders, *The West of England*, p. 69.
69. Gogarty, *The Coast Road*, p.111; Theroux, *The Kingdom by the Sea*, p. 117.
70. Manning-Sanders, *The West of England*, pp. 60–8.
71. Theroux, *The Kingdom by the Sea*, p. 123.
72. Aitch, *A Fete Worse Than Death*, p. 252.
73. Duncan and Gregory, 'Introduction', p. 5.
74. Urry, *Consuming Places*, p. 202.

75. Theroux, *The Kingdom by the Sea*, p. 113.
76. Gogarty, *The Coast Road*, p. 111.
77. Gogarty, *The Coast Road*, p. 126.
78. Theroux, *The Kingdom by the Sea*, p. 115.
79. Gogarty, *The Coast Road*, p. 114.
80. Gogarty, *The Coast Road*, p. 126.
81. Gogarty, *The Coast Road*, p. 121.
82. Gogarty, *The Coast Road*, p. 114.
83. Said, *Orientalism*, p. 206.

9

Cornish Identity
Vague Notion or Social Fact?

Joanie Willett

Introduction

This article discusses recent ethnographic research on 'Cornish identity' (see Appendix). It investigates the degree to which this identity might be considered a 'social fact' by examining the extent, form and depth to which it appears to exist in contemporary Cornwall. The specific purpose of the research project described below was to ascertain whether individuals within Cornwall today felt that there was a distinct sense of Cornish identity, as opposed to or alongside majority 'national' (English or British) identities. As this article demonstrates, the research discovered that a developed sense of 'Cornishness' – often opposed to 'Englishness' and 'Britishness' – does exist within Cornwall, and that this was linked primarily to genealogy and perceptions of Cornish descent. However, it was also found that persons with a more recent association with Cornwall, and who were well integrated into a 'Cornish way of life', could also feel a strong sense of belonging and local identity. This article concludes, therefore, that contemporary Cornish identity, while undeniably complex, is more than a vague notion and can be best understood as a 'social fact'.

Durkheim[1] defined 'social facts' as those things that can be regarded as 'realities'. They exist independently of any conceptual apparatus and the will of individuals, and so can be discovered through empirical investigation. They are not hypothetical but they are of varying strength. For Durkheim, social facts exist on a graduated scale, from being – at the top end of the scale – a 'morphological fact' fully integrated into the 'substratum of collective life', through to 'institutionalized norms' and 'social currents', and on finally to the weaker 'transitory outbreaks' of waves of enthusiasm at the bottom of the scale.

If Cornish identity exists as a social fact, therefore, it can be discovered through empirical research. Likewise, if it does exist, then one might expect it to lie somewhere on the graduated scale proposed by Durkheim. For it to constitute a 'morphological fact', the overwhelming majority of persons within Cornwall would have to view themselves as 'Cornish' and, moreover, this would have to be largely a primary identity. An 'institutionalised norm' would expect that the majority of respondents in any survey would self-identify as 'Cornish', and that local institutions and media would support this. A 'social current' would have a significant minority identifying as 'Cornish', although such a movement might be perceived by the majority as subversive or marginal. A 'transitory outbreak', meanwhile, would see only a very small number of persons calling themselves 'Cornish'. Beyond this, there might be the occasional local event which might prompt a sense of 'Cornish pride', but here Cornish identity would be little more than a 'vague notion', holding little sustained personal meaning for individuals.

Identity and nationalism

There are several ways of understanding identity formation. 'Structural' interpretations see identity as constituting the shared norms and values within a culture or way of life. Here identity is represented as a social product in which identities are 'learned' by members of a cultural group, through a process of socialization. Alternatively, 'constructionalist' approaches see identity as a set of meanings and symbols that are shared amongst a group,[2] a phenomenon that undergoes a process of continual updating, modification and renegotiation through interaction with others against the background of a strong commitment to place.[3] While this also assumes a degree of socialization, there is an implication that identity formation is dynamic and that identities experienced now are likely to be different to those of the past. The third main explanatory paradigm is that of 'postmodernism'. This perspective proposes that there is no 'dominant culture' as such. Instead, individuals adopt the cultural values and thus identities that they have chosen for themselves.[4] By extension, such identities do not necessarily have to be based on specific geographical locations or interpersonal networks,[5] it being argued that in post-traditional societies self-identity is reflexive rather than determined.[6]

The common thread running through each of the above is the view that identities are a group phenomenon; a recognition of individuals having something in common with one another.[7] Erikson[8] has stressed that in addition to this 'commonality' there is also 'continuity' of the group over time. When a group becomes too large for individuals to 'know' all other group members, it begins to develop a wider identity of its own to which all members can subscribe. This group identity is bound by shared beliefs, language or ethnicity.[9] Shared meanings within the group can be compared to 'private jokes' within a family, where an everyday phrase may be considered as 'funny' due to a past event. Outsiders do not understand the joke until they have learned the shared meaning.

Glover believes that newcomers to a community can assimilate into the new identity through a process of learning, a view which complements both 'constructionist' and 'structuralist' approaches. Postmodernism has fewer problems with identity inclusivity, and so has little difficulty in accepting Glover's position. However, the psychoanalytical work of Erikson suggests that socialization within the family may be critical for identity transmission. Nevertheless, he also acknowledges that although individual identity formation follows the identity crises of adolescence, identity development is a part of a life-long process as adults come into contact with new situations. There is, then, common ground between Glover and Erikson, with room for the outsider to acquire a new identity. In contrast, Greer[10] argues strongly that identity is much more fixed, so that (for example) the acquisition of feminine anatomical features does not make a man become a woman. Although this refers to gender identity specifically, it does raise wider questions regarding the extent to which an identity can be learned or otherwise acquired. However, despite these concerns, the theoretical consensus infers that socialization within the family can be modified or overridden in later life, so that individuals may indeed come to identify with a culture different to that in which they were raised. As we shall see, this has important implications for understanding the complexity of contemporary Cornish identity.

'National identity' refers to the identity of a group of people that is brought together by geography, in the sense of occupying or identifying with a specific 'national' territory. This occupancy or identification is essentially 'political' in its implications. Smith[11] agues that nations arise out of shared cultural and political phenomena, deploying myths of national origin, genealogical descent, territory and/or common ancestry as a basis for a political community. However, these forms of identification are sometimes contested, leading to territorial fragmentation as competing 'nations' vie for the same geographical space. This leads to Anderson's classification of nations as 'imagined' communities. As well as 'imagining' their national territories, these communities also 'imagine' their own membership, for 'not even members of the smallest political community will know most of their fellow members, meet them or hear from them'.[12]

'Nationalism' is the assertion of an imagined national community's supposed right to self-determination within its imagined territory. Frequently, contemporary discourses which offer explanations for a rise in nationalist sentiment point to a postmodern lack of social cohesion, where the forces of modernity and globalization have led to a tension between the global and the local.[13] Structuralist explanations regard conflict due to the changing structures of a society as being the root of rising nationalisms. It is also argued that a decline in religion may have led to a search for alternative meta-narratives, such as nationalism.[14] Others continue to point to the existence of unresolved economic, social and political conflicts as the cause of modern nationalisms, or – following a political economy perspective – may interpret nationalism as a device deployed by competing elite groups.[15] Furthermore, it is recognized that nationalisms are not homogenous. 'Self-determination' may mean different things in different contexts. It might be separatist or autonomist, with the desire for an independent nation-state, or it might be federalist or devolutionary, with the wish for more regionally based local decision-making. It might be 'civic', more concerned with institutions and offering inclusivity for all peoples within the territory, or it might be 'ethnic', with membership of the nation being defined by a presumed shared genetic heritage.[16]

The concept of identity is further complicated by the phenomenon of dual, multiple or hybrid identities – the fact that individuals may have many layers of identity, rather than just one, and move between one and another depending on context or circumstance. For example, Moreno[17] found that less than a third of Spaniards expressed a single territorial identity. Instead, individuals tended to hold at least dual identities, such as being both Spanish and Catalan.[18] A similar situation applies in England. The Morgan Stanley study,[19] which investigated the strength of 'county' identities in England, found that the residents of nine counties registered a 'local patriotism' (identification with county identity) of more than 30 per cent, with Cornwall having the greatest such identification at 44 per cent. To measure these dual or multiple identities, Moreno devised a scale that scored the extent of an individual's allegiance to different identities. Subsequently, Anderson used this scale for a study of Scotland and Wales, and found that here too the majority of individuals held dual allegiances, centered around being Scottish/Welsh and British.[20] He also found that in Wales and Scotland readership of UK 'national' newspapers increased 'British' identification, possibly because of the assimilative capacity of the 'national' media. In contrast, readers of 'local' papers were more likely to have a stronger local identity; although Anderson suggests that this may be an effect rather than a cause, as the media is reflective of the identities of its readership. Anderson also found that, especially in Wales, 'local' religious affiliations were also important in fostering 'local' identity.

Cornwall and identity formation

The above discussion has important implications for the study of Cornish identity. Alongside Durkheim's 'social facts', there might also be consideration of Moreno's scale for measuring alternate allegiances. Similarly, issues of 'civic' and 'ethnic' identity need to be explored. So too do those component considerations – such as newspaper readership and religious affiliation – which in Anderson's study were shown to be important in Scotland and Wales, and which we might speculate could be similarly significant in Cornwall.

Moreover, in discussing contemporary Cornish identity, it is important to understand the historical processes that have underpinned its formation over time. Recently, Stoyle has provided a Cornu-centric perspective on early-modern Cornwall.[21] Like Smith, Stoyle recognizes the importance of myths of origin, and shows how Cornish imaginings of their descent from Corineus, comrade-in-arms of Brutus, founder of Britain, fuelled a Cornish ethnicity that saw Cornwall as separate from England. Stoyle concentrates on rebellion and repression in early-modern Cornwall, from 1497 to the events of the Civil War. Kent, meanwhile, identifies a more subtle process of ideological assimilation in this period, with the Cornish cast in the role of the increasingly subservient 'other'.[22] The Cornish language continued to be an important marker of 'difference' at this time, although it was increasingly confined to the far west and the lower classes. Dolly Pentreath, sometimes described as the last Cornish speaker, died in 1778,[23] although there is some evidence to suggest that fragments of the language were still being used into the nineteenth century.[24]

In the eighteenth and nineteenth centuries, this earlier Cornish identity was supplanted by a new, self-confident identity, based on industrialization and centered around mining and Methodism.[25] Methodism became the dominant religious and moral force within the Cornish working and middle classes,[26] and Milden has argued that Methodism became the 'spiritual identity' of modern Cornwall, with nonconformity the symbol of a Cornish radical political identity. This dominance was remarked upon by A.L. Rowse, who observed that Anglican 'church' people in mid Cornwall were a distinct minority by the early twentieth century.[27] But despite the apparent industrial might of the Cornish economy, by the early 1900s a catastrophic decline in mining and the effects of mass emigration had resulted in a culture of poverty and dependency. One consequence was the attempt by the Cornish Celtic Revival, a largely middle-class movement, to try to rebuild 'Celtic Cornwall' anew. These Revivalists resurrected the Cornish language and constructed new symbols of Cornishness. Some, like 'the Cornish national tartan' and 'the Cornish kilt', were very clearly revivalist inventions. Nevertheless, despite their constructed nature, these symbols were adopted by many people in

Cornwall, and their use continues to increase.[28] For example, Gorseth Kernow (the Cornish Gorsedd), formed in 1928, exists today to give expression to 'the national Celtic spirit of Cornwall' by promoting its literature, art, history, music and language, and the flag of St Piran may be found flying all across Cornwall.[29] Yet Cornwall remains one of the economically poorest areas of the United Kingdom,[30] resulting among other things in periodic calls for greater Cornish economic autonomy.[31]

Not surprisingly, given this history and its suggestion of an enduring though changing identity, there is an existing (though small) social science literature on contemporary Cornish identity, some of it based on qualitative and quantitative ethnographic research. For example, Ireland found during his study of two small coastal towns that 'Cornishness' was a 'deeply emotional and personal statement about being part of a living culture' and that a shared sense of Cornishness existed between both locals and in-migrants.[32] Others, however, have questioned the extent to which newcomers can be assimilated to this 'Cornishness', given the scale of recent in-migration: between 1961 and 2000 the population of Cornwall grew by a half, mainly due to in-migration.[33] Nonetheless, research findings reported in 2001 suggested comparatively high levels of Cornish identification amongst 15 to 18-year-olds in Cornwall. This research found that 29 per cent of a sample in this age bracket defined themselves as 'Cornish', and that this identification was more common in the west than in the east. This east–west decay was explained in part by the importance placed by many respondents in the sample upon place of birth: in east Cornwall a great many people have been born in hospitals in Plymouth, just across the Cornwall/Devon border.[34]

Despite these existing studies, none thus far has attempted to represent a cross-section of the population of Cornwall. Nor have existing studies attempted to differentiate between 'civic' and 'ethnic' conceptions of Cornish identity, or the criteria that individuals use to decide their (and other people's) Cornishness. Likewise, existing studies have been unclear whether Cornishness is predominantly a primary or secondary identification, a critical factor in investigating Cornish identity as a 'social fact'. Furthermore, there has been little discussion of the mechanisms of assimilation (should they exist) by which in-migrants might be integrated into local culture, and there is little understanding of in-migrant attitudes to Cornishness. The research reported below, therefore, was undertaken to begin to make good these deficiencies and to pursue the research questions prompted by the above discussion.

Aims and objectives

The study sought to provide a baseline measurement of the extent, form and depth of contemporary (early twenty-first century) Cornish identity, with the aim of determining whether this identity could be considered a 'social fact' according to the criteria proposed by Durkheim. Surveys were made of a sample population across Cornwall, in pursuit of the following objectives:

1. To determine the proportion of the sample which considered itself to be Cornish, and whether this identification was exclusive of being English or British, and to gauge the extent to which Cornishness was a significant part of the identity of those individuals who did not think of themselves as Cornish.
2. To identify those factors that survey respondents felt made a person Cornish: specifically, to consider and compare issues of family socialization, conceptions of history and genealogy, and 'civic' versus 'ethnic' constructions of identity.
3. To investigate whether there was any link between Cornish identity and the extent to which respondents were integrated or institutionalized into local information resources, such as religious affiliation and newspaper readership.

Methodology

Although identity is a multifaceted phenomenon, lending itself to qualitative understanding, for this research exercise a 'constructionist' methodology and qualitative methods seemed impractical. Instead, it was decided to follow an 'objectivist' epistemology, a positivist theoretical perspective and primarily quantitative methods. In using this epistemology, it was assumed that 'truth' and 'meaning' exist independently of consciousness; thus 'identity' is always present, whether an individual is aware of its existence or not. This, in turn, allows for the discovery of 'meaning'. In other words, although identity is not tangible and is located in the mind, an objectivist approach argues that 'Understandings and meanings are objectified within the people that we are studying', and so can be discovered though research.[35]

There is always a risk that quantitative survey techniques might constrain possible responses to fit with pre-conceived categories that the researcher may have.[36] This could adversely affect the validity of the data collected. To avoid this, focus groups were used prior to designing the questionnaire, in an attempt to acquire a deeper understanding of how people in Cornwall see the issue of identity. Adding this qualitative element gave the benefit of 'both worlds', and dealt with the potential shortcomings of a purely quantitative approach.[37]

Method

Design and compilation of the questionnaire followed two focus group meetings. These focus groups contained representatives of different sectors of the community and different areas of Cornwall. After completion of a pilot, the questionnaire research was carried out in the main shopping streets of sixteen towns throughout Cornwall, together with one village in mid-Cornwall, collecting a sample of 150.

Random samples appear to have a greater chance of being 'representative' than other methods of sample selection.[38] However, none of the available sampling frames provided information on all of the inhabitants of Cornwall, so a genuine random sample would have been impossible to achieve.[39] Additionally, use of alternative frames would have necessitated a postal survey, for which the response rate is typically around 20 per cent, making it an inefficient method, even without the risk of increasing non-response error.[40]

Instead, respondents were selected at random in the shopping districts of a number of towns throughout Cornwall. This method also enabled the surveys to be completed immediately, and face to face. However, the researchers recognized that the sampling frame was skewed in favour of people who have the time or inclination to visit their local shopping centres. Some of the surveys were undertaken at weekends, in order to boost the chances of interviewing working people. Even during weekdays the range of individuals abroad was considerable. Nevertheless, a degree of researcher bias was possible, as the interviewer may have been more likely to speak to some types of people than others, or certain members of society may have been more or less inclined to agree to the interview.[41]

There is also the chance that the individuals who allowed themselves to be interviewed during the research process were more likely to have an interest in the issue being investigated, and so be over-represented amongst respondents.[42] This, in turn, may have meant an exaggeratedly high rate of positive responses to questions about Cornish identity, reflecting the willingness of possibly similar individuals to stop and talk about the issue.[43] However, in practice a number of people who claimed no affinity with Cornwall at all, and little interest in the subject, allowed themselves to be interviewed. Fielding and Gilbert, although expressing preference for random samples, also remind us that no one method can create a sample that is truly representative of society.[44]

The sample used in this study is relatively small, especially compared to the minimum of 1500 interviewed by Anderson in Scotland and Wales. However, Fielding and Gilbert note that the British Crime Survey (BCS) generalizes by interviewing between 1000 and 2000 people, out of the UK population of 59 million. Cornwall has a population of 500,000.[45] This investigation interviewed a number ten times fewer than the BCS to cover a community over one hundred times smaller. Additionally, some authorities feel that very large sample increase the effects of sampling error.[46]

Cornwall is currently split into six districts for local government purposes, and these convenient divisions were employed for this research. The number of respondents sought for each district was determined according to the percentage of population each district contributes to the overall population of Cornwall. For example, despite being vastly different in geographical size, the Restormel and Kerrier districts contributed a similar proportion of respondents (30 and 29 respectively), whereas 22 interviews were conducted in North Cornwall even though this district covers the largest area. This approach was an attempt at representing each district as equitably as possible.

Participants of both the focus groups and the questionnaire survey were informed at the beginning of the purpose of the study, and what was going to happen during the discussion and to the collected material. They were given the right to withdraw at any time. Additionally, as recordings of the focus group discussions were to form part of the Cornish Audio Visual Archive (CAVA) collection (co-ordinated by the Institute of Cornish Studies), individuals were asked to fill in consent forms stipulating what could be done with the tapes. This was in accordance with CAVA's ethics code, an effort to ensure that people felt able to speak openly and did not feel that their contributions would be exploited or used inappropriately. Anonymity was also guaranteed as part of this 'informed consent'.[47]

The focus groups

Focus group participants were asked if they considered themselves to be 'Cornish', what they thought 'made a person Cornish', and whether conflicting 'inclusive' and 'exclusive' definitions had the effect of 'devaluing' the experiences of either 'indigenous' or 'outsider' individuals. Respondents were also asked whether they felt that 'being Cornish' was complementary to or distinct from 'being English' or 'British'. Those who described themselves as 'non-Cornish' were asked how they saw themselves in relation to issues of identity and Cornwall.

Five persons attended the first focus group, two men and three women.

One participant lived in the North Cornwall district, the remainder were from Restormel. Only one group member considered him/herself to be Cornish. Another admitted 'a Cornish background' but was not born in Cornwall and so did not feel it 'right' to claim a Cornish identity. The remainder were in-migrants of several years standing. The four 'non-Cornish', although hesitating to claim a Cornish identity, nonetheless felt that 'a love of Cornwall' made up an important part of how they saw themselves. This had significant implications for the questionnaire. For Cornish identity to be a 'social fact', did individuals in Cornwall have to feel that it was their *personal* identity, or, for a significant ('non-Cornish') element of the population, could it be simply an environmental influence which contributed alongside other factors to the way in which they considered themselves? It was suggested in the focus group that persons with 'a deep family background' within Cornwall, and who had been born there, formed an 'aristocracy' of 'true' Cornish people. Intriguingly, their existence was thought to contribute significantly to the considerable appeal of Cornwall to outsiders. Incomers, it was argued, could adopt a veneer of Cornish identity as a part of a wider sense of who they were, an acquisition based on feelings of 'belonging' and 'being comfortable' in Cornwall, but could not legitimately be called 'Cornish'.

The group speculated about there being a 'hierarchy of national identities'. By this it was meant that a 'true' indigenous Cornish person could also classify him/herself as 'British', but not as 'English'. 'Cornish' and 'English' were in this context mutually exclusive. However, those in-migrants who acknowledged 'Cornishness' as an influence in the make up of their identities could quite logically admit this 'Cornish' dimension in discussing their 'national identity', but afterwards self-define as 'English' and then 'British', probably in a sort of rank order. Once again, the factors deemed to comprise 'true' Cornish credentials were being born in Cornwall, having a Cornish lineage, and living in Cornwall. Similarly, a sense of 'belonging' and 'feeling comfortable', together with 'a love of Cornwall', continued to make up the more diffuse sense of 'Cornishness' experienced by incomers.

The second focus group was attended by eight people: two males and six females. Seven were from the Kerrier/Penwith districts and one was from Restormel. Half identified themselves as 'Cornish', a quarter as 'non-Cornish', and the remainder were not sure how to identify themselves. This was because, although they were not 'from Cornwall', they considered that they had no other primary identity to declare.

The discussion in this second group raised the suggestion that people who were confident of 'a Cornish pedigree' were more likely to hold 'exclusive' definitions of what is was to 'be Cornish', whereas in-migrants and others with looser affiliations with Cornwall were more likely have 'inclusive' definitions based on feelings of belonging. However, while it was accepted that 'being Cornish' could be an ethnic identity based on 'pedigree', it was argued by some participants that there were also English persons willing to call themselves 'Cornish' because their identification with Cornwall was now greater than their residual 'English' identity. For such people, their expression of Cornish identity might be a conscious decision to be 'different', arising from a sense of being economically and institutionally marginalized in Cornwall, together with resentment that much of the media portrayed a stereotypical view of Cornishness. In contrast to this more 'civic' sense of identity, however, there were those who continued to insist that Cornish identity was an integral and inalienable part of one's self, comparable to gender. Thus it was not possible for an individual to select an alternative identity, 'because being Cornish is a fundamental part of who you are'. This view also insisted that it was not possible to be both Cornish and English.

The questionnaire

The focus group discussions highlighted the following points that needed to be considered during design of the questionnaire:

- The extent to which a sense of 'Cornishness' could constitute *a part* of an individual's identity.
- The need to establish whether respondents had long-standing family connections with Cornwall, or whether their associations were more recent.
- The extent to which a sense of 'belonging', a 'love of Cornwall', and perceptions of Cornwall as economically and institutionally marginalized, could contribute to a feeling of 'Cornishness'.
- The extent to which people calling themselves 'Cornish' also considered themselves 'English' and/or 'British'.

By asking respondents at the beginning of the questionnaire whether they considered themselves to be 'Cornish', it was hoped to achieve an immediate, 'gut' reaction. Question 2 tried to discover the extent to which 'Cornishness' made up an individual's identity. Both these questions contributed towards the achievement of objective 1. Question 3 presented a range of criteria that might be thought to make a person 'Cornish', and respondents were asked to rank the importance of each criterion as a component of Cornish identity, with a five point likert scale ranging from a 'must' to 'not important'. This was of primary significance for objective 2. However, this proved a complex, time-consuming and thought-provoking process, which some people found difficult. Yet it was considered that this was the easiest way to uncover attitudes towards the components of Cornish identity, and the relative intensities with which they were felt. Moreover, the pilot had not suggested that it would be a real problem.

Question 4 used the criteria from the previous question to discover the type of connections that individuals had with Cornwall, thus furnishing a broader picture of the respondents. Question 5 adapted Anderson's Welsh/Scottish/British analysis to the Cornish/English context, to try to show the level of duality between 'local' identity and the 'majority nation'. The subsequent question introduced 'British' into the equation, and a cross-tabulation was made regarding questions 1, 5 and 6, to uncover the primacy or otherwise of Cornish identity (meeting objective 1).

Question 7 attempted to uncover whether respondents saw Cornwall as just another county or as a region/nation like Scotland and Wales, an inquiry relevant to both objective 1 and objective 3. Question 8 asked what bound the Cornish together (ethnicity, economic marginalization, 'belonging', 'love of place'). It was anticipated that these would be used to cross-reference the results of question 3, and so contribute to objective 2. Questions 9–12 provided demographic information to check the representativeness of the sample. The last two questions were about religion and newspaper readership (objective 3).

Findings

Demographic statistics were checked against those from Cornwall County Council (CCC). This provided the proportions that each district contributed to the overall population of Cornwall. Fortuitously, representations of gender and age within the sample followed those for Cornwall as a whole, although the youngest age band was slightly over-represented and the eldest slightly under. This may be because some older people were physically less able to get into towns, or perhaps that they found it easier to reject the approach of the researcher. The structure of occupational figures used by the CCC was rather different to that used in the research, making it difficult to match the two. However, it was easier to judge the skilled non-manual and professional groups, and in these instances the figures from the sample matched within 2.6 per cent. The latter point aside, age, gender and district were found to be representative, and the first two variables occurred without any intentional manipulation. The results for religion seem to be less representative, suggesting that Methodists were under represented and adherents of the Church of England over.[48] It is possible, however, that non-religious people selected

'Church of England' for convenience, as it is the established church, thus skewing the results.

To recap, the first objective was

- To determine the proportion of the sample which considered itself to be Cornish, and whether this identification was exclusive of being English or British, and to gauge the extent to which Cornishness was a significant part of the identity of those individuals who did not think of themselves as Cornish.

Out of 150 respondents, 58.7 per cent called themselves Cornish, 41 per cent felt more Cornish than English (answering either 'Cornish not English' or 'More Cornish than English'), and 56 per cent considered themselves as Cornish instead of British or English. Intriguingly, some respondents who had not identified as 'Cornish' in Question 1 nonetheless selected 'Cornish' options in the subsequent question, indicating both uncertainty and the importance of *choice* in determining identity. However, for the purpose of this objective, such respondents had to be taken out of the analysis of the data-set. After adjustment the total number of 'Cornish' reduced to 44.6 per cent.

By cross-tabulating the Cornish/English scale with the results of Cornish/English/British, it became clear that only three respondents who felt more Cornish than English classified themselves as British, two of these from the 'Cornish not English' option, while none called themselves English. Further, 36 per cent of the sample consistently identified themselves as Cornish across each of the above measures. This is significant as it suggests that over a third of the sample had a primary identity as Cornish.

Correspondingly, there was a reluctance on the part of those identifying as Cornish in Question 1 to later describe as English, with only 4.5 per cent following this path, whilst 18 per cent were willing to call themselves 'British'. However, when using the Cornish/English scale, 30 per cent of participants answering 'Cornish' for Question 1 saw themselves as 'Equally Cornish and English'. Although 3.4 per cent were willing to say that they were 'More English than Cornish', none registered 'English not Cornish'. Since only 13.5 of the total sample thought of themselves as 'English' when offered the choice between this, 'British' and 'Cornish', and only 29 per cent responded as more English than Cornish, the strength of English identity as a whole within Cornwall could be queried.

51.3 per cent of respondents felt that a 'love of Cornwall' made up all or a large part of who they felt themselves to be. This is interesting, as a third of these persons did not self-identify as Cornish in Question 1. Overall, 73 per cent – or nearly three quarters of respondents – saw Cornwall as more than a county and comparable to Scotland and Wales.

Objective 2 set out

- To identify those factors that survey respondents felt made a person Cornish: specifically, to consider and compare issues of family socialization, conceptions of history and genealogy, and 'civic' versus 'ethnic' constructions of identity.

To analyse the responses to Question 3, frequency tables were created. Each 'must' was weighted 5, 'very important', 4 and so on. 'Not important' was not scored. These were added together to give a final weighted total for each choice. All of the results were then added together, and a percentage given to each criterion to describe its share of the overall score. These are displayed in Table 1 and provide a clear picture of the importance placed on genealogy and family history, although being born in Cornwall (not necessarily with any pre-existing family association) was also widely considered important. 'Civic' identifications were viewed as less legitimate. This outcome matched the opinions of the focus groups. Individuals with family connections to Cornwall were more likely to have exclusive definitions of Cornishness, while there was less tolerance of suggestions that individuals might 'learn' or acquire an identity.

Table 1

Criterion	per cent Importance given
Born and bred in Cornwall	16.1
Born in Cornwall, parents from Cornwall	16
Born in Cornwall	14.9
Born in Cornwall, one side of family Cornish	11.2
Feel an affinity with Cornwall and live here	09.2
Born outside of Cornwall, parents Cornish	08.9
Actively involved in the community	08.6
Lived in Cornwall 10 years or more	07.3
Feel an affinity with Cornwall and not live here	04.9
Live in Cornwall, no affinity	02.7
Total	100

From the above data it could be expected that 'ethnicity' would be considered the main factor that 'binds the Cornish together'. However, the results for this Question (Table 2 below, weightings as per Table 1) reveals a more complex picture.

Table 2

What binds the Cornish together?	per cent
Sense of belonging	30.7
Love of place	30.5
Ethnicity/race/blood	24.2
Sense of economic marginalization	14.7
Total	100

Table 2 appears to offer a more nuanced (possibly contradictory) picture, when compared to Table 1, putting 'ethnicity' into third place. In contrast, the emphasis here is on 'love of place' and 'sense of belonging'. It appears that, despite the apparent importance placed on genealogy and family connection, there were also more 'inclusive' factors at work. For example, widespread acceptance of those born in Cornwall as 'Cornish', irrespective of earlier family association, suggested that there was a long-term 'inclusivity' inherent in contemporary Cornish identity formation.

Objective 3 attempted

- To investigate whether there was any link between Cornish identity and the extent to which respondents were integrated or institutionalized into local information resources, such as religious affiliation and newspaper readership.

Perhaps surprisingly, Methodism was ranked the third most popular religious choice – behind C of E and 'None' – but, as noted above, this may reflect 'C of E' as a default position for those non-practising adherents with only weak religious affiliation. (In this study, 75 per cent of those initially declaring as C of E were non-practising). Moreover, while there was an even split in the 'C of E' category between 'locals' (those born in Cornwall or with strong family associations) and 'in-migrants', almost all those self-identifying as Methodist were also 'local'. In other words, a link between Methodism and Cornish identity was observable.

Table 3.   Religion and identity as a percentage of sample

Religion	Religion as per cent of sample	per cent Cornish in Q1	per cent Cornish in Q6	per cent British in Q6	per cent English in Q6	More Cornish than English Q5	More English than Cornish Q5
Methodist	16.3	25.3	22.9	7.0	10.0	28.8	6.4
C of E	40.1	36.8	43.4	30.2	50.0	39.0	36.2
None	26.5	29.9	22.9	39.5	15.0	22.0	29.8
Other	7.5	6.9	7.2	7.0	5.0	6.8	4.3
RC	6.1	0.0	1.2	11.6	15.0	0.0	19.1
Anglican	3.4	1.1	2.4	4.7	5.0	3.4	4.3
Total	100	100	100	100	100	100	100

Indeed, across all the measures in Table 3 Methodism was the religion most closely linked to Cornish identification, followed by the Church of England and the non-religious. The preference of a small minority to self-define as 'Anglican' rather than 'C of E' was interesting. Overall, the apparent link between Methodism and Cornish identity echoed Anderson's findings, especially in Wales

The connection between newspaper readership and Cornish identity was more clear-cut. On almost every measure, and in the manner demonstrated by Anderson in Scotland and Wales, persons reading just a 'local' newspaper had a stronger sense of Cornishness than those who did not, followed by readers of both the 'national' *and* 'local' press. Respondents who read only a 'national' newspaper had, overall, the weakest sense of Cornishness. This suggested the importance of the 'local' media as a vehicle for sharing and transmitting meanings and values, and also as an important mechanism of socialization through which individuals might learn about local issues and develop an enhanced sense of 'belonging'.

Lastly, the research considered the districts within which the respondents lived. The existing literature, as we have seen, suggested that the eastern districts would have a weaker sense of Cornish identity:[49] an east/west continuum would place Caradon and North Cornwall as having the weakest sense of Cornishness, followed by Restormel, then Carrick, then Kerrier, and finally Penwith with the strongest. A 'Cornish' ranking based on percentage results was given to each district for each question, and a mean taken to give an average score for the districts. Table 4 displays the findings.

Table 4. 'Cornishness' ranking of the districts

District	Overall 'Cornishness' rank () = expected	Average 'Cornishness' rank achieved
Penwith	1 (1)	1.8
Caradon	2 (5/6)	2.5
Restormel	3 (4)	2.8
Carrick	4 (3)	3.5
Kerrier	5 (2)	4.6
North Cornwall	6 (5/6)	5.7

The big upset as far as the expected east/west continuum was concerned, was the relative weakness of Cornish identity in Kerrier and its relative strength in Caradon. Given the history of Cornwall, this is counterintuitive, and it does not reflect other recent work on Cornish identity. There is no clear explanation for this, although part of the explanation may lie in Caradon's proximity to urban areas in Devon (especially Plymouth), and thus a perceived or real threat of cultural homogenization. Intriguingly, over the past 30 years both North Cornwall and Caradon have experienced a similar level of population growth (31.5 per cent and 29.6 per cent respectively) whilst Penwith and Kerrier have experienced smaller increases (20 per cent and 19.5 per cent respectively).[50] This points once more to the complexity of identity formation in contemporary Cornwall.

Conclusion

But do these results indicate that Cornish identity is a 'social fact'? As noted earlier, Durkheim theorized about differing levels of social facts, ranging from the 'morphological facts' that are an integral part of society, down to the 'transitory outbreaks' or occasional waves of enthusiasm.

As we have seen, the results of this study showed that, although just over half of respondents thought of themselves as 'Cornish', this identification formed the primary 'national' identity for little more than a third of respondents. In other words, while this was evidence of a high level of consciousness of 'Cornish' as a primary identity, it nonetheless remained a minority primary identification. However, almost three quarters of respondents saw Cornwall as more than just another county, with a status akin to those of Scotland and Wales. Additionally, a small majority felt that a 'love of Cornwall' and a more diffuse sense of Cornishness made up a large part or all of their identity, a view that was more likely to be held by incomers than those who had already self-identified as Cornish. This suggested that, in addition to a strong 'ethnic' Cornish identity – where being Cornish was seen to be dependent on birth or family association – there was also a more inclusive 'civic' identity where other factors of 'belonging' were important. Taken together, this would indicate that a considerable majority of the population felt a strong attachment to Cornwall.

As in Moreno's study in Spain, and Anderson's in Scotland and Wales, where multiple 'national' identities were shown to exist, this research indicated that in Cornwall there was a highly complex relationship between 'Cornish', 'English' and 'British' identities. As in Wales, Methodism was seen as being an important component of Cornish identity, and – as in Anderson's study of Scotland and Wales – choice of newspapers read had a strong bearing on identity.

Overall, we can conclude that the Cornish identity identified in this study may be considered a 'social fact', according to Durkheim's paradigm. It does not display the high level of integration characteristic of a 'morphological fact', yet is considerably stronger than mere 'transitory waves'. It is certainly far more than a 'vague notion'. Perhaps Cornish identity is best understood as being located within Durkheim's 'institutionalized norms', although, paradoxically, the relative absence of Cornish institutions through which to express these norms presents a conundrum worthy of further research. The Cornish identity is also dynamic, with newcomers socialized and assimilated into the identity. Perhaps surprisingly, perceptions of economic and institutional marginalization are less important than other factors in creating a sense of Cornish solidarity. Here again is an important area for future research. Significant too is the apparent strength of Cornish identity in east Cornwall, a finding that also calls for further investigation.

There can be little doubt that Cornish identity is a 'social fact'. It is complex, dynamic, and a significant factor in the lives of the majority of people in Cornwall. It deserves greater academic attention than it has received hitherto, not least from those seeking to understand the politics of identity in the United Kingdom today.

Appendix: Questionnaire –
Cornish Identity, vague notion or social fact?

1. Do you consider yourself to be Cornish?

Yes		No	

2. Do you feel that a love of Cornwall /sense of Cornishness makes up a part of who you are? Please tick

All of who I am	
Large part	
Significant part	
Small part	
None at all	

3. What do you think makes a person Cornish?

Must	1
Very important	2
Important	3
Little bit important	4
Not important	5

1.	Born and bred (3 generations)	
2.	Born, parents brought up in Cornwall	
3.	Born in Cornwall	
4.	Born outside Cornwall, parents Cornish	
5.	Lived in Cornwall 10 years or more	
6.	Feel an affinity with Cornwall and live here	
7.	Feel an affinity with Cornwall, not live here	
8.	Actively involved in the community (in County)	
9.	Live in Cornwall, no affinity	
10.	Other (please specify)	

4. Which of the above best describes you?

(option number)	

5. Do you see yourself as … Please tick one

Cornish not British	
More Cornish than British	
Equally Cornish and British	
More British than Cornish	
British not Cornish	

6. If you had to choose between being Cornish, British and English which would it be?

_____

7. Do you see Cornwall as a distinct region like Scotland or Wales?

Yes		No	

8. What do you think binds the Cornish together?
   Please rank in order of importance. 1 = most important.

Ethnicity/ race/ blood	
Love of place	
Feeling of economic marginalization	
Sense of belonging	
Other please specify	

9. Are you please tick

Male		Female	

10. Please indicate which age bracket best describes you

Up to 25	
26–40	
41–55	
56–70	
71 and over	

11. Which district do you live in?

Kerrier	
Caradon	
Penwith	
Restormal	
N. Cornwall	
Carrick	

12. Please state the occupation of the main earner in your household

_____

13. Please indicate your religion

Methodist	
Roman Catholic	
Anglican	
C of E	
Other	

Are you

Practising		Non-practising	

14. Do you regularly read a

Local newspaper		National newspaper	

Thank you for your participation!

Notes and references

1. Emile Durkheim, edited by S. Lukes, translated by W. Halls, *The Rules of Sociological Method* (Basingstoke, 1982).
2. See D. Abbot, *Culture and Identity* (London, 1998).
3. A. Cohen, *Belonging – Identity and Social Organisation in British Rural Cultures* (Manchester, 1982).
4. See Abbot, *Culture and Identity*.
5. S. Crook, J. Pakulski and M. Waters, *Postmodernization, Change in Advanced Society* (London, 1992).
6. A. Giddens, *Modernity and Self Identity – Self and Society in the Late Modern Age* (Cambridge, 1991).
7. K. Woodward (ed.), *Questioning Identity; Gender, Class, Nation* (London, 2000).
8. E. Erickson, *Identity and the Life Cycle* (London/New York, 1980).
9. J. Glover, *The Philosophy and Psychology of Personal Identity* (Harmondsworth, Middlesex, 1988).
10. G. Greer, *The Whole Woman* (London, 1999).
11. A. Smith, *National Identity* (Harmondsworth, Middlesex, 1991).
12. B. Anderson, *Imagined Communities* (revised edition, London, 1991), p. 6.
13. See Giddens, *Modernity and Self Identity*.
14. R. Anderson, *National Identity and Independence Attitudes; Minority Nationalism in Scotland and Wales*, Centre for Research Into Elections and Social Trends, Working Paper 86 (2001) www.crest.ox.ac.uk
15. J. Coakley (ed.), *The Social Origins of Nationalist Movements, – The Contemporary West European Experience* (London, 1992).
16. Ibid.
17. L. Moreno, *Multiple Identities and Global Meso-Communities*, Unidad de Politicas Comparadas, Working Paper 02–25 (2002).

18. L. Moreno, A. Arriba and A. Serrano, *Multiple Identities in Decentralized Spain: The Case of Catalonia*, Instituto de Estudios Sociales Avanzados, Working Paper 97–06 (1997).
19. M. Stanley, *Patriotism Study*, Morgan Stanley Consumer Banking (London, 2004).
20. See Anderson, *National Identity and Independence Attitudes.*
21. M. Stoyle, *West Britons, Cornish Identities and the Early Modern British State* (Exeter, 2002).
22. A. Kent, 'Art Thou Of Cornish Crew?' Shakespeare, Henry V and Cornish Identity', in P. Payton (ed.), *Cornish Studies: Four* (Exeter, 1996).
23. See Stoyle, *West Britons.*
24. K. Mackinnon, 'Cornish at its Millennium: An Independent Study of the Language Undertaken in 2000', in P. Payton (ed.), *Cornish Studies: Ten* (Exeter, 2002).
25. K. Milden, *Culture of Conversion* (2001) www.marjohn.ac.uk/cornish-history/conf2001milden/index.htm (accessed 5 April 2004).
26. J. Pearce, *The Wesleys in Cornwall* (Truro, 1964).
27. A. Rowse, *A Cornish Childhood* (London, 1975).
28. B. Deacon, D. Cole and G. Tredidga, *Mebyon Kernow and Cornish Nationalism* (Cardiff, 2003).
29. See Gorseth Kernow (2003) www.gorsethkernow.org.uk, Accessed 20.03.03. Stannary Parliament (20.03.03) www.cornish-stannary-parliament.abelgratis.com. A. Hale, 'Representing the Cornish: Contesting Heritage Interpretation in Cornwall', *Tourist Studies*, 1, 2 (2001), pp. 185–96.
30. Cornwall County Council (2005) www.cornwall.gov.uk/facts.htm, Accessed 20 August 2005.
31. *Cornish Nation*, 23, Autumn (2001).
32. M. Ireland, 'What is Cornishness? The Implications For Tourism', *Tourism, Culture and Communication*, 1 (1998), pp. 17–26.
33. R. Perry, 'The Making of Modern Cornwall 1800–2000', in P. Payton (ed.), *Cornish Studies: Ten* (Exeter, 2002).
34. See P. Aldous and M. Williams, P. Payton (ed.), *Cornish Studies: Nine* (Exeter, 2001), pp. 213–26.
35. M. Crofty, *The Foundations of Social Research* (London, 1998).
36. R. Thomas, 'Surveys', in T. Greenfield (ed.), *Research Methods, Guidance for Postgraduates* (London, 1996).
37. R. Abusabha, M. Woelfel, 'Qualitative vs Quantitative Methods; Two Opposites That Make a Perfect Match (Commentary)', *Journal of the American Dietic Association*, 103, 5 (2003), pp. 564–6.
38. J. Fielding and N. Gilbert, *Understanding Social Statistics* (London, 2000).
39. S. Yates, *Doing Social Research* (London, 2004).
40. S. Arber, *Designing Samples*, in N. Gilbert (ed.), *Researching Social Life* (London, 1993).
41. M. Denscombe, *The Good Research Guide* (Buckingham, 1998).
42. M. Messonier, J. Bergstrom, C. Cornwell, J. Teaseley and K. Cordell, 'Survey Response Biases in Contingent Valuation Concepts, Remedies, and Empirical Application to Valuing Aquatic Plant Management', *American Journal of Economics*, 82, 2 (2000), p. 438.

43. A. Oppenheim, *Questionnaire Design and Attitude Measurement* (London, 1966).
44. See Fielding and Gilbert, *Understanding Social Statistics*.
45. See Cornwall County Council, 2002.
46. V. Jupp and R. Sapford (eds), *Data Collection and Analysis* (London, 1996).
47. B. Antle and C. Regehr, 'Beyond Individual Rights and Freedoms, Meta Ethics in Social Work Research', *Social Work* 48, 1 (2003) p. 135(9) and Yates, *Doing Social Research*.
48. P. Brierley, *Religious Trends 3*, UK Christian Handbook (2003).
49. See Stoyle, *West Britons*; Aldous and Williams, 2001.
50. See Cornwall County Council, 2005.

10

1549

The Rebels Shout Back

Cheryl Hayden

Item we will not receyve the newe seruyce because it is but lyke a Christmas gâme, but we wyll haue oure oldd seruyce of Mattens, masse, Euensong and procession in Latten as it was before. And so we Cornyshe men (wherof certen of vs vnderstâd no Englysh) vtterly refuse thys newe Englysh. (from The Articles of vs the Commoners of Deuonshyre and Cornewall in diuers Campes by East and west of Excettor)[1]

Introduction

As an Australian of predominantly Cornish descent, I was astonished to discover during the course of my study for a Master of Arts degree in Cornish Studies (University of Exeter, 2002) that my ancestral history was notable not only for mining prowess and a colourful tradition of smuggling and piracy, but for a period of rebellion that spanned 150 years and cost hundreds, possibly thousands, of lives. Not only was I bemused by my lack of awareness of events that suggested a significant reluctance on the part of the Cornish to be pulled into line with Tudor England, but I also felt somewhat cross that history appeared to have wiped from the record any notion of ethnically or culturally driven tension between Cornwall and England. In fact, despite being told as a child that my ancestry was Cornish, there was little, if anything, that I was aware of in the far-removed Antipodes to support the unarticulated yet quite clear notion of 'not being English' that was implied by this so-called Cornish heritage.

Suddenly aware of unsung Cornish 'martyrs' and 'heroes', 1 became increasingly fascinated by the unspoken and unrecorded, the great gaps and silences in the historical record that have left them poorly understood, unrecognized and uncelebrated. I was particularly interested in the 1549 Prayer Book Rebellion, or Western Rising, and wanted to know more about its leaders, their thoughts and their arguments, and the beliefs that compelled them to continue to fight until the very bitter end, which included numerous executions — both in Cornwall and in London — and the confiscation of significant amounts of property. Likewise, I was fascinated by the various elements of the rebellion and its aftermaths that, when imagined, had a mythic or poetic quality, particularly the fate of young William Wynslade, who, after the execution of his father and the confiscation of the family estates, was reduced to life as a wandering harper.

Bemused, like Alan Kent,[2] that so little had been done in Cornwall to make heroes of long-lost 'rebels', I began to contemplate the idea of recreating, through fiction, this period of resistance and rebellion as it may have been experienced by the Cornish. The project would inherently 'Kernowcentric', taking the viewpoint that, notwithstanding that they joined forces with a large contingent of Devonshiremen, the Cornish saw themselves as a separate people and were, indeed, seen as different by the English. Also, as a work of fiction, it would delve into the imagined events that may have occurred in the spaces created by history's omissions. To create the novel I imagined, I would need to understand the relationship between and history and fiction, recognize and counteract the techniques employed hitherto by 'history' to ensure that the rebels remained quiet, and to locate places where echoes of their voices may still remain.

Talking up resistance

From the outset I recognized that my creative enterprise would be a story of resistance against, firstly, the English government's abolition of the traditional Latin Mass and the sacraments held to be absolutely integral to worship and, secondly, against interference in Cornish life by the Tudor monarchs' increasingly nationalist approach to government. In this article, therefore, I argue that the Cornish saw the compulsory replacement of Cornish and Latin in church with the English language as a threat to their survival as a people. This is a form of cultural and political oppression some in Cornwall believe continues today: in a school curriculum that ignores the distinctive experience of Cornwall and the Cornish, in governmental refusal to recognize the distinctive features of Cornwall's constitutional status, and in an 'English Heritage organization that excludes the Cornish from the histories of their own heritage sites.[3] Exacerbating the impact of this supposed cultural oppression or marginalization is the outsider's appetite for the 'sanctioned' version of Cornwall: a place that is lost in the mists of its (Celtic) past or 'a romantically different, backward and uncivilized place, the haunt of strange people, smugglers, wreckers and other assorted quaint characters.'[4]

It would seem, then, that to create heroes of Cornishmen who were hanged, drawn and quartered as traitors is today still a highly political and contestatory endeavour. In keeping with this theme, the novel I have created considers alternative views of this period in Cornish history by discussing the rebellion in the context of Cornwall's marginalization,[5] the idea of ongoing ethnic tension,[6] and the notion of particularity in religious practice.[7] It deploys literary and cultural studies theories to analyse representations of this rebellion and Cornish identity in conventional historical documents. It also incorporates analysis of archival material that is new to this area of study. The privileging of marginalized Cornish experience maintains the inherently subversive tradition of cultural studies, which is 'consciously concerned with transforming the practice of producing knowledge, with issue of cultural politics, and with asking cultural and theoretical questions in relation to power.'[8] My fictionalized account of the rebellion would be informed by my analysis in these areas, and my goal of recuperating the 'rebels'' silenced voices began with the use of Cornish voices in the title, *A Christmas Game*, which, as shown above, comes from their description of the new Prayer Book, and continues by contesting British historiography, much of which does little to elevate the rebellion above the status of a skirmish or footnote.

Specifically, however, this article is interested in Hayden White's work on the nature of historical narrative and its relationship to literature[9] and in the subaltern school of post-colonial theory, in particular Ranajit Guha's theory on the prose of counter-insurgency,[10] which provides a useful means for identifying the rhetoric of history and unravelling it in order to then contest it. In this article, I use this approach to interrogate John Hooker's 1564 'eye witness' account,[11] which has informed numerous subsequent accounts, in particular that of Rose-Troup.[12]

In considering the theoretical arguments, this article also draws attention to the oral tradition of history, religious practices, ideas about the power of language, and ethnic ties to the people of Brittany. It also draws on artifacts such as a medieval miracle play, Arthurian legend and the Articles of Demand the rebels sent to the King. And it examines two primary sources from the sixteenth century: one long-forgotten by students of the rebellion and the other never mentioned. The first of these, written in French, was believed by Frances Rose-Troup[13] to have quite possibly been written by the rebel leaders to their King towards the end of the rebellion; the second, written years later by Tristran Winslade, son of William Winslade, a landless and exiled rebel leader, appears to establish a link between the rebellion, the Spanish Court and the second Spanish armada.[14]

The ideas gleaned from these sources subvert the accepted historical discourse that paints the 'rebel' in pejorative terms, and instead presents them as 'heroes' who, according to John Angarrack, 'deserve just recognition [for] few things are more repugnant than the deliberate distortion and systematic denial of the bravery and heroism of thousands of men who, though severely outnumbered, stood their ground to fight seasoned soldiers to the death for a cause they believed in'.[15] The following analysis of the historiography of the rebellion and other recent scholarly work aimed at centering the Cornish experience aims to identify the trends and gaps that could provide the space for the novelist to apply intelligent imagination to the experience of those involved in the rebellion and reclaim some of their voices.

History and fiction

In his critique of Cooper's work on Tudor propaganda and the 'westcountry', Bernard Deacon notes a 'serious lack of historical imagination'.[16] The implied need for imagination in order to understand Cornwall and its history not only underscores Cornwall's marginalization in the historical record but goes to the very issue of what history should be or can be, and to the heart of the relationship between history and fiction.

According to White, '"history" gains the ascendancy over "literature" by virtue of its interest in the "actual" rather than the "possible"'.[17] The 'actual', however, having come from the written record, creates spaces within which historians must use the 'constructive imagination' which tells them 'what must have been the case'.[18] The trouble with chronicled history, White says, can be found in Levi-Strauss's belief that 'we can construct a comprehensible story of the past ... only by a decision to "give up" one or more of the domains of facts offering themselves for inclusion in our accounts. Our explanations of historical structures and processes are ... determined more by what we leave out of our representations than by what we put in.'[19]

While Levi-Strauss points to the absences or omissions integral to history's constructs, White goes further, not only criticizing the status of historical narratives as 'verbal artifact', but describing them as 'verbal fictions, the contents of which are as much invented as found and the forms of which have more in common with their counterparts in literature than they have with those in the sciences'.[20] White, then, not only establishes the blurred distinction between the historical narrative and literature, but provides the space for the historical novelist to go further than employing Collingwood's 'constructive imagination'[21] and to step bravely into the realm of 'empathetic understanding', which Australian author Kate Grenville, in discussing her controversial Commonwealth Prize-winning novel, *The Secret River*, described as 'one way into the lives of people in the past to understand their actions and the choices that they made'.[22]

Understanding the choices made by the 'rebels' and their leaders in 1549 was a prime concern in the fictionalization of the rebellion, as was creating the metaphor by which I would create their world. As Nietzsche claims, the real value of history lay 'in inventing ingenious variations on a probably commonplace theme, in raising the popular melody to a universal symbol and showing what world of depth, power and beauty exists in it'.[23]

The rebellion in history

The historiography of the rebellion can be roughly divided into three broad groups. Most common are those that recount the events through a British history prism focusing on monarchy, government and their policies, which today also includes television documentaries featuring celebrity historians. The second group examines the rebellion in the context of a particular theme, for example in the context of religious reform or its military significance. The third group comprises those histories that centre the experience of the rebels and examine the minutiae of available records to better understand their actions.

The first group – those writing accounts of Edward VI's reign and the Reformation – inevitably include some level of analysis of the rebellion, as it eventually brought down the government and led to the execution in 1552 of Protector Somerset. Many of these accounts, such as Christopher Skidmore's *Edward VI: the Lost King of England*,[24] rely heavily on John Hooker's 1564 account, which (as discussed below) was weighted almost entirely in favour of the government forces. For example, Skidmore relegates details of the first week of the Cornish rising, including Arundell's successful rear-guard defence, to a footnote.[25] Furthermore, his discussion of their list of demands provides no attempt at analysis, but simply comments on their tone with the statement: 'It is easy to see why Cranmer was so incensed by the western rebels.'[26]

Like Skidmore, Jennifer Loach's *Edward VI*[27] focuses on the government's failure to quell the disturbances that swept England in 1549. She states that rebellions are 'readily explicable'[28] and, on the basis that all versions of the rebels' articles of demand 'show a marked contempt for the new Prayer Book, described as a "Christmas Game"',[29] focuses on religion. In doing so, however, she ignores the ethnic references in the very Article she chose to quote, which also says: 'we the Cornishmen (whereof certain of us understand no English) utterly refuse this new English'. She also refers to 'rioting' in Bodmin and suggests that such behaviour provoked the Devonshire disturbances,[30] claims I have found nowhere else in accounts of the rebellion.

Neither of these recent accounts of the rebellion identifies issues of identity or ethnicity as motivating factors, following instead the tradition established by Hooker in the sixteenth century and continued by Rose-Troup, A.L. Rowse[31] and Philip Caraman[32] all of whom, despite centering the Cornish experience, explain the rising almost entirely in terms of religion. Others, such as Barrett Beer, recognize Cornish difference, but then fail to examine it.[33]

Beer belongs to the second group as someone who examines the Prayer Book Rebellion in the context of other rebellions. In doing so he raises the issue of 'Cornwall's sense of political and cultural oppression', and refers to their 'rugged Celtic society'. His analysis, however, is based upon a spatial 'south-west' construct – 'the world of Devon and Cornwall was small, inward-looking, and parochial' – in which issues surrounding ethnicity and identity are absent.[34] More recently, J.P.D. Cooper's *Propaganda and the Tudor State*[35] has used the same approach. Unlike Beer, however, Cooper undermines his own south-west regional framework by paying considerable attention to issues of Cornish identity and culture, with an entire chapter devoted to Cornish miracle plays. Others adopting a south-west or 'west country' approach to the rebellion include David M. Loades[36] and Joyce Youings,[37] both of whom focus on economic hardship as an explanation for the people's discontent.

Also in the second group is Julian Cornwall's *Revolt of the Peasantry 1549*, which examines the Prayer Book Rebellion from a military point of view, and appears to have been motivated by the intriguing issue of 'how close the men of Devon and Cornwall came to reversing the course of the Reformation.'[38] Cornwall identifies local issues as crucial to understanding the rebellion[39] and devotes an entire chapter to the notion of Cornish identity. He says Cornwall 'differed radically from the rest of England. Its people were Celts, speaking their own language'.[40] His detailed dissection of the rebellion pays particular attention to the personalities of the leaders, their circumstances and the strategies they employed. John Sturt's *Revolt in the West: The Western Rebellion of 1549* continues this tradition of military detail, and, while leaning towards a 'south-west' regional treatment, betrays a particular sympathy and admiration for the Cornish leadership.[41]

The third group comprises those historians not only interested in centering the Cornish experience, but in understanding it from the Cornish perspective. Key among these is Mark Stoyle, whose *West Britons* examines a series of Cornish rebellions as symptomatic of on-going ethnically driven resistance to interference by centralist governments. Particularly pertinent to the writing of my novel is Stoyle's declaration of his status as 'a Devonshire man writing about Cornish history'. He sees the Tamar as a distinct boundary, and notes that while relationships have 'frequently been strained over the past 500 years', there exists among Devonians a recognition and respect for 'the various subtle, and not so subtle, signifiers which serve to set the Cornish apart.'[42]

Philip Payton and Bernard Deacon both centre the Cornish experience in their respective interpretations of Cornish history. Payton, in *Cornwall – A History*, examines Cornwall's peripheral status vis-à-vis a politically and administratively dominant England and explains the 1549 rebellion in the context of protest and outrage against a series of incursions and erosions by the Tudor monarchs into a range of 'accommodations' granted to Cornwall in recognition of their 'difference'. According to Payton, the Act of Uniformity, which introduced the Book of Common Prayer in 1549, was 'the epitome of Tudor intrusion.'[43] (2004, 122). By contrast, in *Cornwall – A Concise History*, Deacon examines the rebellion through a prism of identity, examining the religious and ethnic aspects of a range of Cornish identities to conclude that 'if anything, the experience of 1549 produced a sense of common Cornishness rather than reflected it'.[44]

Explanations interested in centering the Cornish experience would appear, then, to point to religious conservatism and ethnic difference as two strands of enquiry essential to understanding the rebellion. Lisa McClain, however, goes even further. In a chapter entitled 'Katholik Kernow' (Catholic Cornwall) she argues that 'Cornwall's isolation allowed the Cornish to nurture their own language, culture and even separate religious traditions both before and after reform.' The difference, she claims, lay in its ties to 'Celtic Christianity' (as opposed to the Roman Church), including a community of saints not recognized by Rome and a strong Cornish belief that the land itself was comprised of intrinsically holy places.[45] In short, the rebellion was fought to protect a religion that was in several respects unique within the British context and a hallmark of Cornish identity, one still apparent today in the keeping of reliquaries such as the skulls of St Probus and St Grace at Probus Church.[46]

While these Cornu-centric endeavours provide great insight into the nature of the rebellion, the recency of highly generalized publications such as Skidmore's show they have made little impact on British history. Indeed, Bernard Deacon, commenting on ten years of a 'new' approach to Cornish historiography, has suggested that there has been insufficient criticism of the current state of Britain's 'four nations' approach to history which 'often gives Cornwall little more space than did "old" English histories.'[47]

It is, therefore, apt to examine the Prayer Book Rebellion through the prism of a theory that will repatriate silenced rebel voices and make them heroes. Fortunately, in the case of this rebellion, while rebel voices are routinely absent from the rebellion's historiography, they have not entirely been erased from the archive.

The distant echo of rebel voices

There are three original sources that carry the voices of the Cornish in relation to the Prayer Book Rebellion. The first is the series of Articles of Demand sent to the King. The dominant conclusion historiography draws from these documents – there were four versions sent to the government, starting with eight articles and increasing to 16 in the final version – is that the protest was entirely to do with religious conservatism; however, the final 16 also included a number of political issues, which, as Julian Cornwall notes, seemed 'preponderantly to have represented the Cornish case'.[48] Of particular note to this project, however, is Article 8 which stated: 'We will not receive the new service because it is but like a Christmas game. We will have our old service of matins, Mass, evensong and procession as it was before; and we the Cornishmen, whereof certain of us understand no English, utterly refuse the new English.'[49] Here, issues of identity come to the fore and Cooper is among the few historians to alert readers to a draft 'answer' to an earlier article which requested that the liturgy be printed in Cornish.[50]

The second original source is the French language pamphlet titled '*La Responce du Peuple Anglois a leur Roy Edouard*'. This was published in Paris in 1550, at which time it was considered seditious in England. As discussed above, Rose-Troup included it as an appendix to her book, believing it possible that it may have been written by rebel leaders. Nicholas Pocock, who believed it to be a response to an unrecorded response by the King to their Articles,[51] describes it as focusing, in polite language, on broad issues of particular interest to the King: their hurt at the King's accusation of rebellion; points of doctrine and matters of precedence; the King's youth and his father's will; and the dangers of alienating Catholic Europe. He claims the rebels' response was 'so sensible and to the point that probably … did not suit Foxe's purposes to produce them'[52] in his book of martyrs, which, as Gasquet and Bishop note, ends with a claim that no one suffered for their religion under Edward VI.[53] The rebels' document ends with a plea to the King to: 'accept your very humble and very obedient subjects, whose desire is to be the dogs appointed to keep your house and your kingdom, and the oxen to cultivate your lands, the asses to carry your burdens … We will pray the Lord God, who holds and turns the hearts of kings where He wills, to watch over and conduct your young age'.[54]

My own translation endeavours also reveal a desire among the Cornish to protect the particularity of their Cornu-Celtic form of Catholicism. In *La Responce*, they plead with the King to understand that:

It is not thus the devil's persuasion, it is not the light-headedness of the people, the simplicity of the ignorant, nor the temerity of the seditious, which caused us to assemble. It is more the particular responsibility each of us owes his friend, the common displeasure at seeing the religion that our ancestors so greatly revered over the vast span of twelve hundred years, is now, at the caprice of two or three, so much changed and reduced by new ways, that the old men among us will die, and the young people will reach extreme old age before understanding that which commends them for salvation.[55]

The reference in 1549 to a 1,200-year-old religious tradition not only appears to support McClain's argument about the particularity of the Cornish church, including, perhaps, still extant quasi-pagan beliefs in the sacred nature of the land itself, but suggests Cornish consciousness of a separate identity going back to the earliest saints.

The third original document was written in 1595 by Tristran Winslade,[56] grandson of executed rebel leader John Wynslade and the son of William Wynslade, who was left landless and penniless and leading the life of a wandering harper in the rebellion's aftermath. Written for King Philip of Spain, the original Latin manuscript informs the Spanish King on how to invade Britain via Cornwall and Devon. It deals with 'top secret' matters and 'goes on to name various Catholic notables of the two counties and the ways in which they could act or use their influence in an uprising to seize control of England'. According to one interpretation, Tristran Winslade also 'requests that if this should take place, that he be restored to the lands and income which his family had owned before they lost all from their devotion to Catholicism'.[57]

Both of these documents demand closer translation and examination, for they are the silenced voices of the rebels, both during and after the rebellion, and have potential to add considerably to our knowledge and debate about Cornish identity and religion during the volatile sixteenth century.

Subverting traditional history

The creative aspect of my project drew heavily on the postmodern belief in the importance of the 'interplay of different heterogeneous discourses that acknowledge the undecidable in both the past and our knowledge of the past'.[58] As my research progressed, it became increasingly 'political' – and so did I – as I realized the extent to which the English have suppressed this part of their history.

The subaltern school of theory, with its origins in Gramsci's work on the Italian peasantry, in which he labelled them 'subalterno' (cited by Pryamvada Gopal as translating as 'subordinate' or 'dependent'[59]), today continues

Gramsci's insistence that 'wherever there is history, there is class, and that the essence of the historical is the long and extraordinarily varied socio-cultural interplay between ruler and ruled, between the elite, dominant, or hegemonic class and the subaltern'.[60]

In the context of rebellion, Ranajit Guha's theories on the prose of counter-insurgency[61] provide an insight into identifying and contesting rhetoric that presents itself as uncontestable truth. Gopal's work is also useful in that it offers an alternative to Spivak's contention that the subaltern cannot speak.[62] Gopal suggests that this can be achieved by 'drawing attention to the small voice of history' and by pursuing an interest in 'the staging of violence and the narrative construction of crime'.[63]

Indeed, Guha is interested in voicing the peasant rebel through 'critical attention to plot, character, authority, language, voice and time'.[64] On the face of it, this model offers a highly appropriate approach to an analysis of any historical account, and is particularly apt when it comes to creating a representation of those whose voices have been silenced. As I struggled to examine issues of Cornish identity in the context of rebellion, these works provided the means for understanding consciousness and motivation[65] and the language of counter-insurgency,[66] which has enshrined the term 'rebel' and other pejorative forms of language as incontestable truths. Indeed, as the writing of this article continues, and as discussed below, I find myself increasingly frustrated at the lack of a suitable word with which to replace the word 'rebel'.

Refuse, scum, and rascals

John Hooker's sixteenth-century 'eye witness' account of the Prayer Book Rebellion provides a legitimate study of the prose of counter-insurgency because, as Julian Cornwall explains, he 'allowed his pen to get the better of him' and started a trend other historians, (including Skidmore as recently as 2007[67]), could not help but follow, as noted above.[68] Hooker's language is particularly relevant to Guha's concept that historiography has been content to deal with the peasant rebel merely as an empirical person or member of a class, but not as an entity whose will and reason constituted the praxis called rebellion. Indeed, the omission is dyed into most narratives by metaphors assimilating peasant revolts to natural phenomena: they break out like thunder-storms, heave like earthquakes, spread like wildfires, infect like epidemics.[69]

Hooker 'observed' the rebellion from within the besieged walls of Exeter and wrote his account 15 years after the event. It is unlikely that he had contact with any of the rebels and, by the time he was writing, almost certain that the political climate of Elizabeth's reign allowed him to give full vent to his Protestant leanings. The following three passages demonstrate the politics and power of omission as established by Guha.

Firstly, Hooker's description of the impact of the Sampford Courtenay villagers' success in forcing their priest to don his full vestments the day after they and the Latin Mass had been banned, tells us that:

> These News as a Cloud carried with a violent Wind, and as a Thunder Clap sounding at one instant through the whole Country, are carried and noised even in a Moment throughout the whole Country: And the common People so well allowed and like thereof, that they clapped their Hands for Joy, and agreed in one mind, to have the same in every of their several Parishes.[70]

Later, Hooker shows us Sir Peter Carew's band of gentlemen attempting to bargain with armed rebels who had manned and fortified two barns on either side of the bridge leading into Crediton:

> Where upon they alighted from their Horses, and after a little Conference had, they agreed to go into the Town on Foot, nothing thinking less that they should be stopped or denied to go in on foot. But when they came to the Rampires they found the contrary; for they not only were denied to come near the Rampires, but utterly were refused to be talked withal: No Offers of Persuasions, nor Motions of Conference at all could be allowed. *For the Sun being in Cancer, and the Midsummer Moon at full, their Minds were imbrued in such Follies, and their Heads carried with such Vanitie, that as the Man of Athens, they would hear no Man speak but themselves, and thought nothing well said but what came out of their own Mouths.* (Hooker's italics)[71]

Finally, Hooker diverts the reader with a description of the rebel leaders. They were 'the Refuse, the Scum, and the Rascals, of the whole Country; and yet such there were in this case, as who rule the Roast [sic], and bore the whole or chiefest sway; and the worse the Man, the greater his Authority among them'.[72]

Even making allowances for the ebullience of sixteenth-century writing, each of these paragraphs is example of the power of the prose of counter-insurgency. The first paragraph uses natural phenomena to de-personify the rebel and gives the reader the impression that some sort of non-human response has occurred in a being bereft of self-awareness and an ability to engage in rational thought. The prose further suggests the bizarre possibility that they were hit by the same decision – apparently to run amok – at precisely the same instant, as though affected by an explosion or infection. Once this discourse establishes 'fact', it becomes easy for historians to follow and denigrate the peasant rebel as an irrational or simple fool who either 'erupts' or is easily misled into following spurious or wicked causes. Equally, it makes it easy for the modern reader to lean towards the government forces, which within such a discourse are rational, logical and righteous.

The second paragraph demonstrates Hooker's sympathy with Carew and his band of gentlemen. The prose fills the reader with confidence that the writer is at one with his subject and has full knowledge of his intentions, which may have been the case after the event, as Hooker was Carew's biographer.[73] Hooker even provides illustrations of their family crests as if to prove their worthiness. The fact, then, that the rebels refused to talk to these right and proper gentlemen appears to have outraged Hooker and apparently justifies the tone of indignation at the idea that they might have adopted some sort of strategy. It is a notion Hooker does not dwell on, as he quickly drops that thread, instead opting to suggest that the rebels' actions were the result of their own vanities (while apparently lacking in self-consciousness) and the forces of nature.

The second paragraph is further understood through an analysis of the 'components of the discourse' (or 'strings of words'), which Guha classifies as either 'indicative' or 'interpretive' (or as reporting or explaining).[74] Such an analysis reveals how strings of words 'interpenetrate and sustain each other in order to give the documents their meaning', thus creating the 'truth'. Hooker's truth – that the peasant rebels were irrational – is created by the imbrication of the report that 'No Offers of Persuasions, nor Motions of Conference at all could be allowed' with the explanation that 'they would hear no Man speak but themselves, and thought nothing well said but what came out of their own Mouths'. As Guha explains, the hiatus between these components is 'necessarily charged with uncertainty and "moments of risk" and every micro-sequence terminates by opening up alternative possibilities only one of which is picked up by the next sequence as it carries on with the story'.[75] In other words, the two elements of discourse are intertwined in such a way that the story spins itself as it is told. Hooker, then, uses the rebels' apparent irrationality to explain their refusal to speak to Carew, thus granting Carew and his actions a hero status that is not supported by facts of his life.

Another contributor to the prose of counter insurgency is the historian's choice of voice. Hooker uses the active voice to describe Carew's party and they are seen throughout this episode to be the ones with consciousness and agency, even when the passive voice tells us they 'were refused to be talked withal'. In this instance, the passive voice denies the rebels their active defiance and any decision-making that might have led them to take such a stance; instead, they are rendered absent or invisible purveyors of an obscure and unreasonable act. The historian's denial of their act of defiance also obviates the need to explain it, and so the rebels' refusal to parley becomes an irrational act that justifies the burning of two barns full of hay, which became a key escalation point in the rebellion.

In the third paragraph, Hooker's rhetoric has shifted from a discourse of natural phenomena to one in which the rebels are bad people who have made a conscious decision to behave very badly indeed. This shift again demonstrates Hooker's preparedness to employ inconsistent rhetoric to convince the reader of his own views.

As noted above by Julian Cornwall, this trend has been perpetuated by other historians. Loades, for example, states that the Cornish had a 'vague intention of marching on London as their grandfathers had done in 1497',[76] while Youings says they were 'by instinct following in the footsteps of their grandfathers'.[77] Caraman, however, finds that 'even before his success at the Mount, Arundell had begun his march towards London, determined to enforce the just demands of the commons and obtain security for their fulfillmen'.[78]

Hooker's prose is also an example of a paradigm in which historians examine human affairs through clearly delineated prisms such as economics or religion, which in turn obviate the need to identify any internal issues that might hint at the existence of rebel self-consciousness. His (or his publisher's) marginal note 'the Cause of this Rebellion was for Religion'[79] establishes a discourse described by Jose Rabasa as neutralizing the world of subaltern insurrection which is 'ruled by the imagination, marvel, civil society, and poetics'.[80]

Guha also identifies the historian's insistence on the use of the past tense as another means of perpetuating a discourse of counter-insurgency.[81] The passing of time between an event and the creation of its written history not only creates a secondary discourse out of a primary experience (as occurred with Hooker's 15-year delay in writing about the rebellion) but it enables the author to '"dechronologize" the historical thread'[82] and destabilize the gaps with uncertainty and bias.

Imagination and empathy

As a practice-led endeavour, the writing process involved in creating my novel *A Christmas Game* constantly bumped against my interpretation and application of the cultural studies theory I was deploying to try to give voice to the Cornish rebels: namely, Guha's theory of the prose of counter-insurgency. Delving into his theory had me constantly questioning the extent to which my own narrative was either supporting or undermining my own goal – to give voice to the rebels – and to find creative ways of contesting traditional means of storytelling. This entwined process I endeavored to record in journal form as a means of reflecting on the way the project unfolded and evolved. This dual process reflects the two strands of discourse identified by Bourke and Nielsen – the use of cultural studies theory and second-order journal practice.[83]

My challenge was to create a story of the Prayer Book Rebellion that would enable the reader to enter the hearts and minds of the Cornish men and women who had engaged in this rising, and to identify and make heard the events and emotions that led them from a peaceful march to open warfare. Guha's analysis enabled me to identify the spaces in the historiography through which their voices could me explored. I found these spaces in the absences or silences in the historical record and in the minutiae of archival material which, as Gopal explains, is particularly pertinent to peasant rebellion as it examines the 'small drama and fine detail of social existence, especially at its lower depths'.[84]

For this project, finding the silences and filling them with rebel voices was a key concern. As Rabasa states, the prose of counter-insurgency neutralizes peasant insurgency by pursuing the 'causes and effects of rebellion',[85] another paradigm that assumes the subaltern (or peasant) to be passive and without self- or class-consciousness. Indeed, there are few accounts of the Prayer Book Rebellion that go beyond an analysis of cause in terms of resistance to State-imposed change or of protest against conditions brought about by government policy, such as religious reform or economic hardship, which are the two most commonly cited causes of the rebellion. This tendency demonstrates Rabasa's argument that the State and its history fail to recognize the struggle of singularity 'because the discourse that resistance articulates remains unintelligible to those who presume that their categories are universal'.[86] This supports Spivak's claim that the subaltern cannot speak; however, as Gopal has demonstrated, it depends who is listening.

In writing *A Christmas Game*, I drew on the widespread belief that the Tudor monarchs were well aware of the ethnically driven tension inherent in their relationships with the Cornish.[87] When my young fictional hero, Margh Tredannack, is interrogated at sword-point by Russell's men and responds in Cornish, one of the soldiers refers to him as an 'ignorant rustic', thus using his own self-assumed superiority to deny him agency. However, as O'Neal has suggested, Spivak's question 'can the subaltern speak?' is perhaps better re-phrased 'When the subaltern speaks, can he be understood?'[88] The answer must surely be 'it depends who is listening.' In this scene, Lord Russell is listening, and as an experienced spy and diplomat, he knows he is hearing an overt expression of ethnically based resistance. He pushes the soldier aside saying, 'Don't for a minute believe that,' and slices Margh's cheek open with his sword. Later that night, this incident plays on Russell's fears: '[Russell] cast his mind to the jostling Cornish ports crawling with papist merchants from France and Spain and Portugal. He saw coves and hamlets alive with dissent. He heard invitations to invade. Quite suddenly, all of Cornwall rushed upon him out of the darkness, a dangerous enemy and a terrible threat.'

The prescience of Russell's thoughts draws on knowledge of the later activities of William and Tristran Wynslade, as discussed above, and draws a direct link between the Prayer Book Rebellion and the two Armadas.

In order to subvert the prose of counter-insurgency, I also identified spaces in the record that provide the rebels with a chance to speak. For my novel, one important gap in the record is how the Cornish reacted to news that the villagers of Sampford Courtenay in Devon had begun a riot by killing a supporter of the new prayer book. The silence created by such gaps in the historical record informs much of the novel in that it opens space for creatively imagined events. In *A Christmas Game* I use this absence of rebel voice to creatively imagine dialogue and debate. It is a strategy used by film director Ken Loach in *The Wind that Shakes the Barley* to allow his Irish rebels the opportunity to discuss strategy, which was 'not only important to the story [but] important to what was at stake at the time ... [and] ... absolutely essential to what we were about, which is because people did articulate these ideas.'[89]

I follow this strategy in the novel to address a range of issues, which are aired in the context of the rage felt by the rebels and the different ways grievances may have been articulated by their leaders and foot soldiers. In terms of their reaction to the violence in Devonshire, I used history's silence to give Arundell the opportunity to express the sense of the confusion I believe they must have felt on learning of this development:

> Arundell dragged his hand down over his face and began striding violently around the room. 'Devon is in uproar. Damn it. This changes everything.'
>
> 'But, Humphry, this is good news!' the mayor said, and conversations broke out all around the table.
>
> Arundell swung around and glared at Bray. 'How can we be sure of that? We don't know what their grievance is, or whether they're even organized. The problem is, they've already become violent. Knowing this, do we want to join them? I would much prefer to proceed peaceably to London and hope to parley with the King.' He paused. 'But if our neighbours across the Tamar are at odds with the King, then perhaps Exeter will be too. As of course it should. And with

Exeter secure, behind us ...' An odd sense of possibility mixed with danger suddenly overwhelmed him.

I also involve my main fictional character, Margh, in the taking of Trematon Castle[90] and the subsequent imprisonment of Sir Richard Grenville at Launceston Castle, an important aspect of contesting the absence of Cornish history from Cornish historical sites. Managed by English Heritage, Launceston Castle's historical display omits the role it played as a prison in 1549, demonstrating this organization's apparent penchant for ignoring the presence of the Cornish people in their own history. I subvert the historical discourse of English Heritage by turning Margh's arrival at Launceston with his prisoners into a celebration, and I further the cause by using the traditional Cornish spelling of the town's name, Lanson, throughout the novel.

'Margh!' he heard. And gasped with delight as Gerent's pale head emerged on the road in front of him. 'A'right?'

Margh leapt from the saddle to embrace his friend. 'Gerent, such tales we heard of your victory at the Mount. You must tell me everything.'

Gerent thumped him on the back. 'But look at you, Captain Tredannack. Prisoners, too!'

'Aye. Sir Richard Grenville among 'em.'

'What glorious soldiering. A happy day, Captain.'

In terms of locating the 'small drama' of history, Eamon Duffy's examination of Morebath's parish records revealed a number of details that helped to bring the rebels to life and 'flesh out' their activities.[91] In this parish, Duffy tells us, the best young men were chosen to join the protest, and they were paid soldiers' rates of 6d per day. Significantly, these records also held a clue to self-consciousness or awareness: the Devonshire rebels, at least, referred to themselves as 'campmen', a term which connotes a sense of peaceful protest or a modern day 'sit in'. This also draws attention to the fact that these people did not see themselves as rebelling, as demonstrated in their post-rebellion response to the King. Prior to the siege, they may have called themselves 'marchers' or even, as Duffy has suggested, 'Christian soldiers', marching as they did, led by priests with holy banners, the Pyx and relics, and singing hymns. According to *La Responce* they had 'assembled' and did not see themselves as rebels. And yet, this is the term I find myself unable to shake off as I write this article. It seems that the power inherent in the prose of counter-insurgency has entrenched its use, rendering everything else inappropriate in terms of describing this conquered army; terms such as 'protestors', 'freedom fighters' or 'liberation army' seem absurd in the context of this sixteenth-century event.

Duffy's examination also highlighted the confused allegiances demonstrated by common people. For example, in Ashburton, 'many must have been sympathetic to their [the rebels'] cause [but] nevertheless sold £10 worth of plate with the whiche money they served the kings majestie against rebells'.[92] Cooper, however, tells us that Russell forced this sale,[93] giving rise to the notion that many people must have been doing one thing while thinking another. This led me to shift the fictional Sir Simon Chiswick's original position of support for Russell – he is one of Russell's many tenants in the area – to one of covert treachery. His ambiguity not only heightened the risk for my heroine, Jenna, but elevated the drama of the storytelling. In one scene, the newly arrived Jenna hears Chiswick and Lord Russell deep in conversation, and she believes Chiswick to be sympathetic to Russell's cause. But after Russell has gone to bed, Chiswick calls Jenna to him:

'Russell says he only has three hundred men. I want you to ride into Honiton and tell me what you see. His troops are bivouacked around the town, with a few at Mohun's Ottery, Sir Peter Carew's place ... Will you do it for me, Jenna? For me.' He coughed and turned his face from her. When he turned back to look at her his eyes were ablaze. 'For our cause?'

'Yes, sir.' The world seemed to sway beneath her.

'You're a good girl, Jenna. The King has ordered Russell to end this outrage and send the leaders to London for punishment. But if Russell truly cannot do it, and cannot convince him that he needs more men, then I need to know.' He patted her hand. 'You'll do it for me? Find out the truth?'

Her mind reeling, Jenna nodded.

Locating anecdotal evidence also helps to contest 'established truths' and open up possibilities to voice the rebels. For example, the character of Lord Russell's key ally, Sir Peter Carew, is open to challenge. While Hooker and a swathe of historians paint Carew as something of a tainted hero, I located on numerous websites an anecdote that makes him something of an idiot. Apparently common knowledge throughout Exeter and Devon, the anecdote tells us that his father had punished him for constant truancy by tying him to either a dog or a sheep and leaving them to roam the streets of Exeter. Russell's jester, Joll – a 'merryman' in Cornish dialect – takes the issue up in a rhyme that reflects the rebels' opinion of Carew, ending it with advice for his master:

'May I suggest, my one true Lord,
What say you now take heed
Of this imbecile's unblest Pa
And put him on a lead.'

I further subvert accepted characterizations by extolling the virtues of the rebel heroes. Far from being 'the worse the Man, the greater his Authority among them', as suggested by Hooker, I draw on the loyalty Arundell commanded from his men[94] and the generosity and bravery attributed to Wynslade[95] and, towards the end of the novel, when Arundell has been captured, I use the Arundell family crest, which featured swallows, not just as a motif for flight, but also to denote his status as a member of the gentry.

While Guha's work on the prose of counter insurgency provided me with the means to challenge such language, an issue arose with the very fact that there were several classes of rebel within the Prayer Book Rebellion. While the Articles of Demand and 'La Responce' provide an insight into the education and language of the priests and gentlemen, I found myself bothered by the realization that the peasant still had not been heard. How, I wondered, would my Sancreed pig-herd, Kitto Trigg, express the need to protest against the prayer book? I used the presence of a small boy to take the challenge to Kitto, who responds uncertainly, but with growing conviction. In another scene, farmer Jan Spargo demonstrates his insight by observing that '*it puts a fire in the belly*' to know what the English think of them.

The poetics of the novel evolved as I endeavoured to contest traditional forms of knowledge and storytelling. The fifteenth-century miracle play, *Beunans Meriasek*, with its overt references to the evil King Teudar, still had resonance for the events of 1549,[96] particularly the section that pits Teudar against the heroic and victorious Duke of Cornwall. Because the political reality of 1549 would have prevented a traditional open-air – *plen-en-gwarry* – performance, my characters perform it in the walled garden at Tredannack.

Arthurian legend also drifts through the pages, with Kitto, awoken from a deep sleep for a march to Feniton Bridges, seeing King Arthur in the glorious battle-ready stance of his captain. Arthurian legend also creates a connection with Brittany through the ship *Broceliande* – the name of Merlin's wood – which takes Margh and Jenna into exile. This connection serves also to subvert the tradition of history's focus on national boundaries, by suggesting that the ethnic ties between the Cornish and the Breton may still have remained strong, particularly during the first weeks of the rebellion's brutal aftermath. I use a Breton character, Guillo, who lives and fights alongside the Cornish characters, to pursue this idea.

I also use the oral tradition of storytelling to interrupt the narrative flow of the rebellion through the voices of the two Williams: William ('Will' throughout the novel) Wynslade and his fictional illegitimate son, young William, who is being raised by Margh and Jenna. Will's voice, chosen because of the poetics inherent in his post-rebellion life as a wandering harper, contrasts with his optimistic rebellion persona, as we hear him from the future when Elizabeth is ascending the throne. Knowledge of his future life of exile and his capture on board the Armada in 1588[97] led me to lace his tone with anger and bitterness as he laments his loss and alludes to his future treachery. Little William's voice reflects the stories he has heard from the family's retainer, Kerra, and the resentment among the Cornish of English interference. He also alludes to the sense he has of the impact of the rebellion on Margh and Jenna.

Other poetic elements came to me in unexpected moments of clarity. The riddle Will sings to Jenna – a verse from Scarborough Fair – is mentioned by Dean as known in the St Columb area of Cornwall,[98] not far from Jenna's home on the Camel Estuary. I was drawn to the lyric 'between the salt water and the sea sand', which suggested the idea of trying to find the impossible – religious freedom, love – but as the novel grew it became symbolic of the marginalization of Cornwall and the cyclical forces of nature found in its most liminal zone – the beach below Margh and Jenna's cottage, on the far western coast. This, in turn, created the scene where a pregnant Jenna is on the beach, raking seaweed to fertilize the soil.

Conclusion

The power inherent within the prose of counter-insurgency ensures that official accounts of insurgencies are saturated by the language of the dominating or conquering force and highly resistant to any language that might attempt to subvert it. The contestatory nature of Subaltern Studies, however, and in particular Guha's analysis of this form of rhetoric, have provided me with the tools to interrogate the historical discourse surrounding the Prayer Book Rebellion of 1549 and to find spaces through which the rebels can become self-conscious human beings and give voice to reason, strategy, fear, and countless other human emotions. To this extent, the subaltern might be heard. Indeed, while writing *A Christmas Game*, I found that by entrenching myself in the rebel camp, I was able to avoid using the word 'rebel' except when writing from the point of view of the government. A search of the 72,000-word manuscript shows I used the word 'rebel' or 'rebellion' 36 times, almost entirely when writing from the viewpoint of the Government forces. Only on three occasions did Arundell use the term, and then only in the context of trying to see events from the Government's perspective. And yet, whenever I moved into twenty-first-century exegesis writing, the dreaded 'r' word was inescapable. To this point in this comparatively short article, the words 'rebel', 'rebels' or 'rebellion' appear more than 100 times – mostly in my own narrative.

The inescapability of the prose of counter-insurgency is further demonstrated by the way this event has been labelled. While commonly referred to as a rebellion by those writing sanctioned versions of history, the Cornish, perhaps in an attempt to contest the assumption that it was illegal, refer to it as a 'rising'.[99] But the word 'rising' is no escape from the prose of counter-insurgency. It is, in fact, one of Guha's 'natural phenomenon' words, denying the peasant insurgent his conscious decision-making. So, the trap is clear: this protest is either an unlawful rebellion or a legitimate but irrational rising. The language of history will not allow it to be both legitimate and rational.

The prose of counter-insurgency, then, appears almost impenetrable. However, by applying the theories of subaltern theorists and commentators to the writing of a work of fiction, I have been able to subvert this overwhelmingly penetrating discourse. The work of Guha, Gopal and Rabasa has provided the tools I needed to analyse, contest and search until I found sufficient contradictions, spaces and archival material to repatriate the long-silenced voices of the Cornish and Devonshire freedom fighters. So while history may never provide space for the passion, the logic, the fear and love that must have driven so many people to fight an army that eventually far-outnumbered them, it may be possible – through the pages of a novel – to hear the echoes of their voices.

Notes and references

1. Published in F. Rose-Troup, *The Western Rebellion* (London, 1913), p. 493.
2. A.M. Kent, 'Screening Kernow: Authenticity, Heritage and the Representation of Cornwall in Film and Television, 1913–2003', in P. Payton (ed.), *Cornish Studies: Eleven* (Exeter, 2003).
3. J. Angarrack, *Our Future is History: Identity, Law and the Cornish Question* (Bodmin, 2002).
4. B. Deacon, 'Foreword', in Alan M. Kent (ed.), *Voices from West Barbary: An Anthology of Anglo-Cornish Poetry 1549–1928* (London, 2002), pp. 13–14.
5. P. Payton, *The Making of Modern Cornwall* (Redruth, 1992).
6. M. Stoyle, *West Britons: Cornish Identities and the Early Modern British State* (Exeter, 2002).
7. L. McClain, *Lest We Be Damned: Practical Innovation and Lived Experience Among Catholics in Protestant England, 1559–1662*, chapter 6 (New York, 2004).
8. A.D. King, *Culture, Globalization and the World System; Contemporary Conditions for the Representation of Identity* (Basingstoke, 1993), p. 3.

9. H. White, *Tropics of Discourse: Essays in Cultural Criticism* (Baltimore, 1978).
10. R. Guha, 'The Prose of Counter-Insurgency', in R. Guha and G.C. Spivak (eds), *Selected Subaltern Studies* (Oxford, 1988).
11. J. Hooker (or Vowells), *The Antique Description and Account of the City of Excester* (c.1564, published 1765).
12. J. Cornwall, *Revolt of the Peasantry 1549* (London, 1977), p. 168.
13. Rose-Troup, *The Western Rebellion*, p. 445.
14. T. Winslade, 'De praesenti statu Cornubiae et Devoniae quae duae Provinciae sunt Hispaniae proximores' (unpublished manuscript, 1595) Hans and Hanni Kraus Sir Francis Drake Collection No 12, Library of Congress. http://www.loc.gov//rr/rarebook/catalog/drake/drake-8-invincible.html. William Wynslade was the son of executed rebel leader, John Wynslade, and according to Richard Carew, spent the years following the rebellion as a wandering harper, living off the hospitality of his father's friends. Carew tells us he was nicknamed 'Sir Tristran' for his way with the ladies (thanks to Dr James Whetter for his interpretation of Carew), and today's Winslades believe the naming of his own son Tristran was a marker of identity to those who knew the family and their Catholic allegiance.
15. T. Winslade, http://www.loc.gov//rr/rarebook/catalog/drake/drake-8-invincible.html
16. B. Deacon, 'Propaganda and the Tudor State or Propaganda of the Tudor Historians?', in P. Payton (ed.), *Cornish Studies: Eleven* (Exeter, 2003), p. 320.
17. White, *Tropics of Discourse*, p. 42.
18. White, *Tropics of Discourse*, on RG Collingwood, p. 46.
19. White, *Tropics of Discourse*, discussing Levi-Strauss, p. 44.
20. White, *Tropics of Discourse*, p. 42.
21. White, *Tropics of Discourse*, p. 46.
22. K. Grenville, quoted by S. White, 'Havoc in History House', *Weekend Australian Review*, 4–5 March 2006 pp. 8–9. Kate Grenville drew on the historical record to create a fictional account of white man's first contact with the Indigenous inhabitants at Wiseman's Ferry. Her novel, *The Secret River*, won the Commonwealth Writers' Prize.
23. Quoted by White, *Tropics of Discourse*, p. 54.
24. C. Skidmore, *Edward VI: The Lost King of England* (London, 2007).
25. Skidmore, p. 310.
26. Skidmore, *Edward VI*, p. 116.
27. J. Loach, *Edward VI* (New Haven, 2002).
28. Loach, *Edward VI*, p. 74.
29. Loach, *Edward VI*, p. 72.
30. Loach, *Edward VI*, p. 70.
31. A.L. Rowse, *Tudor Cornwall* (London, 1941).
32. P. Caraman, *The Western Rising 1549: The Prayer Book Rebellion* (Tiverton, 1994).
33. B. Beer, *Rebellion and Riot: popular disorder in England during the reign of Edward VI* (Ohio, 1982).
34. Beer, *Rebellion and Riot*, pp. 38–42.
35. J.P.D. Cooper, *Propaganda and the Tudor State: Political Culture in the Westcountry* (Oxford, 2003).
36. D.M. Loades, *The Mid-Tudor Crisis, 1545–1565* (London, 1992).
37. J. Youings, 'The South Western Rebellion of 1549', in *Southern History* 1 (1979).

38. Cornwall, *Revolt*, p. 7.
39. Cornwall, *Revolt*, p. 1.
40. Cornwall, *Revolt*, p. 41.
41. J. Sturt, *Revolt in the West: The Western Rebellion of 1549* (Devon Books, Exeter, 1987).
42. Stoyle, *West Britons*, pp. 1–2.
43. P. Payton, *Cornwall: A History* (Cornish Editions Ltd, Fowey, 2004), p. 122.
44. B. Deacon, *Cornwall: A Concise History* (Cardiff, 2007), p. 74.
45. McClain, *Lest We Be Damned*, pp. 172–86.
46. Thanks to Alan Kent for arranging for me to see these.
47. B. Deacon, 'The New Cornish Studies', in P. Payton (ed.), *Cornish Studies: Ten* (Exeter, 2002), p. 33.
48. Cornwall, *Revolt*, p. 114.
49. Cornwall, *Revolt*, p. 115.
50. Cooper, *Propaganda*, p. 64.
51. N. Pocock, *Troubles Connected with the Prayer Book of 1549* (New York, 1884, reprinted by the Camden Society 1965), p. xviii.
52. Pocock, *Troubles Connected*, pp. xviii–xvi.
53. A. Gasquet and E. Bishop, *Edward VI and the Book of Common Prayer* (London, 1928), p. 219.
54. Pocock, *Troubles Connected*, p. xx.
55. Translation of Appendix H, Rose-Troup, *The Western Rebellion*, pp. 451–2. With thanks to Julie Burton.
56. Winslade, 'De praesenti statu Cornubiae', the spelling of Wynslade/Winslade varies from publication to publication. In the twenty-first century, the family uses Winslade, however, my correspondent, Sue Winslade, agrees Wynslade was more frequent in the sixteenth century, and it is also used in a number of accounts of the rebellion. I also opted to use this spelling in my novel.
57. Winslade, 'De praesenti statu Cornubiae'.
58. L. Hutcheon, *The Politics of Postmodernism* (London, 1989), p. 66.
59. P. Gopal, 'Reading subaltern history', in Neil Lazarus (ed.), *The Cambridge Companion to Postcolonial Literary Studies* (Cambridge, 2004), p. 141.
60. Edward Said, in Guha and Spivak, *Selected Subaltern Studies*, p. vi.
61. Guha, 'The Prose of Counter-Insurgency'.
62. G.C. Spivak, 'From "Can the Subaltern Speak?"', in L. Cahoone (ed.), *From Modernism to Postmodernism – an anthology* (Malden, Maine, 2003).
63. Gopal, 'Reading subaltern history', pp. 140–1.
64. Cited by Gopal, 'Reading subaltern history', p. 140.
65. E.g. A. Gramsci, *Selections from Prison Notebooks*, edited and translated by Q. Hoare, and G.N. Smith (London, 1971).
66. Guha, 'The Prose of Counter-Insurgency', p. 53.
67. Skidmore, *Edward VI*.
68. Cornwall, *Revolt*.
69. Guha, 'The Prose of Counter-Insurgency', p. 46.
70. Hooker, *The Antique Description*, p. 35.
71. Hooker, *The Antique Description*, p. 39.
72. Hooker, *The Antique Description*, p. 57.
73. Cooper, *Propaganda*, p. 21.

74. Guha, 'The Prose of Counter-Insurgency', p. 53.
75. Guha, 'The Prose of Counter-Insurgency', p. 55.
76. Loades, *The Mid-Tudor Crisis*, p. 119.
77. Youings, 'The South Western Rebellion', p. 99.
78. Caraman, *The Western Rising*, p. 39.
79. Hooker, *The Antique Description*, p. 33.
80. J. Rabasa, 'On the History of the History of Peoples *Without* History', *Humboldt Journal of Social Relations* 29:1 (2005), p. 209.
81. Guha, 'The Prose of Counter-Insurgency', p. 59.
82. Guha, 'The Prose of Counter-Insurgency', p. 62.
83. N. Bourke and P. Neilsen, 'The Problem of the Exegesis in Creative Writing Higher Degrees', *Text*, Special Issue No. 3 (April 2004).
84. Gopal, 'Reading subaltern history', p. 139.
85. J. Rabasa, 'On the History', p. 209.
86. J. Rabasa, 'On the History', p. 212.
87. As suggested by Mark Stoyle in 'The Recent Historiography of Early Modern Cornwall', in Philip Payton (ed.), *Cornish Studies: Ten* (Exeter, 2002).
88. C. O'Neal, 'The Subaltern Speaks: Ambiguity of Empire in Conrad's 'Karain: A Memory'', *Postcolonial Text*, Vol. 3 No. 1 (2007), p. 2.
89. K. Loach, *At the Movies*, ABC TV (2006) http://www.abc.net.au/atthemovies/txt/s1743486.htm.
90. I wish to thank the lessee at Trematon for allowing me access to this site, which is owned by the Duchy of Cornwall, and also Morley for his enthusiastic guided tour.
91. E. Duffy, *The Voices of Morebath* (New Haven, CT, 2001).
92. Duffy, *Voices*, p. 136, quoting Sir Christopher Trychay, priest of Morebath parish.
93. Cooper, *Propaganda*, p. 68.
94. As suggested by Sturt, *Revolt in the West*.
95. E.g. A.L. Rowse.
96. Whitley Stokes (ed.), *Beunans Meriasek* (1872).
97. Winslade family.
98. S. Dean, *'The Folklore of Cornwall'* (London, 1975), p. 59.
99. Sturt, *Revolt in the West* and Caraman, *The Western Rising*.

Review Article

Cornish Cases and Cornish Social History

Bernard Deacon

John Rule, *Cornish Cases: Essays in Eighteenth and Nineteenth Century Social History*. Southampton: Clio Publishing, 2006, 294 pp., illustrations, ISBN 0-9542650-8-4 (13-digit ISBN: 978-0-9542650-8-3).

In 2002 the publication of Mark Stoyle's *West Britons* was hailed as an exemplar of the 'new Cornish historiography'.[1] *West Britons* collected together a series of articles previously published in various academic journals and added a couple of new essays. As a result Stoyle's important work became more accessible to a wider public. It also adroitly staked a claim for the Cornish experience of the early modern period, between 1485 and the eighteenth century, to be taken seriously as a fit component of the 'New British History'.

Late in 2006 another collection of reprinted and previously unpublished essays appeared which at first glance offered the potential to do for the period from 1700 to 1870 what *West Britons* did for earlier centuries. John Rule has been a prolific historian of the social life of England and a good proportion of his work is based on Cornish empirical material. This reflects the fact that his thesis, completed in 1971, explored the lives of Cornish miners and their communities in the period when Cornwall led the world in metal mining and when up to a third of its labour force obtained their living directly from the mines.[2] The non-appearance of John Rule's thesis in the form of a published monograph must rank as one of the most regrettable losses of Cornish historical literature.[3] Nonetheless, much of the argument of that thesis has re-surfaced over the years in various academic journals and edited collections of conference papers. It is these that are brought together in *Cornish Cases*.

The doctoral genesis of this book, now more than a generation ago, indicates that caution is in order if we wish to view *Cornish Cases* as an example of the 'new Cornish historiography'. On the one hand Roger Burt claims in a typically provocative foreword to this book that John Rule is a 'progenitor of what is now seen as the "new Cornish historiography"'.[4] Yet both Burt and, to a lesser extent, Rule appear to base their understanding of the 'new Cornish historiography' solely on the calls from a decade and a half ago to make the study of Cornish 'difference' the *raison d'etre* of Cornish Studies.[5] The parallel aim of setting Cornish history in context and placing it in a comparative framework seems to have been ignored by Roger Burt in his foreword.[6] There, he rightly states that to understand Cornwall it is necessary to see its uniqueness from a perspective that encompasses other unique and special localities in order to give it a comparative meaning. However, he then proceeds to make the more questionable assertion that 'greater benefits … can be derived from the very act of stepping beyond the county into the great national and international centres of learning'.[7] In a more measured way John Rule brings a perspective gained from his career at one of those centres of learning – Southampton – to suggest the limitations of the 'new Cornish historiography'. He glosses the latter as importing the methods and subjects familiar to other historians and adopting an explicit inter-disciplinarity and theoretical stance.[8] However, this bare summary misses the ongoing discussion, and it might be said criticism, that has taken place within the Cornish Studies field around the 'new Cornish historiography' and our approach to understanding the past in Cornwall.[9] For instance, in 2002 I called for, among other things, a greater focus on micro-history in Cornish history.[10] It is perhaps here that the potential of John Rule's work becomes plain. For, as Roger Burt observes, it can be seen as an example of that micro-history, firmly tied to a close reading of the sources but using them to draw out generalizations of greater relevance grounded in the comparative academic literature.

Anyone expecting this book to do for the eighteenth and nineteenth centuries what *West Britons* did for the sixteenth and seventeenth and provide an off-the-shelf manifesto for the new Cornish history of those centuries will be disappointed. Most of the essays here were originally published around a decade ago and even those published here for the first time seem from their references to have been composed in the mid-1990s. As such, much will be familiar to anyone who has made a serious study of eighteenth and nineteenth century Cornwall. However, in his introductory chapter, John Rule does engage directly with the 'new Cornish historiography'. But he does so from a critical position consciously outside it. I have suggested elsewhere that a key feature of the new Cornish Studies more generally was a normative stance that views Cornwall and its people as suitable subjects of study in their own right and, furthermore, accepts the importance of a Cornish standpoint on knowledge.[11] While providing many insights into the Cornish past, *Cornish Cases* is not an example of this. Unlike Mark Stoyle's enthusiastic embrace of the 'new Cornish historiography', John Rule remains more sceptical, slightly suspicious of what he concludes is its overarching purpose – a search for difference. Nonetheless, I shall return to this aspect at the end of this review article and suggest that, while personally somewhat reluctant to be co-opted into the 'new Cornish historiography', Rule's work contains a number of aspects that are of major relevance to the new Cornish history.

That said, this collection conveniently draws John Rule's important body of work on Cornish subjects together in one place. More importantly, it raises issues and analogies that practitioners of Cornish history might fruitfully pursue. As I shall argue, both the 'new Cornish historiography' and the social history tradition in which John Rule's earlier work was located can be seen to have their limitations. However, this book implicitly provides a map with which we can find our way to a more nuanced historical approach that transcends those limitations and prefigures the potential shape of Cornish history.

In the rest of this review article I intend first to put John Rule's work in the context of the disintegration of the 'traditional' British social history of the 1960s and 70s from which it emerged and the changes that have taken place in that sub-discipline since the 1980s. I then summarise the content of the book and discuss some of the lessons it holds for historians of eighteenth and nineteenth century Cornwall. Finally, I review its implications for the new Cornish history, where it offers a potential route away from a 'histori-ography' dominated by the events of the early modern period and towards a more inclusive Cornish history.

Returning to the roots: the British social history

In his introductory chapter John Rule returns to his roots. First, he revisits the influence on his work of E.P. Thompson, his doctorate supervisor at Warwick in the late 1960s. Thompson was both the inspiration and the most accomplished practitioner of a school of social history that emerged in 1960's Britain. These historians set out to discover more about the lives of working people and understand their political activities. They were themselves often the sons (though not at this stage the daughters) of working-class parents who, with the expansion of the British university system in Harold Wilson's Britain, saw the citadels of privilege that had jealously guarded the gates of academia begin to crumble. Seizing this opportunity they set about with a will, in Thompson's words, to rescue their class from 'the enormous condescension of posterity' that had previously characterized a history dominated by high politics and the ruling elite.

The majority of British social historians of the 1960s and 1970s shared a set of assumptions about the centrality of material facts in explaining social changes and about the importance of social conditions conditioning workers' experiences. Those experiences produced social classes. Even non-marxist historians adopted a vaguely determinist perspective and took the existence of social classes and their creation during the industrial revolution for granted.[12] Debate revolved around the extent of class consciousness, the timing of its appearance and the delineation of the resulting class structure rather than around the existence of class as the main structure constraining and conditioning the lives of people in Victorian Britain.

However, in the 1980s, reflecting the turn to individualism and conservatism in contemporary politics and the emergence of new feminist and poststructuralist theories, both the methods and assumptions of British social history began to come under sustained attack.[13] Gareth Stedman Jones initiated a growing chorus of dissension. Class was not, he argued, just a social phenomenon rooted in material conditions, but a question of culture and to a large extent a linguistic creation. This was taken further by historians such as Patrick Joyce and James Vernon in the 1990s, who viewed class as an ideological and discursive construct and one that was not in fact central to the world view of those living through the nineteenth century.[14] Despite a vigorous counter-attack by marxist social historians, the centrality of class in historical accounts of the nineteenth century began to weaken and dissolve as historians turned to more cultural approaches to explain the lives of working people and away from a fixation on the history of political movements and trade unionism, the staples of the labour history that had emerged as a sub-genre of the British social history.[15]

By 1993 even Thompson himself was admitting that class was 'a concept long past its sell-by date'.[16] The bitter disputes of the 1980s and early 1990s have now died away, leaving a social history landscape where narratives, consumption and complex plural identities have replaced a single-minded focus on class as the primary social identity of everyday life. The content of social history has in consequence widened as attention has shifted away from the workplace and from class as the principal explanatory factor in discussing topics such as family life, education, leisure or religion. That does not mean that class and the role of material conditions have entirely disappeared. The more recent contributions of British social historians may argue for multiple and more contingent identities but these include narratives of class, and class can still be seen as key identity at certain times and in certain places.[17]

John Rule avoided the frenetic and sometimes heated debates of the 1980s about the nature of social history, preferring to continue his work documenting the lives of working people from the archives, building on his Cornish thesis to become a respected social historian of the eighteenth century whose remit included the whole of England and whose interests ranged from crime to the history of the fishing industry.[18] In the course of this, his work retained the tenor of Thompson's approach, adopting the latter's 'socialist humanism' while rejecting the strict economic determinism of more doctrinaire marxists. This career is recounted in the first part of the introductory chapter to this collection, where a historical approach grounded in a thorough engagement with evidence and combined with a close reading of the texts, with at times 'attentive disbelief', is re-affirmed and the postmodernist critique of history politely but firmly rejected.[19] While accepting the need for studies of identities other than class, Rule's position remains one that views social consciousness as arising out of lived experience. But, as most of the essays in this volume were written more than ten years ago, they inevitably reflect an earlier more unambiguously Thompsonian perspective and can be read as examples of that influential 'Warwick School' of British social history.

While in that sense an affirmation and confirmation of his Thompsonian roots, the volume marks a return to another set of roots. In the second part of the introduction John Rule returns to his Cornish family roots with a disarming account of his own family background in Redruth. With grandparents and great grandparents born in Redruth, St Just, Helston, St Day and Truro among other places, and with the inevitable examples of emigration in his family story, he firmly establishes his Cornish voice, grounded in the communities of west Cornwall. It is those communities and the lives of those who struggled to live, work and survive among the burrows and engine houses of the west that have been the principal subjects of John Rule's historical research on Cornwall.

The Rule thesis: quietism and its causes

Baldly stated, the marxist historiographical tradition foregrounds the link between the economy on the one hand and social movements and cultural knowledge on the other. The former determines the latter, even though that determination may be indirect and 'in the last resort'. Given that, for a marxist, the economic organization of any society is explained by the struggle between classes, its social and cultural superstructure can always be read off from its economic base. Thus in a feudal society, the dominant class is composed of landlords who exploit the peasantry. The religious, legal and administrative structures of such a society work in the interests of landlords and combine to oppress the peasantry. Similarly, in a capitalist society the levers of the economy are reserved for the capitalist class, who in their search to maximise profits, exploit the working class. Education, media, religion and other social and cultural aspects ultimately serve the interests of capitalism and its ruling class. This admittedly gross over-simplification of marxism is the tradition out of which Thompsonian social history grew, although that social history tradition gave considerable agency to the working class in creating their own institutions and culture.

Such a model brings its own set of predictions. If the economy is governed by capitalist precepts then workers will ultimately generate a consciousness of themselves as an exploited class. This will lead to the organization of political parties and trade unions through which they will protest their working and living conditions. Labour institutions are thus the inevitable outcomes of the social experience of labour. The centrality of class to a marxist interpretation resulted in an over-fixation by British social historians on one central issue – the rise of unions and the Labour Party. For a marxist, as capitalism matured, the emergence of unions and socialism would be the expected by-product. As Britain was the world's first industrial society then it should also, logically, contain the strongest and most advanced workers' organizations. But it did not, a problem that marxist historians then spent much time trying to explain.

The socialist humanism of E.P. Thompson and John Rule meant that they investigated a wider range of social phenomenon than just labour organization, including crime, leisure and religion. Moreover, their commitment to an empiricist methodology tempered the teleology of the marxist model. Yet there is still a sense in John Rule's work that the counter-factual question of why labour organization did not conform to the pattern predicted by marxism is an important issue that requires examining. Thus, much of John Rule's writings on Cornwall focused on the issue of why Cornish miners, despite being one of the oldest and best established of the UK's industrial communities in the early nineteenth century, did not generate their own trade unions or get involved in early political movements such as Chartism.

For example, chapter 9 of *Cornish Cases* explains the failure of the two Chartist missionaries to Cornwall in 1839 – Robert Lowery and Abram Duncan – to tap support for the People's Charter among the miners. Miners were 'too conservative' and too committed to a 'prior political economy', a 'moral economy' which blamed middlemen and merchants rather than their employers at times of penury. This 'moral economy' included regular and uncommonly large food riots led by miners at times of high prices, but the focus remained on high prices rather than low wages. Chapter 2 describes the food rioting that was endemic in Cornwall from 1727 to 1847 and is a valuable addition to the literature, not previously published although much of the empirical material can be found in John Rule's 1971 thesis. Rule concludes that food riots in Cornwall triggered some of the largest crowd actions anywhere in Britain and were an example of the miners constituting a separate community. Food riots continued later in Cornwall than elsewhere because they were effective in achieving their aims and because the older 'moral economy' (as opposed to the new-fangled market economy) remained a powerful concept.

Nonetheless, despite their predilection for noisy 'riot' (although in reality food riots had become highly ritualistic and relatively disciplined affairs by the 1780s) John Rule still describes the society of which they were part as 'quietist'. His key argument is found in Chapter 10, first published in 1992, on the 'configuration of quietism'. Cornish miners are described as 'quietist' not because they were particularly quiet but because they did not get involved in trade unionism, Chartism or strike action, as might be expected from a marxist perspective. Rejecting a single cause explanation, in this article Rule brings together a number of factors in a multiple-cause explanation, seeing quietism as the outcome of a 'cumulative impact of a number of factors'. Nevertheless, the Rule thesis both in this chapter and elsewhere in *Cornish Cases* gives special attention to two factors. The first was the labour organization of the mining industry and the second the role of Methodism.

Chapter 4 investigates why tributing was held by contemporary mid-nineteenth century observers to be the 'perfect wage system', producing an ordered workforce free from the taint of unions and strikes that disfigured other industrial communities. Its main effect, according to John Rule, was the disappearance of the employer and the absence of a boss-class, something that slowed the development of class consciousness.[20] While re-asserting the centrality of tributing in the experience of mining communities, Rule does however provide evidence that it was not as competitive and perfect as contemporaries claimed. 'Imperfect' practices such as collusion in bidding for working pitches, 'kitting' or mixing ore from different pitches, and ore stealing are documented and may be the tip of an iceberg of fraud more characteristic of the actual working of the system.

This wage system combined with a second factor, the domination of Methodism, to hold back Cornish miners' class consciousness. Three of the chapters in this book are centrally concerned with the role of Methodism in the mining communities. Chapter 3 argues that Methodism was a folk religion that provided real solace and consolation for the community. This was its negative effect, diverting potential protest over exploitation and high mortality into issues of personal redemption. Personal redemption took on a collective aspect when multitudes were 'saved' at the same time. Periodic mass revivals were the means through which Methodism in Cornwall gained membership from the 1780s through to the 1860s with the greatest revivals in 1799 and 1814 transforming Methodism from a minority sect into the dominant denomination of Cornish religious life. Chapter 6 argues that revivals are best explained not by exogenous factors such as war, pestilence or high food prices but from the internal dynamic of local religious culture. Rule here closely follows the argument of David Luker who places Methodist revivals in the context of a society where Methodism had become the cultural norm.[21] Chapter 7 reprints an older contribution of 1982 which recounts the positive and competitive opposition offered by Methodism to potential political activism. Methodism provided positive opposition by being locked into pre-existing popular beliefs and folk superstitions and competitive opposition by underpinning the mass teetotal movement which swept through Cornwall after 1839. While teetotalism in Cornwall awaits its historian, Rule's view of popular Methodism as an example of an older folk tradition might be usefully contrasted with David Luker's work which explained it in terms of a combination of the old and new, bridging the community values of moral economy eighteenth century Cornwall and the individualism that spread in the nineteenth.[22]

The chapters in this book, therefore, provide an accessible restatement of John Rule's conclusions about the social life of Cornish mining communities in their heyday. However, from a broader Cornish history perspective, we might pinpoint a number of problems with this approach. Detailing these allows us to discern the outlines of a future research agenda for Cornish social history.

Limitations of the thesis

Qualifications relating to the arguments that surface in this collection of essays can be grouped as involving interlinked issues of content, context and comparison. In terms of content, and purely on an empirical level, both the definition and the details of the 'configuration of quietism' might be questioned. John Rule graciously acknowledges in the introductory chapter earlier doubts expressed about this concept.[23] But even if we were to accept the notion of 'quietism' for a moment, room for debate remains over the relative importance of the proposed factors. Chapter 5 of *Cornish Cases*, for example, calls for more research on the 'mixed economy of welfare' in the nineteenth century, on savings, charity and the strategies families adopted to cope with misfortune. In particular, the role of collateral aids in Cornish mining districts – smallholdings, potato patches, access to fishing boats – may be more critical than previously thought.[24] Here, more comparative work involving the social experience of Cornish miners in the New World mining frontiers would seem worth the investment. Despite the presence of tributing and Methodism, for example, Cornish workers in South Australia seemed willing to both establish trade unions and take energetic strike action when needed.[25] Was the presence or absence of the collateral aids along with the dense social relations that girdled and penetrated the older Cornish communities in the west of Cornwall the key factor?

Turning to context, a second line of attack echoes those wider criticisms levelled against the traditional British social history more generally; the concern with labour and class consciousness limits the breadth of issues that the social historian studies. John Rule is clearly aware of this and concedes the point.[26] But if social and cultural history has moved beyond its earlier narrower concern with class and class consciousness, then the bulk of the work collected here should more strictly be seen as of valuable historio-graphical interest, charting a particular approach to Cornish social history, rather than being an exemplar of what that social history might entail. For instance, issues of the chronology of change in Cornish communities and the genesis of the distinct occupational communities studied here could repay further investigation.[27] How, for example, did the shift occur from the miners in 1839 who did not know the difference between a Chartist and a pilchard or mackerel to those newly enfranchised miners in 1885 who demonstrated a keen interest in politics and who were hailed as one of the most democratic communities in the British Isles?[28]

We can sometimes underplay or ignore aspects that do not fit our preconceived frameworks. Chapter 8 in this book reminds us of the existence of small-town radicalism in Cornwall through an account of John Spurr's activities in the 1830s. Spurr was a vociferous cabinet maker who led opposition in Truro to the town's conservative elite, unthinking supporters of established church and local landlords. Spurr had had enough of things by 1839 and left for London, eventually emigrating to Australia in 1850. But his voice was not the only note of political dissent in the towns of west Cornwall as the survival of Chartist activity in Camborne, Falmouth, Hayle, Helston, Penzance and Truro in the 1840s hints at.[29] Furthermore, even in mining communities, there is now more evidence of the presence of institutions associated with a modern class society than was available in 1971. For example, when discussing the wage system in a chapter originally published in 1997 John Rule writes that 'miners lacked the experience of the independent mutual finds, which played a clear role in the development of artisan trade unions'. However, in the next chapter, published first in 2001, Rule reports research that concludes that friendly society membership in Cornwall was 'more common than has been assumed'.[30] Friendly society membership at the beginning of the nineteenth century was both relatively high when compared with other regions and concentrated in mining parishes.

This type of evidence serves to chip away at the quietist thesis. That thesis can be subjected to more doubts if we move away from the mining communities and do more to compare them with others, both in Cornwall and further afield. John Rule insists that miners made up a distinct occupational community in Cornwall but this claim cries out for some close exploration of the boundaries between mining and other occupational groups in the nineteenth century, for example through reconstituting life histories, examining afresh the issue of dual or multiple occupations or investigating marriage patterns. Even at its height in 1861, mining did not employ just over two thirds of the Cornish workforce. While many of these would have been economically dependent on the fortunes of the mines this still suggests that at least half of Cornish people were not inhabiting communities dominated by mining. Just as the political attitudes of miners need to be studied alongside political attitudes of craftsmen and artisans and other town dwellers, so the patterns of life in mining communities need comparing with those in market towns or in other rural communities that were occupationally less homogenous, or if homogenous, populated by families engaged in farming or fishing. In this volume Rule provides an example of this wider field in Chapter 11 which is a straightforward economic history of the fishing industry in Cornwall and Devon.

In short, there needs to more holistic work which can draw the conclusions from John Rule's social history together with the research of other scholars such as Ed Jaggard on the political life of late eighteenth and early nineteenth century Cornwall.[31] Furthermore, a more holistic approach could be allied with a more comparative approach. Explicit comparisons are required with coal mining communities in the rest of Britain and with metal mining communities in the north of England and overseas before we can reach confident conclusions about the uniqueness of Cornish mining communities.

Towards a new Cornish social history

John Rule is actually well aware of the limitations of the work on the social history of Cornwall and makes incisive calls in the introduction to *Cornish Cases* for more research and more writing on the social history of the period after the sixteenth century. One under-worked lode is the demographic history of seventeenth and eighteenth century Cornwall. It is noticeable that family reconstruction work on Cornish parishes is absent from the major accounts of demographic change that have issued from the Cambridge Group on population.[32] Yet in the later seventeenth and early eighteenth centuries it appears that Hundreds in the west were growing rapidly at a time when population in England and Wales was stagnating.[33] The mechanism of this calls for research and Rule suggests the possibility of parish register studies in this period and also more comparative work on rates of illegitimacy, bridal pregnancy and patterns of mortality in the critical eighteenth century when communities in Cornwall were amongst the first to experience the traumas and opportunities of the social changes accompanying industrialization.

The last chapter in the book, the most recently written and one previously unpublished, is in many ways the most interesting. Chapter 12 is a study of gender and feasting in the nineteenth century based on the evidence of the Cornish drolls collected by Bottrell and Hunt. In a fascinating account of representations of feast days in these folk stories John Rule draws out how Feast Day had changed by the mid-nineteenth century. When gentry patronage and its 'carnivalesque' aspects declined, the Feast meal became the domestic centre of celebration. As its functions changed Feast Day had a concomitant gendered effect as the women of the parish played a central role in the success or failure of this domestic self-provisioning. This chapter opens up a whole area of research into the texture of everyday life in nineteenth-century Cornwall which is at present largely untapped and is a striking example of what a social history sensitive to textual evidence can achieve.

Furthermore, in the introduction we read of what might have been. John Rule's intention was to write an over-arching monograph of Cornish mining and fishing communities. This would have combined the history of these communities and extended the boundaries of the new Cornish history, in the process meeting the criticisms raised here concerning context and comparison. Regrettably, illness has cut this project short. Nonetheless, the concluding sentences of the final pages in this book, at the end of some very useful 'Bibliographical and Historiographical Notes', repeat John Rule's confidence that a substantial corpus of sources exist from which to write an ethnographic study of this period.[34] All that is required are the historians of sufficient imagination to meet the challenge he sets.

Cornish Cases thus provides a signpost for the future direction of the new Cornish history. I have already argued that the 'new Cornish historiography' is yoked too closely to the new British History.[35] The latter is fundamentally about the process of state formation, escaping nation-centred approaches in order to examine the relations between the different peoples of the British 'archipelago'. The new British history claims to look for common trends and experiences and is distinguished from national histories which focus on the making of nations.[36] But precisely because of its focus on state formation that produced a state centred on London and the south east margins of the archipelago the new British history has come under attack from Irish and Scottish historians as merely a continuation of the old anglocentric history and for over-emphasizing similarities at the expense of difference.[37] There is also still little evidence that the new British history is giving the Cornish experience any more then token space.[38]

In any case, the new British history, because of its concentration on one period of the past to the exclusion of others, is too restrictive and confined in its topics of interest to accommodate Cornish history. The paradox is that Cornish history is much more than British history. The experience of the diaspora for example links it to the project known as Atlantic history.[39] From this perspective the events of 1549 for example might make more, or different, sense by being set in a context of that expanding marchland of European 'civilisation' which, moving out of its core regions, engaged in savage and authorized brutality to impose itself on native peoples. The slaughters of 1549 in Cornwall (and Devon) could then be contextualized by comparison with those in that other Atlantic frontier across the Celtic Sea – Ireland – in the seventeenth – and the Americas from the seventeenth to the nineteenth centuries. Cornwall's location at the southern littoral of the Celtic Sea also reminds us that there have been long-lasting maritime links southwards as well as northwards, also generating experiences that may owe little to British state formation.

If the new British history is too meagre a canvas on which to paint the new Cornish history, then how do we enlarge it? Here, the trajectory of British social history offers a revealing model. It is now generally accepted that traditional social history in Britain was over-concerned with a single identity – that of class. Class is now viewed as one amongst a number of multiple identities with which in different times and in different contexts people in Britain have identified. Cornish history too has been over-concerned with a single identity – that of ethnicity. While understandable in view of the persistent ignorance and occasional patronizing disdain that still besets some English academics on being confronted by Cornwall, it is time to move to the multiple identities of Cornwall both contemporary and historic. Amongst these ethnicity will remain as an at times important identity but will not necessarily be *primus inter pares*.[40]

In this search for multiple Cornwalls and a diversity of experience we begin to mirror John Rule's path away from a focus on mining communities alone to an all-encompassing ethnographic history. The addition of a variety of different methods – ethnographic, quantitative, textual – and a plethora of topics will achieve two further goals. First, it will bridge the gap between the 'theoretically led historical inquiry' that has been the hallmark of the new Cornish history and the ethnographic studies of Cornish cultural life that Amy Hale eloquently called for in 2002. By providing the new Cornish history with a variety of methods it will also, secondly, meet the suggestion of Malcolm Williams that Cornish Studies involves a deliberate 'triangulation' of methods, not confining itself to one or two approaches but seeking new angles on old subjects.[41]

I have argued here that John Rule's book may only tangentially be included as part of the 'new Cornish historiography', unlike Mark Stoyle's *West Britons*. This is partly because of John's suspicions of the normative project of Cornish Studies but also because most of the essays in the book predate the 'new Cornish historiography' and are examples of a parallel historiography with different roots. However, it may well offer a better road map for the future of the new Cornish history. It is certainly a worthy addition to the corpus of literature on the social experience of the Cornish in past times, admirably succeeding in rescuing the Cornish labouring communities of the industrial period from the 'enormous condescension of posterity'. For that reason alone it deserves to be on the bookshelves of anyone with a serious interest in Cornish history.

Notes and references

1. Mark Stoyle, *West Britons: Cornish Identities and the Early Modern British State* (Exeter, 2002). Philip Payton, 'Introduction' in Philip Payton (ed.), *Cornish Studies: Ten* (Exeter, 2002), p. 11.
2. John Rule, 'The Labouring Miner in Cornwall c.1740–1870', unpublished Ph.D. thesis (University of Warwick, 1971).
3. The same applies to Gill Burke's thesis on the Cornish miner in the later period – Gill Burke, 'The Cornish Miner and the Cornish Mining Industry 1870–1921', unpublished Ph.D. thesis (University of London, 1981). Together, these two dissertations provide the raw material for a comprehensive social history of Cornish mining communities but this material has not yet been fully quarried.
4. John Rule, *Cornish Cases: Essays in Eighteenth and Nineteenth Century Social History* (Southampton, 2006), p. vii.
5. Philip Payton, 'Introduction' in Philip Payton (ed.), *Cornish Studies: One* (Exeter, 1993), pp. 2–3.
6. For this definition of the aims of the 'new Cornish historiography' see Philip Payton, 'Cornwall in Context: The New Cornish Historiography', in Philip Payton (ed.), *Cornish Studies: Five* (Exeter, 1997), pp. 9–20.
7. Rule, *Cornish Cases*, p. viii.
8. Rule, *Cornish Cases*, p. 17. Here, he explicitly rejects the application of the concept of proto-industrialization to Cornwall, on the grounds that this concept should include a demographic dimension through stimulating population growth. However, this is at odds with other definitions of proto-industrialisation (see for example Steven King and Geoffrey Timmins, *Making Sense of the Industrial Revolution: English economy and society 1700–1850* (Manchester, 2001), pp. 39–41). By the criteria offered in King and Timmins Cornish mining certainly qualifies as proto-industrial. Even were we to demand that it stimulated higher fertility then there is other work that strongly suggest it had exactly this effect in the far west of Cornwall in the late seventeenth century – see David Cullum, 'Society and Economy in West Cornwall, c.1588–1750', unpublished Ph.D. thesis (University of Exeter, 1993), pp. 285–8 and Jonathan Barry, 'Population Distribution and

Growth in the Early Modern Period' in Roger Kain and William Ravenhill (eds), *The Historical Atlas of South West England* (Exeter, 1999), pp. 110–17.

9. For example Bernard Deacon, 'The New Cornish Studies: New Discipline or Rhetorically-defined Space?' in Philip Payton (ed.), *Cornish Studies: Ten* (Exeter, 2002), pp. 34–6, or Bob Keys and Garry Tregidga, 'Past, Present and Future: A Review of Cornish Historical Studies', Cornish History 2002 (online journal accessible at www.marjon.ac.uk/cornish-history).

10. Deacon, 'The New Cornish Studies'. For micro-history see Pat Hudson, 'Industrialization in Britain: The Challenge of Micro-history', *Family & Community History* 2 (1999), pp. 5–16 and for an excellent example of micro-history in practice Barry Reay, *Microhistories: Demography, Society and Culture in Rural England, 1800–1930* (Cambridge, 1996).

11. Deacon, 'The New Cornish Studies'.

12. For example Harold Perkin, *The Origins of Modern English Society* (London, 1969).

13. For the best account of this see John Host, *Victorian Labour History: Experience, Identity and the Politics of Representation* (London, 1998), pp. 8–59.

14. Gareth Stedman Jones, *Languages of Class: Studies in English Working-Class History, 1832–1982* (Cambridge, 1983); Patrick Joyce, *Democratic Subjects: The Self and the Social in Nineteenth-Century England* (Cambridge, 1994), pp. 1–7; James Vernon, 'Who's Afraid of the "linguistic turn"? The Politics of Social History and its Discontents', *Social History* 19 (1994), pp. 81–97.

15. For the defence of class see Bryan Palmer, *Descent into Discourse: The Reification of Language and the Writing of Social History* (Philadelphia PA, 1990). For a flavour of the debate see the contributions in the journal *Social History* triggered by David Mayfield and Susan Thorne, 'Social History and its Discontents: Gareth Stedman Jones and the Politics of Language', *Social History* 17 (1992), pp. 165–88.

16. Cited in Andrew August, *The British Working Class, 1832–1940* (Harlow, 2007), p. 1.

17. August, 2007; Geoff Eley and Keith Nield, *the Future of Class History: What's Left of the Social?* (Ann Arbor, MI, 2007).

18. The books that established his reputation were *The Labouring Classes in Early Industrial England 1750–1850* (London, 1986); *The Vital Century: England's developing economy, 1714–1815* (London, 1992); *Albion's People: English Society 1714–1815* (London, 1992).

19. See also the historiographical notes at the end of Rule, *Cornish Cases*, p. 291.

20. Rule, *Cornish Cases*, p. 104.

21. David Luker, 'Revivalism in Theory and Practice: The Case of Cornish Methodism', *Journal of Ecclesiastical History* 37 (1986), pp. 603–19.

22. Unfortunately, Luker's important and comprehensive history of the growth of Methodism in Cornwall is only available in his thesis – 'Cornish Methodism, Revivalism and Popular Belief, c.1780–1870', unpublished D.Litt. thesis (University of Oxford, 1987).

23. For these see Bernard Deacon, 'In Search of the Missing "Turn": The Spatial Dimension and Cornish Studies' in Philip Payton (ed.), *Cornish Studies: Eight* (Exeter, 2000), pp. 219–21 and Bernard Deacon, 'The Reformulation of Territorial Identity: Cornwall in the late Eighteenth and Nineteenth Centuries', unpublished Ph.D. thesis (Open University, 2001), pp. 238–41.

24. See Damaris Rose, 'Home Ownership, Subsistence and Historical Change: The Mining District of West Cornwall in the late Nineteenth Century', in Nigel Thrift and Peter Williams (eds), *Class and Space: The Making of an Urban Society* (London, 1987), pp. 108–53; Deacon, 'The Reformulation of Territorial Identity', pp. 249–56; Peter Tremewan in this volume.

25. Philip Payton, *Making Moonta: The Invention of Australia's Little Cornwall* (Exeter, 2007), pp. 97–129.

26. Rule, *Cornish Cases*, p. 15.

27. For a suggested revision of the received chronology of nineteenth-century Cornish history see Bernard Deacon, 'Proto-industrialization and Potatoes: A Revised Narrative for Nineteenth-century Cornwall', in Philip Payton (ed.), *Cornish Studies: Five* (Exeter, 1997), pp. 60–84.

28. For the fish reference see Rule, *Cornish Cases*, p. 208. For the political culture of the central mining district in 1885 see Bernard Deacon, ' "Conybeare for ever!" ' in Terry Knight (ed.), *Old Redruth: Original Studies of the Town's History* (Redruth, 1992), pp. 37–43.

29. Rule, *Cornish Cases*, p. 219.

30. Rule, *Cornish Cases*, p. 105. For the distribution of friendly societies see Martin Gorsky, 'The Growth and Distribution of English Friendly Societies in the Early Nineteenth Century', *Economic History Review* 51 (1998), pp. 489–511. Cornwall also had a more than its fair share of the first wave of cooperative societies in the 1850s – see Deacon, 'The Reformulation of Territorial Identity', p. 265.

31. Edwin Jaggard, *Cornwall Politics in the Age of Reform, 1790–1885* (Woodbridge, 1999).

32. Edward Wrigley and Roger Schofield, *The Population History of England, 1541–1871: A Reconstruction* (Cambridge, 1989), pp. 40–2.

33. Cullum, 'Society and Economy in West Cornwall'; Barry, 'Population Distribution and Growth'.

34. Rule, *Cornish Cases*, p. 294.

35. Deacon, ' "Conybeare for ever!" ', p. 37.

36. Steven Ellis, *The Making of the British Isles: the State of Britain and Ireland 1450–1660* (Harlow, 2007), pp. xvi–xix.

37. Murray Pittock, *Celtic Identity and the British Image* (Manchester, 1999), pp. 98–100; Nicholas Canny, 'The Attempted Anglicization of Ireland in the Seventeenth Century: An Exemplar of "British history" ', in Ronald Asch (ed.), *Three Nations – a Common History? England, Scotland, Ireland and British Bistory, c.1600–1920* (Bochum, 1993), pp. 49–50.

38. See the references to Cornwall in Ellis, *The Making of the British Isles*. Here the index entry is 'Cornwall and Devon' and the Cornish are not described as one of the peoples of the British archipelago.

39. Bernard Bailyn, *Atlantic History: Concept and Contours* (Cambridge, MA, 2005).

40. This repeats my call in Deacon, 'The New Cornish Studies', to move from a study of Cornwall to a study of Cornwalls.

41. Amy Hale, 'Cornish Studies and Cornish Culture(s): Valuations and Directions' in Philip Payton (ed.), *Cornish Studies: Ten* (Exeter, 2002), pp. 240–51; Malcolm Williams, 'Discourses and Social Science in Cornish Studies – A Reply to Bernard Deacon' in Philip Payton (ed.), *Cornish Studies: Eleven* (Exeter, 2003), pp. 14–23.